INSIDE SPORTS

How do people become involved in sports? What can their experiences teach us?

These are two of the many questions asked by this unique collection of personal stories of people involved in sport. Told by researchers who have interviewed participants and observed what happens in the setting where people play sports, the contributions not only show how sport studies contribute to the wider study of society, but also describe the difficulties and challenges faced when doing research of this kind.

Inside Sports is divided into four main sections reflecting the social processes and developments over time that make up the experience of sport for most people, however diverse their circumstances may otherwise be:

early experiences: being introduced to sports
experience and identity: becoming an athlete
deep in the experience: doing sports
transition experiences: facing life beyond the playing field

In its extensive coverage of the sporting experience from within, as well as its discussion of research methods, *Inside Sports* will be essential reading for all students studying sport in society.

Jay Coakley is Professor of Sociology at the University of Colorado at Colorado Springs and is author of *Sport and Society: Issues and Controversies*. **Peter Donnelly** is Director of the Centre for Sport Policy Studies at the University of Toronto.

INSIDE SPORTS

*Edited by Jay Coakley and
Peter Donnelly*

London and New York

First published 1999
by Routledge
11 New Fetter Lane, London EC4P 4EE

Simultaneously published in the USA and Canada
by Routledge
29 West 35th Street, New York, NY 10001

Typeset in Baskerville by
BC Typesetting, Bristol
Printed and bound in Great Britain by
TJ International Ltd, Padstow, Cornwall

British Library Cataloguing in Publication Data
A catalogue record for this book is available from the British Library

Library of Congress Cataloging in Publication Data
Inside sports/edited by Jay Coakley and Peter Donnelly.
p.   cm.
Includes bibliographical references and index.
1. Sports–Social aspects.   I. Coakley, Jay J.   II. Donnelly, Peter.
GV706.5.I55   1999
306.4′83–dc21   98-36508
                                                                      CIP

ISBN 0–415–17088–5 (hbk)
ISBN 0–415–17089–3 (pbk)

CONTENTS

CONTENTS

CONTRIBUTORS

Patricia A. Adler and Peter Adler We received PhDs in sociology from the University of California, San Diego. Peter is a Professor of Sociology at the University of Denver and Patti is an Associate Professor of Sociology at the University of Colorado, Boulder. We have written and worked together for almost thirty years. Our interest in the sociology of sport began in the mid-1970s when we examined the role of momentum in sport and its effects on athletes' motivation, arousal, and emotional states (see P. Adler, *Momentum*, Sage, 1981). Our study of elite college athletes (Chapter 16) explores the socialization of young men into the world of NCAA Division I basketball. Our most recent project focuses on the social worlds of preadolescent children. Our work on "Afterschool Activities" looks at children's experiences in these adult-organized realms, and the way they bring adult values into children's lives at the same time as they contribute to the increased class stratification of society (see P.A. Adler and P. Adler, *Peer Power*, Rutgers University Press, 1998). We have served as editors of *Journal of Contemporary Ethnography* (1986–94) and as the founding editors of *Sociological Studies of Child Development* (1985–92).

Becky Beal Sport participation has always been central in my life. It captures my feelings and facilitates my friendships. As an undergraduate, I took my running and my studies seriously, but I never thought to integrate the two. With a history degree (Pomona College, 1985), I expected to be a high school teacher and coach. But taking a required course in the sociology of sport from Dr George Sage changed my path. His course enabled me to connect my academic interests with my sport experiences. This ideal match inspired me to obtain a doctorate with an emphasis in the sociology of sport at the University of Northern Colorado (1992). Now I teach in the Department of Sport Sciences at the University of the Pacific in Stockton, California.

Janet Saltzman Chafetz I am a Professor and Chairperson of the Department of Sociology at the University of Houston where I've taught since 1971. My areas of interest are sociological theory and the sociology of gender. Much of my work has focused specifically on developing a better theoretical understanding of how systems of gender inequality both continue to reproduce themselves and also to change. I wrote *Sex and Advantage* (1985), a book on gender stratification theory, *Gender Equity* (1990), a book on how systems of gender inequity maintain and change themselves, and recently edited a *Handbook on Gender Sociology* (1999). I'm now working with a colleague who is doing research on immigrant religious institutions.

Jay Coakley I became hooked on sociology as an undergraduate student-athlete in the 1960s. After receiving an MA and PhD in sociology at the University of Notre Dame I began to teach and do research on sport and leisure. Since then I have written six editions of *Sport in Society: Issues and Controversies*, a sociology of sport textbook, and been the editor of *Sociology of Sport Journal* (1984–9). My teaching and research interests as a professor at the University of Colorado in Colorado Springs have focused on using sociology critically to understand sports as a part of people's lives.

Todd Crosset I spent most of my undergraduate days in a pool at the University of Texas, training for national championships. After receiving a degree in philosophy in 1982 I went to Brandeis University for graduate studies. I was unprepared and overwhelmed by the sociology theory, including critical and feminist theories, during my first year in graduate school. I survived by applying theory to the world of sports because it was what I knew best. One paper on sport led to another and finally to a PhD dissertation on sport. I coached while doing my research, and I now teach in the Sport Management Program at the University of Massachusetts.

Anna Dacyshyn After I graduated from college and retired from competitive diving, I wasn't sure what I wanted to do. Despite my passion for sport, some of my experiences as an athlete had been disappointing. I pursued a Master's degree in sport psychology at the University of Toronto, partly to understand my experiences in sport and because I wanted to make sport more healthy and enjoyable for future athletes. I learned that psychology should be studied with sociology because an individual's experience is intimately linked to the social environment in which s/he exists, and athletes can only be as sound as the culture of which they are a part. Now I am back to diving, this time as a coach. I divide my time between coaching and my new passion for dance.

Alison Dewar I am a physical education teacher turned professor turned lawyer. I was drawn to sport early in my life because sport was one place to feel great about who I was as a budding feminist and lesbian. After teaching for a couple of years I got the travel bug and moved from Scotland to Canada where I did graduate work and became interested in feminist sport sociology. Eight years of teaching in universities in Ohio and Canada convinced me that I needed a change so I decided to try my hand at the law. That's where I am now, trying to work for social justice in a different forum. I am currently working at a small law firm that represents unions, and I am trying to work out how to stay involved in sport.

Peter Donnelly Most of my undergraduate years in England were spent away from campus rock climbing. I started graduate school at the University of Massachusetts in sport psychology to understand my own risk-taking experiences. Psychology was unable to produce the answers and I realized that I needed to understand the social context of risk taking. Since that time my sociological interests have diversified. I've edited two books, and the *Sociology of Sport Journal* (1990–4), and I am now Director of the Centre for Sport Policy Studies at the University of Toronto. But I'm still interested in the subculture of sports like rock climbing, and the social context of risk taking.

Douglas E. Foley After two knee operations, I quit playing tight end and shooting guard for the University of Northern Iowa and became a serious student. Upon graduation, I began teaching and coaching in an Iowa high school, only to hear the call of President Kennedy to join the Peace Corps. Two years in a Philippine fishing village inspired me to finish a PhD in anthropology at Stanford. Since 1970 I have been at the University of Texas in Austin where I teach and write about the US civil rights movement and race relations. Because the races play sports together, I still hang out in gyms and locker rooms to see if they get along any better than they did when I was a kid.

Mark A. Grey Like most high school athletes, I enjoyed playing sports, but I liked the status that came along with it even more. After I started studying anthropology, I began to realize how high school athletes achieve their status and why some athletes have a higher status than others. I still play soccer, but just for fun. Still, I often consider the role of sport in social and ethnic relations. These days, I spend most of my days studying farms. But if I had it all to do over again, I might have chosen to study sports instead. Perhaps there is still time.

Cynthia A. Hasbrook I took my first sociology of sport course in 1972, while completing my MS degree at California Polytechnic State University, San Luis Obispo, and teaching and coaching at the secondary level. Sport sociology struck a cord with me, and in 1979 I left secondary education and coaching to pursue a PhD with a specialization in sport sociology at the University of Illinois at Champaign-Urbana. Since obtaining my doctorate, I've taught sociology of sport courses and conducted research at the University of Wisconsin-Milwaukee. Currently I am Professor and Chair of Human Kinetics and served as editor of the *Sociology of Sport Journal* (1995–8).

Alan G. Ingham As a youth I ran track and then played soccer with a semi-pro team, and with the youth system at Manchester City (England). My teachers thought I was too concerned with athletics and playing drums in a rock and roll band, but bright enough to study physical education in college. It was there that I discovered sociology. I came to the USA in 1968 and completed a PhD in sociology at the University of Massachusetts. I have been the president of the International Sociology of Sport Association and co-edited (with John Loy) *Sport in Social Development*. My sociology focuses on social class, professional sport and community, and the problems of failure in sport. I am a Professor of Sport Studies at Miami University, Ohio.

Alan M. Klein I'm just a ballplayer who didn't make it past his Junior College baseball team. Everything else in my life followed from that. I got into radical 1960s politics as much because of the principles involved as through the realization that it was easier to find a date at an antiwar rally than at my ball games. It was years before I could reconvince myself that sports were not a diversion away from politics, but when I came back I was able to use my critical sociological and anthropological perspectives in my work. I've done three full-length fieldwork studies since 1980 – a six-year study of competitive bodybuilders in Southern California, a three-year Dominican study of baseball and cultural politics, and a study of nationalism on the US–Mexican border as it is played out through baseball. All have been published as books.

Joseph A. Kotarba A BA from Illinois State University and an MA from Arizona State University helped me focus my dissertation research at the University of California at San Diego on the sociology of health and illness. A highlight of that project was spending the summer of 1978 in the locker room and dug-out with the San Diego Padres, investigating sports injuries and pain management. My current interest in the sociology of sports is also driven by coaching and parenting Little League All Stars at first base (Chris) and short-stop (Andrew), and a girls' All Star point-guard (Hessie).

Bette McKenzie I have experienced sports in a unique and personal way. My father was a pro hockey player with a reputation as a fighter. Watching him take part in such a rough sport did not deter me from playing. In fact, sports kept me in school, and I came to rely on them as a source of identity and social acceptance. When I married a professional football player I was introduced to the "behind-the-scenes" culture of professional sports on an adult level. Now I enjoy weightlifting, running, and ironman competitions. Sport remains a major component of my lifestyle and self identity.

Michael A. Messner I spent most of my free time through high school shooting hoops and dreaming of becoming a professional athlete. Drawing on my experience as a "failed" athlete, and as a youth league coach and referee, I later became a sport sociologist. I am now Associate Professor of Sociology and Gender Studies at the University of Southern California, and have written *Power at Play: Sports and the Problem of Masculinity*, and other books and articles on gender and sport. My 5-year-old son Sasha just started playing soccer, while my 9-year-old son Miles plays baseball and electric guitar (though not simultaneously).

Kitty Porterfield What 44-year-old woman with a Radcliffe degree, college-age children and a full-time job, active in her community and an inveterate traveler who had never participated in organized sports would train to become a competitive rower? I did, and my life view changed for ever. Today, I am the Director of Communications for the Fairfax County Public Schools, the twelfth largest in the country. It is a job that requires skills which I honed on the race course. My husband and I live in Northern Virginia, under the watchful eye of our three grown kids.

Christopher Stevenson My undergraduate degree in England was in zoology, but I was really just playing water polo. During my Master's programme in exercise physiology at the University of British Columbia in Vancouver I took a sociology course as an elective – and my eyes were opened. I went to Stanford and did an MA in sociology and a PhD. My research interests have included the careers of athletes, the dilemmas of Christian athletes and, most recently, various aspects of masters' swimming. I am the current editor of the *Sociology of Sport Journal* (1999–).

Derek A. Swain As an undergraduate at the University of British Columbia, I was the student manager of two national championship basketball teams in 1970 and 1972. I became a physical education teacher and, after graduate school, a college athletic director and basketball coach. My interest in the psychological dynamics that contribute to both individual and team performance later expanded to general human performance and interaction. While studying for a doctorate in counselling psychology, I linked sport with my interests in career development processes. I currently work as a counsellor at a secondary school in Vancouver and maintain a small private practice as a registered psychologist.

Nancy Theberge All my degrees are in sociology: a BA (1970) and PhD (1977) from the University of Massachusetts and an MA (1972) from Boston College. It was during my doctoral studies that I began to work in the sociology of sport. Unlike many sport sociologists, I have no experience in organized sport or training in physical education. I did, however, grow up in a family with a passion for sport and as a child I followed with great interest the fortunes of professional teams, especially the Boston Red Sox. As a sociologist, I studied gender and sport. My doctoral dissertation was a study of career patterns on the Ladies' Professional Golf Association Tour. Then I studied women in coaching. Most recently I've studied women's ice hockey, and focused on women's experience of physicality.

Shona Thompson As an undergraduate student I wanted to become a teacher, I specialized in physical education after an older friend told me it would be fun. It was fun, so I travelled from New Zealand to study physical education at the University of Alberta in Canada. There I became fascinated by a "new" subject called sport sociology. My career goals shifted and now, twenty-five years later, I teach the sociology of sport in a Sport and Exercise Science Department at Auckland University. The research reported in this book was done in Australia, where I lived for several years.

Wendy Thompson I met the man I would marry while we were in high school in Canada. When we graduated I went to university to major in physical education, and he went away to play professional ice hockey. Sociology of sport courses helped me understand what we were experiencing in our personal lives. We married while I was an undergraduate, and I went on to complete a Master's degree in the sociology of sport. I worried that my husband's career in hockey could end abruptly, and I wanted to be prepared to work. After earning my degree I felt secure enough to start a family. I am currently a full-time mother by choice. "Wendy Thompson" is a pseudonym. I don't want what I say in my chapter to jeopardize my husband's status on his National Hockey League team.

Anita White Sport has been an important part of my life for as long as I can remember. I've played at all levels, the peak experience being to captain the England Field Hockey team to World Cup victory in 1975. I've coached, organized, and studied sports, and taught in a Sport Studies program. Now in my role as a Director of the English Sports Council I work to make a difference in how sport is delivered and experienced in England. My studies in the sociology of sport, working with people like George Sage and Jay Coakley, gave me valuable insights into the sport process. These help me in my job. I have also been very involved in the Women and Sport movement in England and internationally, again drawing on my experiences and studies to change sport for the better.

Philip White Following a career as a varsity rugby player during my undergraduate studies, I moved on to play at a highly competitive level for the town of Otley in

Yorkshire, England. In hindsight, I tolerated the extreme violence and the toll it took on my body in return for fleeting glory and an occasional mention in the newspapers. Since that time and throughout my academic career, I have remained enmeshed in the game as a provincial and national level coach, despite remaining ambivalent about the macho culture of rugby and its often unnecessarily high level of violence. As a Professor of Kinesiology at McMaster University in Canada, I teach and do research in the area of sport and gender, and I coach the men's varsity rugby program.

Kevin Young My interests in researching sport emerged both from 'doing' sport at school and university (primarily soccer and rugby), and from learning how to think sociologically while pursuing undergraduate and graduate degrees. Though I teach mostly in the criminology area, I continue to study, teach, and think about sport sociologically. I have co-edited *Sport and Gender in Canada* (with Phil White), have served on the editorial boards of the *Sociology of Sport Journal* and *Avante*, and the executive board of the North American Society for the Sociology of Sport.

PREFACE

A primary goal in most sociology of sport courses is to acquaint students with theory and research on sport in society. Of course, those of us who teach these courses hope to achieve this goal in ways that make sense to our students and create in them a sense of excitement about what they can learn about culture and society when they study sports.

Many of us use one of the introductory sociology of sport texts as required reading in our courses. But we often use additional articles or books to give students a taste of the research we do on sport-related topics, or to give them an inside look at what happens in connection with particular sport experiences or within a particular sport context. When we choose these additional articles and books we often consider whether we want students to read research that is published in academic journals or whether we want them to read more popularized accounts of sports and sport participation written by athletes or journalists. When we (Peter and Jay) have faced this choice in our own courses we have wished there was a book that introduced research in the sociology of sport in a way that was directed at beginning students and written to provide them with an interesting and informative learning experience. This collection is designed to satisfy that wish.

Inside Sports contains twenty-two chapters, each of which has been written for the introductory sociology of sport student. None of them presumes that readers have had a previous sociology course. Twenty of the chapters are written by social scientists. They summarize their research projects and highlight some of their most interesting findings in a straightforward and personalized manner. Two of the articles are written by women who do not identify themselves as social scientists, but who have unique insights associated with their sport experiences as an athlete or as a member of a family containing a professional athlete.

Every person we asked to write a chapter for this book accepted our invitation. Most of them teach sociology of sport courses and they were eager to take on the challenge of presenting their research to beginning students in their own classes. All the authors enjoyed this challenge. The result is that we have assembled a collection that puts our students in touch with research in the sociology of sport and presents research findings in an accessible and exciting way.

Taken together, these chapters give readers an opportunity to move *Inside Sports* through the insights and concepts provided by sociology. Reading them not only puts readers in touch with the excitement and dynamics of sport participation, but also connects them with the challenge and excitement of doing sociological research and discovering things about human beings, social relationships, and social life.

ACKNOWLEDGMENTS

We thank Steve Mosher, Department of Exercise and Sport Science at Ithaca College, for providing the four sets of film annotations that are included in the "Learning exercises and resources" that follow the chapters in each part. Thanks also go to Mari Shullaw, Geraldine Williams, Geraldine Lyons and Penelope Allport, the editors who guided this book to and through production.

We also appreciate the athletes, coaches, spectators, parents, spouses and partners who provided information and experiences to all of us who have completed the research projects summarized in the chapters that follow. It is only with their cooperation that we are able to look *Inside Sports*.

Jay Coakley, Colorado Springs
Peter Donnelly, Toronto

INTRODUCTION

This is a book about what happens in the world of sport and physical activity. It consists of twenty-two stories about the experiences of people who play sports or support the participation of others. These stories are unique because they are told by researchers who have interviewed sport participants or observed sports up close. The settings chosen by the researchers range from baseball fields to rugby fields, from golf courses and schoolyards to gymnastics gyms and hockey rinks.

When we in the sociology of sport do research, we view sports as social activities that make up a part of our everyday lives. We also see them as settings for our social relationships, and as activities that influence our ideas about social life, including our expectations about how social life should be organized. Finally, we see sports as settings in which people have experiences that inform their own sense of who they are and how they are connected to the rest of the world. In fact, the notion that sport participation is related to processes of identity development is central to many of the stories told in this book.

The stories in this book were chosen to represent some of the ways in which sociologists learn about sports as a part of our social lives. The research for each chapter was collected by ethnographic methods: in other words, the researchers used fieldwork, observations, in-depth interviews, or some combination of these three methods of gathering data. These are not the only methods used to study people's experiences in sports and physical activities, but research based on them is often reported in forms that enable us to move inside the sport setting and feel close to the action and emotions experienced by the participants. This makes learning about the social side of sports more interesting, and demonstrates what makes sociological research exciting for many of us in the field.

Learning by reading research

When we first considered research projects to include in this book, we started with a long list. It was not easy to narrow it down to the twenty-two we eventually selected. The final choices were based on our evaluation of the quality of the research and our sense that students would find it fun to read about what the researchers did and what they discovered in their projects.

Each chapter represents good examples of research based on observations, interviews, and interpretive analysis. These methods of doing research happen to be the ones we prefer, and enjoy using, when we study sports as social phenomena. We have also done studies using empirical or quantitative research methods, and we feel strongly that

research employing numerical measures and statistics is very useful as we try to understand social life and the social significance of sports in society. But when it comes to encouraging our students to be interested in and excited about studying sports, we have found interpretive research to be especially helpful. Interpretive research leads to more intimate and personal depictions of the social side of what happens in sports and physical activities; it enables us to look at sports from the inside, through the experiences of the participants.

Students often find it easier to identify with and respond to descriptive and interpretive analyses. Our intent is to encourage all the readers of this book to think about, respond to, and criticize what each chapter tells us about sports and how people live their lives in and around organized physical activities in society today.

It is appropriate to use your own experiences as starting points when you read, think about, respond to, and criticize the chapters in this book. However, we want you to use them to move beyond your personal experiences, and develop ideas about social life that are based on a more broadly informed sense of the experiences of others and how those experiences are related to the social world in which they occur.

To assist you in this process all the authors have written opening statements in which they give personalized descriptions of their projects and why they did them. You should read them to discover the stories behind the stories told in the research projects on which the articles are based. Each contains information about many things including: what led these authors to undertake their studies; what problems they encountered; why they used qualitative research methods; and what practical applications their work might have for those of us interested in sports as social phenomena. Because the chapters are about the human side of sports and physical activities, we want you to see the human side of research as well. Therefore, the opening statement at the beginning of each chapter is designed to give you an idea of why and how research in the sociology of sport is done and why it is important.

Four dimensions of sport and physical activity experiences

The chapters are organized into four parts:

- Part 1   Early experiences: being introduced to sports
- Part 2   Experience and identity: becoming an athlete
- Part 3   Deep in the experience: doing sports
- Part 4   Transition experiences: facing life beyond the playing field

These four parts represent major topics on which qualitative research has provided particularly rich data and insights into important social processes that make up sport experiences in different settings for different people. For example, the studies in Parts 1 and 2 (Early experiences and Experience and identity) identify the processes and circumstances that enable people to, or constrain people from, becoming involved in sports and physical activities. These studies do more than simply telling us who plays certain sports. Instead, they tell us about how people are introduced to sport participation and how that participation comes to be meaningful in their lives.

The studies in Parts 2, 3 and 4 (Experience and identity, Deep in the experience, and Transition experiences) tell us about other processes through which athletes produce meaning in, and derive meaning from their sport involvement. The ways that people produce and reproduce particular cultural meanings – often contradictory meanings – as they play sports is shown in a variety of settings, and considered in the light of a wide range of personal and social experiences associated with the lives of people who come to see themselves as athletes.

The social and cultural context in which people play sports and become athletes is important in each of the four parts and all of the chapters. For example, as you read each chapter you will see that sport experiences can be understood only in the social and cultural contexts where they occur. These contexts include the following: an organized youth ice hockey program in the USA, elite international amateur sports in Canada, dusty baseball diamonds in the Dominican Republic, a high school in a small town in Texas, a high profile intercollegiate basketball team in the USA, a women's professional golf tour, and top professional sports in North America.

The final chapter of each part contains a story about the people who support and make possible the sport participation of others. These people include those who drive child athletes to practices and games, those who do volunteer work and fund raising, and those parents and partners who provide athletes with emotional, social, and material support as they train, play, and then retire from active competition.

At the end of each part there are "Learning exercises and resources" designed to complement the chapters. In these four sections we have provided "Projects and discussion topics," annotations of films and an annotated bibliography of books and articles that are related to the chapters. The books and articles included in the bibliography were chosen because they represent additional examples of qualitative research that highlight experiences *Inside Sports*.

We hope you will connect with and relate to many of the experiences described in these studies. As you do, we also hope that three other things will happen. First, we want you to practice being critical as you read and think about the research done by social scientists. That is, we want you to ask questions about what the researchers did and what they found in their projects. Second, we want you to gain insights into your own social worlds, especially those involving sports and physical activities. That is, we want you to learn more about how the organization of sports influences people's experiences. Third, we want you to develop a greater appreciation and knowledge of social life and how it is studied in the sociology of sport. That is, we want you to be willing and ready to undertake your own first attempts to study social life *Inside Sports*.

Part 1

EARLY EXPERIENCES
Being introduced to sports

How do people first come to be involved as active participants in sports? Most of us learn basic physical skills and play our first physical activities in the context of our families and childhood peer groups. But our first experiences in organized physical activities and sports may occur in many different settings. These settings often include physical education classes in elementary school and adult-controlled youth programs in our school or community. First experiences in organized sports generally occur during childhood, but they can occur at any point in the life course.

The chapters in Part 1 provide stories about early experiences in physical activities and sports. In Chapter 1, Cynthia A. Hasbrook describes how children in elementary school develop ideas about physicality and give meaning to their own physical abilities and skills. As a physical educator, she knows that our bodies are central to our sense of who we are, and that we learn about ourselves and the world around us as we participate in physical activities, including sports. Her study of boys and girls from different racial and ethnic backgrounds shows that physical activities are always socially and culturally "situated." This means that we cannot understand the personal and social significance of physical activities or sports unless we know about the social and cultural context in which the experiences occur.

Hasbrook's data indicate that children give meaning to their physical abilities and skills at the same time as they learn about what it means to be male or female. Ideas about gender are learned through social relationships and through representations of masculinity and femininity in the media and the social world in which children live. Hasbrook notes that the children in her study learn about their own bodies and what their bodies can do in terms that highlight differences rather than similarities between boys and girls. This learned notion of difference accounts for why some little girls do not play sports even though their physical skills are equal to those of boys. Similarly, it accounts for why most boys participate freely in many of the physical activities and sports that occur in elementary school. This "difference-based" approach to gender creates a social context in which some boys feel that they have "social permission" to put down the physicality of girls, and in which boys are more likely than girls to express themselves in physically assertive performances for their classmates.

Hasbrook observes that children's ideas about masculinity and femininity are socially constructed and reproduced as they present and move their bodies while they are at school. For example, young boys learn that their status depends on showing others that they are physically strong and willing to be physically aggressive. At the same time, many girls learn that being physically strong and aggressive has few social benefits for them. Some girls, especially girls bigger and stronger than their classmates, challenge these ideas by expressing their strength and being aggressive in their relationships with boys. This sometimes leads boys to fear them and girls to hide behind them, but these girls also experience forms of teasing and social rejection. Over time, strong girls are marginalized. At the same time, certain physical activities, including many sports, come to be defined by the children as "boys' activities."

Finally, Hasbrook emphasizes that the meanings given to physicality and expressions of physical abilities and skills vary with the social class and racial/ethnic backgrounds of the children. In other words, physicality is constructed through relationships that are influenced by gender, social class, and race and ethnicity. This is why ideas about physicality vary from one group to another in a society and from one society to another.

The connection between playing sports and learning about masculinity and femininity is the central theme in Chapter 2 by Alan G. Ingham and Alison Dewar. As Ingham watched his son play ice hockey and interact with his teammates on an organized competitive hockey team for 13- to 14-year-old boys, he became concerned with what these boys were learning about what it meant to be a man in sports and in society at large. Alan teamed up with Alison Dewar, then one of his colleagues in the Department of Physical Education, Health, and Sport Studies at Miami University. They brought the boys from this team together to have them talk about their experiences. Alison facilitated these discussions because she was trained in the use of interviewing and because the boys did not know her on a personal level as they knew Alan.

Many issues were explored during Alison's conversations with the boys. When the conversational data were analyzed, both Ingham and Dewar noted patterns of comments and inferences that revolved around playing sports and being a man. They concluded that as these boys played competitive hockey they were exposed to a narrow set of ideas about masculinity. The boys, however, did not see this as a problem. In fact, they eagerly used these ideas as a basis for how hockey should be played and for how they should assess themselves and their peers as they made their own transitions into manhood on and off the ice.

Ingham and Dewar make the case that contact sports in North America serve as a setting in which honor and shame are used to reproduce a form of masculinity in which power over others and the ability to dominate are primary bases for status and prestige. To the extent that boys apply this narrow definition of masculinity in their own lives, they idealize toughness and come to view anyone who is vulnerable or weak as unworthy of their respect. When this occurs, the locker rooms of men's contact sport teams become places for the expression of homophobia and negative attitudes toward girls, women, and anyone defined as weak or effeminate. At the same time, playing fields become sites for expressions of violence by those men who use this narrow definition of masculinity as a basis for their own identities. In this way, these men and their fellow athletes become potential victims of their own ideas about masculinity. Ingham and Dewar are depressed by their findings. They conclude the chapter by asking all of us to think about how sports might be constructed to prevent this waste of human potential.

Chapter 3 is written by Mark A. Grey, an anthropologist (and soccer enthusiast) who spent two years as a part of a research team that studied a Kansas town where immigrant workers from Asia and Latin America were recruited to meet the labor needs of a booming beef industry. He and the other researchers focused on the complex patterns of ethnic relations associated with this influx of immigrant families into a traditional Midwestern town populated by white people from Euro-American backgrounds. To learn about the dynamics of the relationships between the established residents of the town and the new immigrants, Mark did his observations and interviews in the local high school where many of the sons and daughters of the immigrant workers became students.

After he gathered field notes and talked with numerous people at the school, Mark discovered that the dynamics of ethnic relations in the town largely depended on two things:

- the ability of the immigrants to speak English;
- the willingness of immigrant students to participate in the traditional American sports offered through the varsity high school sport program.

Established residents of the town expected the new immigrants to fit into the culture that they had created in their community. They did not anticipate that the cultural practices and interests of the new immigrants would change their traditional ways of doing things in the town.

Grey discovered that the new students and their families could prove their willingness to become "real Americans" and be accepted by the established residents by supporting and participating in the traditional varsity sports at the high school. But these sports did not fit the cultural experiences and interests of many of the new students. They often preferred soccer instead of football and basketball. When the new families did not support the varsity sports, the established residents, including many teachers and coaches, were confused. When the new students expressed an interest in playing soccer, even though it was only a club sport with few resources, the established residents and most people at the school felt threatened. Established residents thought that if they "gave in" to this "foreign interest" it might erode the cultural foundations of social life at the school and in the community at large.

Grey concludes that in the case of this town, sports actually interfered with democratic inclusion into the school and the town as a whole. The lack of interest in the traditional sports offered through the school, combined with the interest in the "foreign" sport of soccer, contributed to the social marginalization of immigrant workers and their children. Grey's study shows how the decisions to play sports and the meanings given to sport participation are sometimes tied to complex social issues such as race and ethnic relations.

Chapter 4 is one of two autobiographical articles we include in the book. Kitty Porterfield never trained or competed in any sport until she was 44 years old. She grew up before Title IX took effect in the USA (the federal legislation that makes gender discrimination illegal in all schools that receive any funds from the federal government), so she had few opportunities to play sports outside of physical education classes in school. After nearly twenty years of watching and promoting the sport participation of her three children, Kitty decided it was her time to train and compete. Inspired by her children's involvement in rowing, she bought a boat with the goal of testing her own physical limits as a rower. She tells her story in an engaging and insightful manner. She explains what was involved in being a "crew mom" and making sure that her children had opportunities she never had. She also tells us how difficult it was for her to begin training and to enter her first race in her forties.

As Porterfield describes her feelings of accomplishment and pleasure as an athlete, she gives us a vivid inside view of sports. Her story illustrates how she integrates sport participation into the rest of her life, and how her job and family set limits on her participation. As with the elementary school children studied by Hasbrook and the boys studied by Ingham and Dewar, Kitty Porterfield's experiences and the meanings given to them can only be understood in the social and cultural context in which she lives them. Not only is her age important, but so is the historical point in time in which she grew up.

The last chapter of Part 1 is written by sociologists Janet Saltzman Chafetz and Joseph A. Kotarba. Chapter 5, like the final chapter of each part, is unique because it focuses on the experiences of those who support the sport participation of others in their families. Chafetz and Kotarba did a case study in which they analyzed the social and cultural implications of the role of upper-middle-class little league mothers who supported the involvement of their 11- and 12-year-old sons during a prestigious post-season baseball tournament.

Janet's son played on the team, so she had immediate access to all of what parents, especially the mothers, did to support their sons' early sport participation. She recorded information about what the mothers did, what the fathers did, and how much time, energy, and money were devoted to young boys who came to believe that they did in fact, as boys playing sports, deserve these expenditures of resources.

As Saltzman and Kotarba analyzed the data from the case study they found that the mothers of the players worked long hours on highly organized committees and sub-committees. Through these committees the mothers were responsible for maintaining "team spirit" and designing the consumption experiences of team members and team families. The mothers bought food, fixed meals, drove to restaurants, provided pre- and post-game meals, bought snacks and treats, bought and made other rewards and mementos associated with playing in the tournament, and made sure that the boys could go to movies and play video games in their "off-time" away from baseball. Some mothers organized some of the "baseball sisters" into a cheerleader squad, and others made sure that all the boys on the team had special door decorations for their homes, pins for their shirts, and scrapbooks commemorating their experience. Fathers occasionally helped at practices, but mostly enjoyed attending games, eating food prepared by their wives, and commenting on the sport performances of their sons.

Chafetz and Kotarba concluded that the nearly month-long tournament was the site of a set of experiences that reproduced clearly the notions that women are good wives and mothers to the extent that they facilitate enjoyable family consumption revolving around the leisure and sport experiences of their husbands and sons. It was assumed that these mothers, if they were really good mothers, would expect nothing in return. Through this experience the unspoken message to the boys on the team was that they were "son gods" whose sport participation would be supported by their families, but primarily by their mothers. In this way, the little league experience became a social site for "doing gender" and "doing social class" in a particular way. It maintained what the men, women, boys and girls in the town of "Texasville" came to believe, day after day, was normal and good.

In summary, these descriptions of early experiences illustrate that there is clearly a "social side" to becoming involved in sports. Early sport experiences are part of larger social processes that make up people's lives. The meanings given to those experiences are tied to how people define themselves, their relationships with others, and their connection with the larger social world in which they live their lives.

1

YOUNG CHILDREN'S SOCIAL CONSTRUCTIONS OF PHYSICALITY AND GENDER

Cynthia A. Hasbrook

First graders, Ann and Katherine, were "good at sports." When they played with us, I could tell they liked sports. Yet, they seldom chose to play. Why not? It puzzled me. After all, I reasoned, they were good and liked playing as much as I did. Why was I the only first grade girl who always played "one-fly up" and "kickball" with the boys?

By the end of first grade, we all knew who the "good" players were. We gathered each recess, selected two of the "best" players as team captains and, in turn, captains chose up teams. The least skilled players were always chosen last, and these players always seemed to be the same few boys. Knowing I would hate to be chosen last, I wondered why these boys would want to keep playing with us. In second grade, they no longer joined us and were labeled "sissies" and "girls."

By third grade, Katherine and Ann stopped playing with us altogether. While other girls did not seem to care for sports, it was evident that Katherine and Ann still, though secretly, liked sports. I was sad for them and puzzled as to how they could possibly give up doing something they did so well and liked so much.

Often scholars study what personally interests them and do so by using philosophical and theoretical perspectives with which they are comfortable. I have spent much of my academic career exploring several facets of those very questions I first asked myself as a youngster growing up in the 1950s and 1960s. While they may seem like simple questions, they have become more and more complex with each new study I have undertaken.

Initially, my research examined how childhood and adolescent sport involvement was influenced by a person's social class background and by significant others such as parents, peers, and siblings. I relied on a positivist approach and quantitative methods. I collected numerical data by using paper and pencil questionnaires that asked young people to report basic demographic information such as age, number of brothers and sisters, mother's and father's levels of education, and how many sports they played. The young people in my samples were also asked to recall who influenced them to become involved in sports. I then statistically analyzed my data and reported my findings in a number of published papers.

After several years of doing this type of research, I began to ask questions that could not be answered adequately with data collected through paper and pencil questionnaires. I wanted to go inside the experiences of children and learn what encourages or discourages their involvement in physical activity. I wanted to understand why and how children link physical activity and gender, and I wanted to know personally the children I was studying. I wanted to go beyond the numbers generated from questionnaires. But I had not been trained to go into the field and do qualitative research. Therefore, I spent two years learning to do ethnographic research that I could use to study the lived experiences of children as they engaged in physical activities and incorporated movement into their sense of who they are and how they are connected with other people.

As I reviewed the work of others, I found few ethnographic studies exploring children's social interactions within school settings. I also discovered that there were no such studies exploring young children's physical activity and gender. Fortunately, I was able to use a semester-long sabbatical leave to begin a study of how a group of first grade children developed ideas about their own physicality and gender. The study turned out to be a three-year project in which I followed the children through their third grade year of school.

To date, two papers have been written from the three-year project: the first (Hasbrook 1997) focuses on the children during their first grade year and specifically examines how girls' and boys' physicality and gender are constructed and linked; the second (Hasbrook and Harris 1998) examines how the children, as first and second graders, rely on their physicality socially to construct masculinity(ies). I invited Othello Harris of Miami University to join me in data analysis, interpretation, and writing of this second paper so that it would represent and benefit from the perspective of a black man as well as a white woman. This chapter describes the overall project and some of the most important information reported in these two papers.

The project

The project was conducted at a predominately black, inner-city elementary school (three-year old kindergarten through fifth grade) serving approximately 425 children (71 percent African-American, 13 percent Asian American, 8 percent Latin American, and 8 percent Anglo-American) from predominately lower income backgrounds (70 percent). I observed and interacted with the children during classroom instruction, lunch, restroom breaks, recess, and special events such as assemblies and field trips for four-month periods during the children's first, second, and third grade years. Observations were conducted three to four days per week during the first grade year, and one to two days per week during the second and third grade years. Observations commenced at the start of each school day and ended each afternoon as the children boarded buses to return home.

At the outset of the project, the first grade classroom teachers introduced me to the class by my first name, and I offered the children a partial, undetailed explanation of my project. My role as a participant observer did not fit a single category such as "friend." Although I entered the project with the intention of establishing a non-authority, friend role with the children, I quickly discovered that this would be impossible. Observing during classroom instruction time required that I should not distract the children. Yet, my mere presence created a disruption. Even when class was in session, the children took every opportunity to talk with me, hold my hands, sit on my lap, touch my hair, clothes, jewelry, sit near me, or walk with me. While the classroom teachers had some control over this situation, I also had to discourage the children from focusing on me. This was accomplished by talking with the children at the beginning of the second day of the project and, together, establishing some ground rules.

The ground rules we established, which prohibited the children and me from interacting during classroom instruction, required enforcement on my behalf as well as the teachers' and inescapably placed me in a position of authority. In addition, the children saw me as an adult and on some occasions would call me "teacher," expecting me to intervene in their arguments, stop fights on the playground, or help them with various classroom assignments. Initially I tried to resist these roles and explain that, although I was an adult, I was not a teacher but simply a friend. Most of the children could not comprehend such a distinction and were confused by my unwillingness to stop their playground fights or help them with schoolwork. I sensed that I was losing their trust and respect as someone truly interested in them and their well-being. Thus, I assumed a fluid set of roles that included at times being friends with the children and privy to their thoughts, understandings, and secrets, at other times being a rather remote observer, and at other times assuming a position of authority. This seemed to work, and by the end of the first month of observation the children understood that although I was an adult, I was not a teacher. We became closer, yet I was always distinguished as an adult; perhaps most clearly illustrated by many of the children insisting on calling me "Miss Cindy." In addition, several children told me I was "like their grandmother" and one child often called me her "second mother." The children were also cognitively mature enough to categorize me as white, and my race probably affected what I observed as well as what some children allowed me to see.

As first graders, the children did not yet possess very well developed verbal skills. Thus, I relied not only on what they told me and talked about with one another, but on a number of non-verbal sources of expression including stories they wrote, pictures they drew, and facial expressions, gestures and postures. I also conducted group interviews in the hopes that the children might talk more in groups than they did with me one-on-one. Three to four children were placed in same-gender groups and interviewed to seek additional information and clarification regarding their physical activity preferences, ideas concerning what types of physical activity were "appropriate" and "inappropriate" for girls and boys, and understandings of terms and phrases used by some of the children. Interviews were audio-recorded using a microcassette recorder and later transcribed.

Initially, the children were fascinated with and greatly distracted by my research equipment (notebook, mechanical pencil, tape-recorder, and 35mm camera). To accustom them to this equipment, I allowed them to write in my notebook and look at what I was writing. They often asked what I was writing about, and I responded by reading them selected excerpts from my notes. I let them tape-record their voices and take photographs of one another.

Nearly five hundred, single-spaced, typewritten pages of field notes were collected during the course of the three-year project. Five types of field notes were made:

- an abbreviated account of daily observations and impressions;
- a more developed account of daily observations;
- daily descriptions of methodological concerns, problems, and ideas;
- ongoing observational insights and questions;
- a provisional running record of data analysis and interpretation.

As observational data were gathered, notable and recurring interactions were identified that yielded categories of focus for further observation and informal interviewing.

Project terminology

In this chapter I use three terms that can have various meanings:

- social construction;
- gender;
- physicality.

I want to share the specific meanings these terms have in this project.

Social construction

Social construction refers to the processes or ways by which the children developed meanings and understandings of physicality and gender. Through interaction with one another, the children established and reinforced what is physically involved in establishing a gender identity as a boy or a girl. That is, through their own actions and behaviors, they created an unstated but well understood set of rules or code concerning the ways girls and boys "should" and "should not" move. For example, when a boy cannot throw a ball well he is often teased for "throwing like a girl," thereby establishing and reinforcing the rule that boys should be able to skillfully throw balls. When a girl walks with a long stride, arms moving back and forth in a wide arc, she may be accused of "walking like a boy." This works to socially construct, or establish, reinforce, and reproduce a rule concerning how girls should not move.

Gender

Gender is an everyday aspect of children's social relationships. Children organize much of their daily interaction and activities to signify, reflect, and express themselves as boys or girls. For example, first through fifth graders most often physically separate themselves by gender when they line up, eat lunch together, or gather on the playground. Here gender is not simply a variable or a social role; it is social practice that emerges as children learn how to "do" gender in their everyday lives. An analogy might help to clarify gender as social doing or a social construction. A house is usually a four-sided building with doors, windows and a roof and may be thought of as an object or a variable. When children "play house," however, the meaning of "house" changes to signify a set of activities and social relations occurring among family members living in the house. Just as children learn to play house and, in the process, socially construct and reproduce a set of family relations, girls and boys learn to separate themselves into same-gender

10

groups and physically move in gender-specific ways that help to socially construct gender.

Physicality

Physicality is multifaceted. It is posture and gesture and involves ways of moving. Physicality is not simply a function of the biological body. It takes shape in connection with social factors such as gender, social class, race and ethnicity. Physicality involves two things:

1 How one moves.
2 The sense of who one is and how one is related to others as he or she moves and communicates with others through movement.

For example, over time children learn to associate different physical movements with their ideas about masculinity and femininity. The long-term result of this is that most people possess an exquisite knowledge of rules and a well-practiced and developed repertoire of gestures, postures and movements related to who they are as women or men.

Our social class, race and ethnicity also influence physicality. For example, several scholars point out that many Black men and some Black women, particularly those from lower social class backgrounds, adopt a certain set of physical gestures and postures denoting toughness, control, and detachment. They suggest that such physicality is a means of responding to and coping with institutionalized racism (Harris 1992; Majors and Billson 1992).

The focus of this project was on physicality among a culturally diverse group of young children. Physicality is at the heart of all physical activity, including sports. If we are to understand children's decisions to become involved in sports, as well as the meanings such involvement may have for them, then we need to understand how children from diverse social settings form ideas about physicality and gender and link the two concepts.

Some project findings

The children I talked with and observed formed ideas about, or socially constructed, physicality and gender simultaneously and reciprocally. They learned to define gender in terms of differences between girls and boys (masculinity *versus* femininity) at the same time as they developed ideas about physicality and used them to guide and interpret their own movements and those of others. They relied heavily on the notion of difference between boys and girls to construct and reinforce gender in their lives. However, some children also engaged in behaviors that challenged and contradicted traditional, dominant ideas about physicality and gender that are based on notions of difference between girls and boys.

Constructing physicality and gender as "difference" between girls and boys

Although there were not noticeable differences between the first grade girls' and boys' physical abilities and skill, they most often engaged in different types of physical activity

11

that helped to construct and reinforce masculine and feminine identities and physicalities. Boys tended to engage in contests of physical strength and performances of athletic skill, and unprovoked physical aggression that girls rarely engaged in. Boys also often verbally "put down" girls' physicality, while it was most unusual to observe a girl putting down a boy's physicality.

Contests of physical strength and performances of athletic skill

One example of boys engaging in a contest of physical strength involved Nicholas lifting his classroom chair up to head level with one arm and exclaiming: "Look at this!" A classmate, Wallace, responded saying: "Anybody can pick up that chair." He and a third boy, Peter, then took turns trying to lift the chair (neither was successful). Another example involved José placing a crayon under his index, ring and little fingers and over the middle finger of one hand and then striking his hand, palm down, on the table in front of him and exclaiming: "See, I broke it." Martin and Wallace noticed this, and then each successfully broke crayons in a similar fashion.

Several boys from various class, racial, and ethnic backgrounds engaged in performances of athletic skill. The concept of "performance" is used here because boys typically engaged in such behaviors as if they were acting out a movement for the sake of display rather than for the sake of the movement itself. They called attention to their performances, engaged in them individually, and often competitively performed them to determine who could best execute the movements. For example, boys often went through the motions of shooting or dunking a basketball, occasionally using a tennis ball, stuffed animal or Lego as the ball. A wastepaper basket or some other open container served as the basket, and boys would take turns or simultaneously shoot or dunk as they compared their skills. They often fantasized about being famous athletes like Michael Jordan or Shaquille O'Neal. Boxing and martial arts movements were often displayed. On one occasion, a boy assumed a boxing stance with fists up, and shadowboxed, and proclaimed: "Look, I'm Mike Tyson." On another occasion, four boys began performing martial arts kicks and punches and made the following statements: "I can do it better," and "That's not how you do it." One of the boys, Bareep, told me he was "practicing for the Olympics."

Most of the girls did not engage in contests of physical strength or performances of athletic skill. Nor did they fantasize about athletic performances or being a star athlete. Many of the African-American girls, however, engaged in two types of physical activity; dance and a small group game called "Let's Get the Rhythm." These activities were not engaged in by boys or by white, Hispanic or Asian girls. On occasion a group of girls would gather together, begin singing a song and simultaneously dance. They did not compete with one another nor call attention to their performances; rather they danced together for the sake of dancing. For example, "Let's Get the Rhythm" was a game in which a small group of girls would stand in a circle, holding hands and sing a repetitive phrase that started out as: "Let's get the rhythm of the arms." They would then drop hands and go through a set of dancelike movements with their arms. This routine would be repeated several times, each time with a new part of the body replacing the formerly named part (e.g. "Let's get the rhythm of the legs").

Unprovoked physical aggression

Several boys tended to be physically aggressive toward inanimate objects, less "popular" or lower social status boys, and girls. Such physical aggression was usually unprovoked and took the form of shoving, pushing, hitting, and chasing. The intent of this aggression was most often intimidation, self-assertion, and demonstration and maintenance of one's status and dominance over others.

In the "reading classroom" there was a carpeted area with three child-sized stuffed bears resting against the wall. The children played with these bears when assigned to the area for "quiet reading." A number of boys punched, mimicked strangling, and wrestled with the bears. Only two of the less mature, smaller boys cuddled with the bears, and each of them hit the bears on occasion. In contrast, girls treated the bears with nurturing affection as if they were their friends or young children to be cared for. Girls would snuggle with the bears, pretend to put them to bed by tucking them in and kissing them good night, or feed them by offering make-believe cups of drink and pieces of food.

African-American boys from lower income families who possessed high social status among their peers often physically threatened and accosted lower status boys who tended to be non-aggressive, smaller, of differing racial and ethnic background, and/or have physical and cognitive disabilities. A field note entry provides an example:

> During recess, Marcus decides to chase Eddie for no apparent reason. Dennis sees what's going on and joins Marcus in the chase. They wrestle Eddie to the wet blacktop and Marcus punches him hard again and again. Dennis punches him too, but more like he's "going along" (not very hard). Eddie is angry and sticks up for himself, trying to fight back and run, but winds up soaking wet, very tired, and crying. When Marcus and Dennis stop chasing Eddie, they spot Trang and chase him. They wrestle him to the ground and Marcus hits him. Trang, like Eddie, fights back but can't hold off both boys. Trang winds up standing and soaking wet. He looks angry, confused and hurt all at once. Marcus gets very close to him and yells (hateful) in one ear: "Chinese boy."
>
> (First Grade, February 1993)

African-American boys from lower income families who possessed high social status also exhibited physical aggression toward girls. The following two field note entries describe how Chantel, Regina, and Rakella, popular high status girls in the first grade, were physically threatened and/or accosted by high status boys:

> Now the class is going to fine arts. The fine arts specialist has taken a leave, so there is a new teacher who is much stricter. Martin comes into the classroom late and approaches Regina at her seat and says: "Get out of my seat!" He makes a half gesture with his forearm and hand as though he's going to hit her. Regina immediately and calmly obliged, showing no resentment or anger. The seat was not Martin's.
>
> (First Grade, March 1993)

13

The kids are back at their tables. Jamel gets up from his seat and walks over to Chantel's table, picks up a box of felt markers, and takes one out. Chantel protests, Jamel puts down the marker, hits Chantel in the back of the head with his hand, and walks back to his table. He starts punching Rakella in the arm. Rakella does not react to the punching. Jamel continues to hit her harder and harder trying to get a reaction out of her – she absolutely does not react. She finally slides her chair away from his, but he slides his over and continues to punch her about as hard as he can. The teacher becomes aware of the situation and stops it.

(Second Grade, May 1994)

The boys' behavior was not challenged and seemed almost acceptable to Regina, Chantel, and Rakella as well as the other girls and boys in the class. Social permission was accorded these boys to exert physical power and control over the girls. Such exertion of physical power and control over girls (and social permission for it) is not difficult to understand. Many of the African-American children were growing up in families with men and older boys who face racial discrimination and its effects daily. Many such men and boys adopt masculine identities that express resistance to their marginal and subordinate status and assert power and control over women (Ghaill 1994).

It is important to note that not all African-American boys adopted such an aggressive, dominant masculinity. Those from more "privileged" middle and upper income levels with access to conventional symbols of masculinity were less likely to exhibit this masculinity (Harris 1992). It is also important to point out that a few girls would not have tolerated such aggression and acts of subordination. They would have immediately responded physically and verbally to Martin's or Jamel's physical aggression. These girls, however, were seldom physically challenged by boys and never physically challenged by the most dominant, high status boys. High status boys avoided interactions in which girls could physically challenge their status and dominance. The boys' recognition of some girls' potential abilities to physically challenge and overcome them partially contradicts traditional ideas about gender. Yet, because the boys avoided situations where girls might physically dominate them such contradiction was kept in check and traditional gender (and power) relationships maintained.

"Putting down" girls' physicality

Boys intentionally and publicly made girl–boy comparisons in play, game, and other physical activity related contexts that "put down" and discredited girls' physicality. Such public put-downs positioned boys as physically superior and girls as inferior. They "constructed" dominant masculine and subordinate feminine forms of physicality, and reinforced gender in terms of difference. For example, one day the children were working on math papers at their tables. Four children were assigned seats at each table, and at most tables there were two girls and two boys. The teacher directed the students to clean up their tables, which involved one child from each table taking materials back to a classroom counter. As an incentive for cleaning up, the teacher told the students that the first table to finish cleaning up would receive a reward. At one of the tables, Chantel got up to take materials to the counter. Bereep, excited and wanting to win, stood up, put his hand on Chantel's arm to stop her and exclaimed: "I can run faster, I'll go!" She sat back down, without apparent reservation or dismay, allowing Bereep to run to the counter. Bereep was considerably shorter than Chantel and definitely not faster.

In another example, during a physical education class the children were directed to form five-member, mixed-gender teams for a set of relay races. The teacher asked the children to sit down in straight lines once they had formed their teams. One team consisting of three boys and two girls initially formed their line with the two girls, Su Ling and Chie, seated in the first and second positions. Martin and Wallace, noticing this seating arrangement, stood up and got Su Ling and Chie to move to the end, placing the boys in the front of the line. The two girls were two of the more socially and physically reserved members of the class. However, neither was physically unskilled. Showing no physical or verbal resistance, they quietly moved to the end of the line. After class I asked the girls why they had moved to the end of the line and they told me: "Because the boys wanted us to; we didn't care." Ethnographers have noted that certain types of sports and physical activities are not widely valued or recognized in the cultures of Asian immigrants, especially among girls. Thus, it is not surprising that Su Ling and Chie offered no resistance and agreed to move to the end of the line in a competitive relay race. I also asked Martin why he and Wallace had moved to the first two positions in line and he said "because we're faster than those girls."

Challenging traditional ideas about gender and physicality

Madeline was ten to twelve inches taller than most of the other children and two feet taller than some. She was heavy and outweighed each of the other children by at least fifteen pounds. She was strong and physical and wrestled with and easily overcame boys willing to wrestle with her.

The most popular boys carefully avoided wrestling with Madeline. These boys made fun of her by calling her names that reflected their attention to and concern about her size and physicality. On one occasion when Martin had watched Madeline wrestle another boy, totally controlling him by sitting on him, Martin loudly proclaimed to the class that she "sounds like a whale." On another occasion, the children were sitting on the carpet listening to a story. Madeline moved to sit next to a group of boys that included Martin. Martin did not like this and announced: "Madeline is a tomboy." Madeline seemed crushed by the remark, put her head down, moved away to a space by herself, and was uncharacteristically quiet the remainder of the afternoon. I asked Martin what the word "tomboy" meant and he responded: "Madeline looks like a boy."

Madeline's physicality, especially her ability to physically subdue her male peers, contradicts and challenges traditional ideas about physicality, gender, and gender relations. Such ideas include: girls are not supposed to be big, strong, powerful, or physical; such attributes are shameful and a source of offense to others, particularly boys; girls who display strength, power, or physicality when interacting with boys may be disliked, chastised, and/or marginalized.

Conclusions

The children simultaneously and reciprocally constructed physicality and gender by establishing, reproducing and reinforcing embodied differences between girls and boys. Both the type and meaning of boys' and girls' physicality differed. Social constructions of physicality and gender were often complex because differing social class, race and ethnic backgrounds gave varying cultural meanings to physicality, gender, and relationships between gender and physicality.

Some girls by virtue of their size, strength, physical skill, aggressiveness, and/or decisions to engage in activities viewed as "boys' activities" actually challenged and contradicted traditional ideas about the meaning of physicality and traditional notions of gender as *difference* between girls and boys. The boys tried to minimize these challenges and contradictions putting down and discrediting the most competent girls. The boys also tried to avoid situations in which a girl might challenge their own physicality. The boys worked hard to maintain traditional notions of gender as *difference* between them and the girls.

The kind of study that I have done with elementary school children is relatively rare. Few sociologists have studied the lived experiences of children from and "inside perspective." Although sociologists conducted a few quantitative studies of childhood sport socialization in the 1970s and 1980s, there has been little work on this topic during the 1990s. My goal for this project is to enhance our general understanding and appreciation of children's physicality and its significance in the social construction of gender.

Educational practitioners, particularly current and future elementary school teachers interested in gender equity issues and programs, may find information from this project useful. For them, it is especially important to know what happens inside the physical activities of the children they teach.

References

Ghaill, M. (1994) *The Making of Men*, Philadelphia, PA: Open University Press.

Harris, S. M. (1992) "Black masculinity and same sex friendships," *Western Journal of Black Studies* 16: 74–81.

Hasbrook, C. A. (1997) "Gendering practices and first graders' bodies: physicality, sexuality, and bodily adornment in a minority inner-city school," unpublished manuscript, University of Wisconsin-Milwaukee.

Hasbrook, C. A. and Harris, O. (1998) "Wrestling with gender: physicality and masculinity (ties) among inner-city first and second graders," *Men and Masculinities* 1(2).

Majors, R. and Billson, J. M. (1992) *Cool Pose*, New York: Lexington Books.

2

THROUGH THE EYES OF YOUTH

"Deep play" in PeeWee ice hockey

Alan G. Ingham and Alison Dewar

Initially, I (Alan Ingham) was engaged with the hockey program as a parent although, in gender stereotypical fashion, it seemed like my spouse, J.C.I., was doing more of the driving, dropping off, and picking up of our son than I was. Spending time at the rink, on the road, watching games, occasionally visiting the locker room, serving on the town's youth hockey association's board, I was primarily "hanging around." At first I thought I could spot all kinds of flaws in both the coaching and organization of my son's teams, even though I had never skated in my life! Eventually I resigned myself to the fact that I could not do anything about the coaching, and I focused my attention on the team organization and the interpersonal relationships between the boys.

As I watched my son and his teammates, it seemed to me that there was more conflict within the team than between the team and its opponents. Why was this, I asked. Why did team members abuse each other verbally and physically? The observations I made from just "hanging around" did not provide sufficient information. I felt that the boys had to speak for themselves. But I was working on projects of a theoretical nature, and I had little first-hand experience doing ethnographic research. So I turned to my colleague, Alison Dewar, to help me explore systematically the experiences of the boys on the team. She could do the ethnographic interviews that we needed in order to understand some of the things I had observed. Thus, most of the data used in our first research report came from her work with the boys.

Interviewing boys, boys in the process of becoming men, presented an interesting challenge for Alison. Gaining their trust was not really a problem because she was acquainted with some of the boys. Feigning ignorance of what boys do at the age of fourteen was more difficult for Alison because she had studied gender issues for a number of years. What we did was to take my observations, use them as focus points for the development of open-ended questions, while trying to not let our presuppositions influence the boys' responses. Because I had been hanging around the boys over several seasons and had developed "outsider" explanations for their behaviors, I was not involved in any of the interviews.

After the first series of interviews were completed, Alison left Miami University, so the study was never completed as we had planned when we started. Reported here is a summary report of what is best described as a pilot study involving a few of the boys. This report comes from a longer paper that we presented at the North American Society for the Sociology of Sport's meetings in Washington, DC, 1989. We hope others may pick up from where we left off. There is much more published work in the area of masculinities than when we initiated this project, so we expect that other research will present findings that go beyond our findings in this study.

There is more to the game of hockey than meets the eye, especially when the view is refracted through the lenses of 14 year olds. They know that the game has a content and form because of the coaching they receive. But they also know from their lived experiences that there is a deeper game – a complex, social relational affair both on and off the ice. Intuitively and cognitively they have knowledge that connects the game to wider cultural practices. In short, they are aware of what it takes to obtain status, honor or prestige, and, conversely, how it feels to be shamed or embarrassed.

We think that sociologists' intellectual and socio-political biographies are intrinsically involved in choosing and framing the research questions that stir their passion. We mention this because we started this project after I used conversations with my son to see PeeWee ice hockey through the eyes of a participant. (PeeWee is the name of the division in which 13 and 14 year olds play organized competitive ice hockey.) We took the issues raised by him and added our own interests anchored in sociology, psychology and pedagogy. The primary reason for our study lay in my observations of interpersonal violence (both symbolic and physical) as I watched practices, went on road trips, and sat through games as a dedicated spectator. I asked: "Why did so much interpersonal conflict occur on a team that was supposed to be a coordinated and cohesive unit when engaged in competition?" Many ideas surfaced, but Alison and I thought it was important to let the boys speak for themselves, give their rationales for their behaviors, and then try to make sense of their responses from what we knew about social relations theories. In short, we tried to let the boys' insights lead our interpretations rather than imposing our interpretations on their behaviors.

In this chapter we focus on one theme, *hegemonic masculinity*, that is, the form of masculinity that comes to be dominant within a group or society. My initial observations led us to pose many questions. Alison asked questions about equipment as a status symbol and about coaches' instructions concerning "hitting" and "making respect." She asked about the ways that conflicts on the ice spilled over into other contexts such as school and socializing with friends. She asked about moms and dads and their involvement in the masculinization process and how playing time affected the boys' self-concepts. But when we selectively coded the data from the interviews, the theme of "masculinities" emerged as the underlying explanation for much of boys' assertive and aggressive behaviors on and off the ice.

Here, it should be noted that we labeled many of the boys' responses with the concept of "hegemonic masculinity" and used it as our storyline because "what it was to be a man" figured so heavily in their accounts. It could be that their focus on masculinity was an age-related, developmental thing. After all, it is at the PeeWee level (ages 13–14) in the USA that athletes first encounter the "checking" game and, in their ambiguous boy–man status, confront the anxiety of status passage into manhood as linked to the labeling process that occurs in connection with their behaviors. "Goon," "tough," "wimp," and other labels were key in this passage. Also, PeeWees are caught in the transition from doing sport "for fun" to doing sport "as work." Discipline of the mind and the body becomes more salient at this point in young athletes' lives, at least in the minds of the coaches. Drills supersede "play." It is at this point in their lives that these boys learn to labor, to do "men's work," especially if they progress from the club to the all-star team. As they progress in age or performance levels, the use of dispraise and sarcasm by coaches also seems to increase. Maybe dispraise and sarcasm weed out the men from the boys – "if you can't stand the heat, get out of the kitchen." Thus, there were both external and internalized inducements that encouraged the boys to be concerned with what it took to be a "real man" in today's society.

Hegemonic masculinity and victimology

Even today, there is a concept of manhood that is contoured by residual and dominant standards of heterosexuality and the idea that a "real man" is assertive, aggressive, competitive, lustful, and violent. Mark (Jacko) Jackson, the bad boy of Australian rules football, probably epitomizes the standards with these words: "I'm not an animal, I'm an individual but I fought with no fewer than eight of the other team's eighteen players on the field and was badly disappointed that I couldn't catch the other ten." Media representations of masculinity, with an emphasis similar to the one in Jackson's quote, rub off on the boys. This is illustrated in the following exchange that occurred in an interview between Alison and one of the boys:

Alison: I mean hockey is a rough, rough game . . . from the sidelines looking at it. I've never been in it.
Player: It's like in the top five in the world in roughest sports. I mean because Aussie rugby is the toughest.
Alison: Because they have no padding?
Player: No padding and they fight. That would be cool. I know it would be.

Life in modern society may no longer involve the dramatizations of the passage from boyhood to manhood that often exist in the formal initiation rites found in many traditional societies, but that does not necessarily eliminate the "felt want" of many would-be "men" to find ways to exhibit the transition by proving that they are "real men" on a fairly regular basis. It is the notion of "felt want" which reinforces the values of a particular form of masculinity. The felt want for masculinity begins early in the biography of a hockey player:

Alison: How did you get started?
Player: I saw an ice rink. I'd never seen an ice rink in my life. I went to the ice rink skating. Mother said, like well you have to do figure skating first . . . So.
Alison: Oh, how did that feel?
Player: So I did figure skating. It's OK, I didn't mind. I didn't even mind the insults and stuff I got from the kids.

Alison:	What did they say?
Player:	Stuff like, "Oh you little pansy, you play hockey but you figure skate on the side."
Alison:	So if you guys figure skate, then the first thing they say is you're a pansy.
Player:	If you don't play hockey.

This "felt want" for masculinity continues as the status criteria used in school combine with the boy–man quests for esteem in the hockey subculture. This connection was evident during the interviews as Alison talked with one of the boys about how he first started playing hockey. His teammate joined in and "interpreted" what being a hockey player meant in his mind:

Alison:	How did you get started?
Player:	I started from him.
Alison:	So you saw him playing.
Player:	Yes.
Alison:	So you wanted to try this.
Player:	Yes. I followed his games and then started getting interested in it and he started teaching me how to skate.
Teammate:	Turned him from a pansy into a *normal* person. From a football player into a hockey player. You play football if you want all the ladies. You play football. If you just want to play a sport, you can pretty much take out all of your aggressions and still do well and play hockey.

Sociologists have long made the case that we are born male or female, but we learn to be a man or a woman. Our sex is a biological given, but our gender is a social construction. What emerges then is a concept of hegemonic masculinity, not as a male role, but as a particular variety of masculinity to which others – among them women, young and effeminate as well as homosexual men – are subordinated (Carrigan *et al.*, 1985). Because a particular version of masculinity is socially constructed as the preferred version of masculinity, prestige or status is acquired by conforming to the "ideal" type. Prestige is allocated to men by acclamation and victimization. This process not only socializes boys and men, but also serves as a basis for social control in the society at large. A man's identity is thus connected to a fear of departing from the hegemonic standards. Even if only a small number of men conform to and, thereby, reproduce a narrow definition of what it is to be a "real man," the hegemony of a narrow definition can induce many males to reaffirm the power of this definition through acts of complicity (Carrigan *et al.*, 1985). These acts of complicity may involve fictitious sexual conquests, fictitious victories in fights, and fantasies such as "this senior in high school is hot for me and I'm only a freshman."

Over twenty years ago, a respected sociologist explained the dynamics of this process in the following way:

> To perform and be ranked at the highest levels . . . demands both talent and dedication which only a few can muster. Such "heroes" are given more prestige or admiration because both the level and type of performance are rare and

evaluated highly within the relevant group. Most admirers recognize that such performances are possible for only a few.

(Goode 1978: 67)

Goode is referring to skill, but in this chapter we are referring to *machismo* in which males rank different masculinities in terms of their relative prestige. These masculinities are then contested even between those who play different heavy contact sports. This was highlighted in the following interview segment when one of the players explains that playing hockey requires more "real toughness" than playing football:

Alison: It's sort of interesting because we often think of hockey as being quite a tough kind of sport, so I would have thought that the girls absolutely thought that it was great – that hockey players were great . . . No?

Player: Only because they make football rougher than hockey. They don't understand the concept that just because they make contact in football every two seconds that it's rougher than hockey. Ever notice that a fight in football is slapping the helmets. They slap each other's helmets. Like in hockey, gloves hit the ground, helmets come off and blood spills.

We will return to the "girl" question later. At this juncture we note that "toughness" – a will to engage in violence – is entrenched in our hockey adolescents, and that the structured, prestige hierarchy of school sports connects with the prestige hierarchy of masculinity.

Alison: What happens to the kids, the guys, who don't play basketball, football or hockey?

Player: You'd better learn how to fight!

We followed up on this player's response because many males get through the adolescent years without being involved in a fight. It seems that males are victimized by hegemonic masculinity, but some escape the actual physical consequences of violence to the body. Why is this? Do the macho males simply ignore the brains, nerds and geeks because there is no prestige in taking them on – so you beat up on a wimp, who cares? Leave the "brains" alone, they are weird anyway. According to the logic of hegemonic masculinity, "real men" get "Cs." For example:

Alison: What happens if I'm a bookworm?

Player: A bookworm – you don't get a girl.

Alison: So you've got to learn to fight to prove yourself or play a sport.

Player: Either that or you have to be a person who's liked by everyone. Otherwise you're considered a nerd or geek and no one will talk to you.

Alison: What's a nerd or a geek?

Player: A kid who doesn't play any sports. I mean all they talk about . . . a book/ author they read last night. Then there are the tennis players and golfers.

Teammate: Soccer players. No the soccer players are like the same as us – no actually they're more popular than us.

Alison: So tennis players and golfers are like . . . ?

Teammate: Geeks! There are some popular ones who play other sports. But after that they're like geeks. That's how football and basketball players consider hockey players. [We] hockey players just look up and say "play tennis."

So the prestige sports (i.e., revenue producing sports that are heavily promoted at high schools) contour and shape definitions of masculinity. For example, those who play heavy contact sports often ridicule non-contact sports and those who play them. In social psychological terms they use sarcasm as identity degradation. They make caustic remarks about fellow males whose sport participation does not demand true manly behavior according to the definition of masculinity they use to assess themselves and their own behaviors.

There is skill involved in this masculinity approval game. Identity work is involved in the quest for esteem and the earning of deference from peers and others in the community. This was clear in the way the hockey players talked about how respect was earned among teammates:

Alison: On the team you played for, what's the thing that you admired most?
Player: Taking shots [read: being able to take a hard hit from an opponent].
Teammate: Your shot, your goal average, how well you can kick ass. You have to hit hard. You have to be able to put five kids in a crying position before the end of the season.
Alison: Is that right? You've got to show that you're tough and can take it out there?
Player: There's some that'll call you pussy even if you do. I've put about fifteen kids down and a couple of them had to be carried off, and [he] put like five down. He [another boy] put a lot down. I mean these aren't rough hits. I mean they're not like rough like in sticks up.

Thus, our respondents know the fine line between legitimate and illegitimate acts of violence, but it appears to us that the boys construe the walking of the fine line as a refined skill. As one boy put it: "These are legal hits but they hurt." We shall return to this point, but one player's comment fits nicely here. It relates to crossing the fine line:

Player: If you're caught. I'm pretty good at eluding refs from what I do because . . . it's not like major action [that could bring a big penalty] but it hurts.

As we noted earlier, proactive violence leads to reactive violence. Much of the proactive violence is instrumental violence – a means to an end, a way to win, and a way to socially construct an identity that will bring respect and "moral standing" among peers. Much of the reactive violence develops from this instrumental rationality. It is affectual or emotion-based violence in that it satisfies emotions such as anger. This combination of the instrumental and the affectual produces a spiral of violence. The instrumental use of violence is "part of the game" "you must intimidate your opponents!" "Learning how to take it" as well as "learning how to give it out" is part of "being cool." But walking away from intimidation engages the dilemma: "Are you cool or are you a wimp?" Managing cool from the vantage point of the narrow, but hegemonic, definition of masculinity produces, perhaps, the "don't get mad, get even" syndrome, as noted in this interview segment:

Alison: You don't get mad, you get even. That's the way you play hockey. Can you explain that to me?

Player: Well if you get mad, you're the one in the [penalty] box.

Alison: OK, I see. So if you pull your gloves off?

Player: Either way, if you stick them back, you're the one in the box. They [referees] only see the return. They never see the first. So what you do is you wait a couple of shifts, you get them in position, then you give them back what they gave you.

But getting back without receiving a penalty is something of an art.

Alison: So there's a fine line between getting a penalty and getting back? If you get mad you're going to get a penalty.

Player: If you get mad, you snap your cord out. You'll be sitting [in the penalty box] for a couple of minutes. Depending on who the refs are, you can actually get back to a certain extent before they'll even blow the whistle.

Alison: How do you get back without getting a penalty?

Player: When a goalie sticks his stick out . . . when a goalie does that to me . . . when you know he's going to do it the next time . . . so you just raise your stick. Like I was taught this up at my camp. No one had taught me this before, but the defense coach, he coached Junior A, told me a way. What you do is you wind and take a short slap shot which means, instead of doing a bailed hay shot you come to your waist, let it go, but what you do is a curved motion like you were just following through, and you just lock your arms.

Whether grounded in affectual or instrumental terms, violence begets violence. The problem, as we noted previously, is that the quest for social esteem and the social process of according deference are important bases of social control in social groups and society at large. They produce conformity within the hockey subculture as it connects to the prevailing standards of hegemonic masculinity within North American culture. Failure to conform to these standards results in embarrassment, and embarrassment is involved not only in the contest of character; but also in the contest for character. The two sides of the social control coin – honor and shame – produce an extraordinary system of influence which, in turn, produces mutual pride in conformity and a real fear of rejection if one does not conform. This, we believe, reproduces the cycle of violence that is so much a part of hockey in North America.

Alison: Your all-star coach?

Player: I love my all-star coach. He beat up on me and sent me down the boards like this [demonstration].

Institutionalized violence and subcultural violence thus connect in a normative prescription for behavior. Australian sociologist Bob Connell helps to explain this connection and what it means for how men think about their own bodies and how it influences the dynamics of gender relations in society:

Prowess . . . becomes a means of judging one's degree of masculinity. So the concern with force and skill becomes a statement embedded in the body, embedded through years of participation in social practices like organized sport . . . The meanings in the bodily sense of masculinity concern, above all else, the superiority of men to women, and the exaltation of hegemonic masculinity over other groups of men which is essential to the domination of women. The social definition of men as holders of power is translated not only into mental body images and fantasies, but also into muscle tensions, posture, the feel and texture of the body.

(Connell 1987: 85)

In short, hegemonic masculinity is not only a caricature of heterosexuality, but it also promotes homophobia. This leads us to our last points concerning the boys' status anxiety as it connects to the penis and *"scoring* with the ladies". These topics were mentioned unexpectedly by the boys in this interview exchange:

Alison: What is interesting to me that as a girl, as a woman, you never know what goes on in the locker room. Sometimes it's better you don't.

Player: He came into the locker room with a 6″ wide cup. It was about this big [hand show] I mean it covered half his legs too. The day before that he had one this big [hand show] . . . it was sort of golf ball size. "RY, you're not near his size. What are you doing?"

Alison: So there's big pressure?

Player: I mean if somebody goes . . . What's wrong with you do you wear a small cup? It's like, well you can wear a small cup that fits nicely and does the job or you can wear a big one that rubs your legs raw.

Alison: Well one of the things you mentioned, "pencil dick." I mean does a lot of that go on? You guys tease each other a lot by the sounds of things, all about cups and stuff.

Player: Yeah. Actually cups aren't *the* big thing.

Teammate: No. Girls! Like RA asked, "Is she still a virgin, or did you have to get her drunk?" Stuff like that.

Alison: None of this shocks me.

Player: You have been around enough hockey players.

Alison: The stuff I teach is about how women are often treated as sexual objects and they're often sort of the butt of jokes in the locker room. We think it has changed a little, right? Because of equality, but clearly it hasn't changed at all.

Player: Right.

Teammate: If you're the most caring guy in the world . . . like we really won't take advantage of a person . . . But we still crack jokes.

Player: I mean like small jokes about someone else, someone else's girlfriend. I mean it's just normal, just to piss the guy off.

Alison: That's how you guys relate [to each other] then?

Player: No, it's how you get a guy pissed off.

Alison: Tell me more about the locker room. You guys fight your own team?

Player: Remember the time you jumped that one kid?

Teammate: I jumped on RA and I jumped M, too. One time because he was running his mouth. So the kid was joking, but it's a touchy subject. One time RA comes up and goes – like I had just broken up with K, and he goes, "Oh well she's just a stupid bitch" and I went, well . . .

Alison: So he called her a stupid bitch?

Player: And the next day he asked her out.

Teammate: And she went out with him. Which means he was on the floor again next day.

Alison: So you fight over girls then?

Player: Girls are a touchy subject in the locker room. M with one . . . "boner."

Alison: What does that mean? I don't know the language.

Player: Screwing at age 14. M walked in with a big smile on his face.

So the cycle of violence, in this case intra-team, is connected via the penis, the competition for women, and the use of women, to enhance one's social esteem in the peer group. A woman becomes a prestige marker for men. The conquest over a woman who ranks high on the male-defined desirability scale is an objective to be pursued, sometimes at the expense of interpersonal and intra-team cohesion. While it may have been established that violence on the ice does not induce violence off the ice, the competition for heterosexual status spills over into interpersonal and school relations via the objectification of and competition for women. Yet, when we get to the bottom line, females can be sacrificed. Their importance is secondary, even though sexual conquest is crucial. The boys confirmed this with the following statements:

Player: We make time for the ladies, but apart from that . . .

Alison: OK. So if you've to spend time – you've got to spend time on hockey, time for girlfriends, and time for schoolwork, if one of those three had to go, which one would go first?

Player: Girls!

Alison: OK. So girls would go before hockey, clearly?

Player: Yes. Everything would go before hockey.

Is the heterosexuality status game subordinated to the game per se? Is the play more important than the "deep play?" We do not think so. The behavior and the comments of the boys show that there is clearly a subcultural socialization process in ice hockey that reproduces both a hegemonic definition of masculinity and homophobia. The homophobia is clearly expressed in this interview segment:

Alison: You were able to hit. What about other things that are interesting in sport? People always feel that if you play sport that you're a real man. What would happen if one . . . is there anything about sort of baiting guys who people think are gay? Or what would happen if there was someone who was gay on your team?

Player: If someone was gay on our team? They'd be dead. I played football last year and this one kid came up to me . . . wow! "The only reason you're playing football is so you can see the guys undressed in the locker room."

Alison: You lost it?

Player: So the guy's a fag. As long as he stays away from me, I don't care.

The challenge of transforming culture

We end this chapter with a few questions. How do we, as practical sociologists, assist male adolescents to transcend the narrow, but hegemonic, definition of masculinity in North American culture? How do we assist them in a way that will thereby alleviate the social pressures which produce spirals of violence? How do we assist them in a way that will alleviate the "felt want" to be superior over other men, and alleviate the related "felt want" to be superior over women and young, old, or effeminate males? How do we overcome homophobia? Practical transformation does not occur simply through intellectual discourse. How do we convert our esoteric theoretical knowledge into practical strategies that enable us to deconstruct hegemonic masculinity in ways that could lead to a real reconstruction of masculinity in gender egalitarian terms?

We know that language has power, but the power of language is practical power only if the user of the language has power. Presumably, I (Alan) have some power over my own son. In fact, my son knows about my social democratic politics, my support for feminist moral and political claims, and my acts of resistance to hegemonic masculinity. But if I was unable (apparently) to effectively combat hegemonic masculinity in my own house because the male peer group had "outposts" in my son's head, how do we eliminate hegemonic masculinity over the larger terrain of social relations? (We use "outposts" here to refer to an ideological predisposition that is formed in people's minds after repeatedly hearing and seeing messages that support dominant cultural definitions in a particular society.)

Paradoxically and ironically, given how we object to males victimizing males, we might have to start with the "prestige male" in the culture. The boys gave us this clue:

Alison: What would happen . . . You're in the locker room and people are making all these jokes "have you got any yet," "have you got any pussy" and "you're a 'pencil dick'." What would happen if someone said, "look guys this is pretty bad." Would they laugh at you?

Player: Well if B stood or if I stood up and said it they'd probably shut up.

Alison: So it depends on your status on the team. Why would they listen to B?

Player: He has 14″ biceps!

Who do boys/would-be men listen to? It seems that they listen to "real men." If we are trying to undermine hegemonic masculinity, and boys are listening to the very men who epitomize hegemonic masculinity, we have a situation akin to the fox guarding the chicken coop. Even if we tried to train the fox, we would probably be unsuccessful. Coaches may be of little help here, especially if they think it is their mission to separate the men from the boys. And as for professional hockey players, the role models – aren't they paid to fight? Doesn't fighting bring in the crowds? Even those who do not fight have goons on their teams to protect them and sustain their careers. Isn't this seen as necessary according to the logic of hegemonic masculinity?

As long as respect and retribution are seen as "normal" parts of ice hockey, men will be victims of their own hegemonic masculinity as will all that they touch. This includes the boys whom they coach and father, the women with whom they live, and those who are weak and vulnerable in their worlds. This, to us, seems to be a depressing waste of human potential.

References

Carrigan, T., Connell, R. and Lee. J. (1985) ''Toward a new sociology of masculinity,'' *Theory and Society* 14: 551–604.

Connell, R. (1987) *Gender and Power*, Stanford: Stanford University Press.

Goode, W. (1978) *The Celebration of Heroes: Prestige as a Control System*, Berkeley: University of California Press.

3

PLAYING SPORTS AND SOCIAL ACCEPTANCE

The experiences of immigrant and refugee students in Garden City, Kansas

Mark A. Grey

When I flew home from wrapping up my dissertation research in Southern Africa, my wife met me at the airport. She had some rather interesting news. A few days prior to my return, she said, "Some guys called from Kansas and they want you to work for them." The next thing I knew, I was working in Garden City, Kansas, in the South-western corner of the state. I became so intrigued by what was happening there that my career took a fundamental change in direction. Although I finished my dissertation about school graduates in Swaziland, I never went back to Africa; there was too much exciting, research to do in the rural American Midwest.

When I tell my students that my research in rural America can be just as exciting and rewarding as it was in Africa, they are often incredulous and look at me strangely. But my experience in Garden City taught me two important lessons about being an anthropologist:

- that valuable anthropological research can be done in domestic settings and travel to foreign and exotic lands is not always necessary;
- that some of the most important questions about ourselves and our society can be answered through qualitative research, but only if we are willing to ask them.

As I found in Garden City, it was the questions that people did not like to ask that usually revealed the most about them and their community. In Garden City – like so many rural American communities – I found that some of the most difficult questions people did not like to ask were about the role of sports in their lives and schools.

This research grew from a two-year study of the Garden City community that took place between 1987 and 1989. I joined a team of five anthropologists and one geographer. Since I had a particular interest in schools, I was assigned to study ethnic relations in Garden City High School (GCHS). Since GCHS was the town's only high school, I was able to study a sort of micro-model of the entire community.

While my colleagues studied particular populations, such as Southeast Asian refugees, Anglo packinghouse workers and Latinos, I was able to examine the interaction of all the community's diverse populations in one setting.

Although I examined the institutional setting for accommodating immigrant and refugee students – such as the school's English as a Second Language (ESL) program – it soon became apparent to me that sports played a significant role in ethnic relations as well. For many in the school – students, teachers and administrators – participation in mainstream sports became a kind of litmus test to determine whether immigrant and refugee students were serious about assimilating into American culture. Throughout the school year and its various sports seasons I was able to observe how advocates of sports used them to determine status in the school and community. Because of their lack of interest in most established sports, immigrant and refugee students were seen as outsiders.

Interestingly, my own sports interests affected my status as well. As a soccer enthusiast, I noted how established residents viewed newcomers' (and my) interest in that game suspiciously. To many, particularly football backers, soccer seemed to be a threat since it was relatively new to the community. To many staff and students, soccer seemed to threaten the very American nature of sport. Yet to others the lack of a soccer team sent a clear message to newcomers that they were not welcome.

This study was published in 1992 as "Sports and Immigrant, Minority and Anglo Relations in Garden City, Kansas High School" (*Sociology of Sport Journal* 9(3): 255–70). The research, however, has influenced my thinking about sports for nearly ten years. I can never just go to a high school game of any kind now because I spend most of my time looking for clues about status in the school and community. With the exception of a good soccer game, I consider most of the sports I watch as *ritual*, and not simply games.

I have also found that this perspective provides a number of ways to provoke arguments in class. When I teach my courses on the social context of schooling or rural sociology, nothing makes students more animated than a critique of school sports, and in particular their role in dividing up status. Of course, most students from small-town Iowa simply took sports for granted and accepted them as an expected and integral part of school life. But when I use the Garden City High School study to demonstrate how sports can provide a status system that often discriminates against minorities and others who do not participate, many students often see things about sports that they had never observed before.

Garden City, Kansas

Western Kansas is a flat, featureless land. There are few points that extend above the horizon other than huge wheat silos that dot the countryside every twenty miles or so. It can be hot, dry and windy. There are no lakes to speak of, so the fishing is lousy. There are not a lot of people, and the nearest large city (Denver, Colorado) is several hours away.

Yet in the middle of this apparent desolation, the economy thrives. Agriculture has long been the central feature and wheat fields extend as far as the eye can see. In the past, oil and gas exploration also contributed, but the more recent boom for the local economy has been cattle and beef production. The highest concentration of cattle production and beefpacking in the world is in Southwestern Kansas. Within a hundred-mile circle, there are four major beef plants and millions of cattle in large commercial feed lots. At the center of this great circle is Garden City, the shining buckle on the Kansas beef belt. The Garden City area hosts two large beef plants, including the world's largest plant operated by IBP, Inc. This plant alone can slaughter and process 5,000 cattle per day. With this kind of capacity, Garden City has become surrounded by large cattle feeding operations: within a 50-mile radius of Garden City, there are more than 1.5 million cattle.

When the huge IBP plant opened in 1980 there were plenty of cattle, but the local population was not large enough to provide the thousands of workers required to operate it. The only solution was to import workers from outside Southwestern Kansas. Throughout the 1980s, thousands of newcomers came to Garden City. Indeed, the community's population grew by 50 percent in a five-year period, making it the fastest growing town in Kansas at the time. Its current population is about 25,000.

Although the number of newcomers was important, what was more significant was the ethnic nature of this new population: many (if not most) of the newcomers were Southeast Asian refugees and Latino immigrants. In a few short years, Garden City went from being a bicultural town with Anglos and established Hispanics, to a multicultural and multilingual community. Of all the institutions that were affected by this changing demography, Garden City schools were the hardest hit. Total and minority enrollments grew rapidly. More schools had to be built and new programs were started to address the needs of students who did not speak English.

Changing Relations Project

In light of the changes experienced in Garden City, the Ford Foundation funded an in-depth study of ethnic relations called the Changing Relations Project. Six social scientists were involved, including myself. We each took different parts of the community to study and I worked in the community's only high school, Garden City High School (GCHS).

The purpose of the overall study was to determine the nature of relations among the town's diverse ethnic populations. Generally speaking, there was a great deal of accommodation among groups; that is, they "got along" not because people actively sought each other out but because they left each other alone. Despite the expectations of pessimists, there was very little conflict. Individual families created connections with members of other ethnic groups, but there was no community-wide social integration.

Although the different ethnic groups kept their social distance in the community, there were two institutions that brought them together on a continual basis: work and school. Meatpacking plants have a high degree of cultural diversity and we observed some interaction among workers from different cultures, but there was one problem: packing plants are very noisy and workers wear ear protection. This and the physically demanding nature of the work meant that workers could not really carry on conversations throughout most of the workday.

Schools, of course, are much more conducive to holding conversations, but did this necessarily mean that different ethnic groups developed close relations. It certainly did not in GCHS. In many ways the high school reflected what was going on in the community that surrounded it. Here in the school were representatives of the community's ethnic groups, but just because they all shared the same space did not necessarily mean that they would become friends.

When I first started my research in GCHS I expected that the primary barrier keeping new immigrant and refugees students separated from the others would be language. In 1988–9, there were ten different languages spoken in the school. To some extent, this prediction proved correct and understandably so. It would be difficult for people to become close friends if they could not communicate well.

But the more time I spent in the school, the more I began to realize that differences in languages did not adequately explain the lower status of most minority newcomers. Indeed, even those new minority students and the established resident Hispanics who spoke English well often suffered from a relatively low status. Something else was going on and I suspected it had something to do with sports.

To find out, I started spending as much time as I could at games, watching practices and interviewing teachers, administrators, coaches and students – athletes and non-athletes alike. This ethnography of GCHS was balanced by observation and interviews. It was also informed by participant observation. I became a part of the school as much as I could: I played pick-up basketball with teachers, went to lunch with the students and met some of the staff for dinner or beers in the evenings. I even helped construct the booster club's float for the homecoming parade. I attended as many school functions as I could, including pep rallies in the gym, and traveled with some of the teams to away games.

Throughout the year I spent at GCHS, each little thing people told me or that I observed gave me another piece to a larger puzzle. In some ways, I became a part of school life and people got used to me hanging around. But once in a while they could not believe that some of the things they thought so commonplace could interest me the most. For example, I shall never forget watching a large wrestling tournament one evening in the main gym and taking notes. A teacher noticed my note-taking and came over to me with a puzzled look on her face: "What on earth do you find so interesting in a wrestling meet?" What I found so interesting in her question was the implication that nothing of significance could be found in something so "normal," so matter of fact.

This was exactly the point that emerged from my research: sports were considered so normal that people either did not see – or did not care about – how they helped to create a status system. Sports, it seemed, were just another natural way for different students to assume their inherent place in the community. The only way to realize this was through an extensive personal study of the school using observation and interviews. In many ways, the interviews and observations greatly complemented each other.

Sports and student relations

Like most rural high schools, interscholastic athletics were an important part of school life. The high status of sports was not just found in the school, but in the community as well. Curiously, I found that sports were not necessarily touted for the idea that they can be fun and promote physical fitness. Instead, sports were often justified as another form of extracurricular activity that would help students develop an identity with the school and maintain their interest in academics. In GCHS, participation in sports was also promoted as a way to bring down the school's notoriously high drop-out rate. Some teachers and administrators were also convinced that a winning football team would lower drop-out rates. How? Because students would take more pride in the team – and therefore the school – and want to stay part of something they felt proud of.

Although sports were publicly approved because of these qualities, I found that they were often really used by students, teachers, administrators and community members to assign students a particular status in both the school and community. For those students who played on high profile sports like football and basketball, their status was quite elevated. But those students who did not play sports and who even rejected sports were often suspect.

Immigrants, refugees and sports

Most teachers and administrators expected that a certain number of students would not or could not play sports. That was "OK," because either these students could find some other school-based activity or they belonged to the subclass of "losers." Immigrant and refugee students, however, were often looked at differently. Because they were new to the school, and the society for that matter, people often gave them an initial benefit of the doubt. But it was also clear that there were only a few ways that these newcomers could demonstrate that they wanted to become real members of the school and, by extension, "Americans."

One way these newcomers could demonstrate this willingness to assimilate was through learning English. Some of the refugees already spoke English, particularly if they had learned it in their home countries or if they had been in the USA for several years. Other newcomers were learning English in the school's English as a Second Language (ESL) program. Some Anglo students appreciated this, but were often impatient with the pace of the newcomers' progress.

Beyond learning English, however, my research indicated that participation in sports was also a critical test for determining the newcomers' willingness to assimilate. Although no one used these terms exactly, there always seemed to be an assumption that sports were some kind of universal language appreciated by all cultures. What most people in the school did not realize, of course, was that different cultures often appreciated different kinds of sport forms and that they often interpreted the purpose of sports differently.

Many people in the school considered sports the door they opened for newcomers to gain entry into school life, but the terms were often uncomfortable for newcomers. Here was a way for immigrant and refugee students to gain entry into the mainstream of school life. Established resident students and teachers found the widespread refusal of newcomers to accept this invitation confusing. Implied in this invitation, however, were two important matters:

1   If newcomers were to be accepted in the school, it would be on the terms of the mainstream teachers and students.
2   Acceptance in the mainstream also required immigrants and refugees to forget about the sports which were important in their home cultures.

Both of these attitudes were exemplified in remarks by the head football coach:

We don't get a whole lot of Oriental-type kids involved [in athletics] . . . but we keep making the attempt to involve those kids. They just haven't grown up in a culture where that's an important part of their life and they probably don't feel they are included in that, but if we could try to break the ice and get two or three in it, I think athletically they would have a lot of talent and they would probably do well and it might open the door for others.

(Grey 1992: 262)

What, exactly, is the coach saying and not saying in this quote? First of all, he recognizes the cultural dimension of newcomers' lack of interest in American sports, but does not suggest that these different cultural perspectives are legitimate. Nor does he say that the school should change its sports programs to accommodate these different cultural interests. It is apparent that he is interested in two things:

- getting more newcomer students in sports so they can develop an appreciation for American culture;
- immigrants and refugees could contribute to established sports teams with their athletic talent.

This whole business about whether the school should accommodate the sports interests of immigrants and refugees was particularly telling. The sport that interested most male newcomers was soccer. In the years before my arrival, GCHS had a soccer club. It was not a "team" that had regularly scheduled games with other schools. As a club, it did not have a paid coach but a sponsor, usually a member of the teaching staff who was willing to spend the time to make it work. During the year I was in GCHS, however, the teacher who usually sponsored the soccer club – and appreciated the new students' interest in this sport – was away. No other teacher among the seventy in the school was willing to sponsor the club and it died.

When I talked to people about their attitudes towards the soccer club, I found out a great deal about how people felt about this sport and, more importantly, how the soccer club was considered a troublesome development. Clearly the soccer club was a way for the school to accommodate the sports interests of Southeast Asian refugees and Latino immigrants. It was a very public way to recognize these cultural differences and a sanctioned way to allow these differences to express themselves. But many people were very uncomfortable with the existence of the club for exactly these reasons. They believed that allowing a soccer club somehow threatened the established sports. But how? The vast majority of students who played soccer did not play mainstream sports, so soccer was not a threat in terms of taking athletes from other teams. In addition, there was very little interest among mainstream students in playing on the club, so they would not be pulled from other sports either. Finally, the club received virtually no funding from the school, so it did not pose a threat in these regards either.

So what did people find so threatening about the soccer club? I found that the real reason most people did not want a soccer club was this: if the school provided this accommodation for the cultural differences of immigrants and refugees, then the usual way people gave students a status in the school and community – through mainstream sports – was in jeopardy. The polite term used by people when they talked about soccer was that it was a "non-established" sport. By allowing this sport in the school, most people would have been forced to use a different calculus to assign an appropriate status for newcomers. Perhaps more importantly, it would have also meant that the school was changing to meet their culture rather than forcing them to become more like us.

There were two particular ironies to all of this. First, the soccer club was the one school activity that involved many refugee and immigrant students. School administrators emphasized the importance of extracurricular activities in students' lives, but the soccer club somehow did not qualify. It did not matter that students wanted the club. What mattered to most teachers and students was that the soccer club was too much of a cultural accommodation and therefore did not legitimize the status quo. In other words, this particular activity did not reinforce the values that school personnel wanted their activities to express.

The other particular irony about attitudes towards the soccer club concerned its role in assimilating newcomers. When the club was active, many school personnel who were uncomfortable with it did find one positive element: participation in the club required students to speak English. Here is how the football coach put it:

> One of the big things [about the soccer club], which was a good thing last
> year . . . was the deal that while you are there at soccer practice or in
> the game, everybody has to speak English regardless of what country you're
> from . . . Well that turned out to be a positive thing for the kids in that they
> had to practice using expressions and so on that maybe they normally wouldn't.
>
> (Grey 1992: 263)

What the coach is saying here, of course, is that he did not value the soccer club because it accommodated the sports interests of immigrants and refugees, but because students were required to speak English. One irony of this, of course, is that students from various countries and who speak a variety of languages would probably want to speak a common language in order to work well together as a team. As I know from countless pick-up games of soccer, players do not have to speak the same language in order to play.

Sports and democracy

Many of the people I met in GCHS believed that sports were the "great equalizer" that could democratize the student body and therefore society. In many respects this is an extension of the schools-as-great-equalizer argument. Schools – and sports – are supposedly blind to class and ethnic differences. What matters is the willingness to become involved and work together for the success of the team and school. What counts is the willingness to try.

For some members of the GCHS student body, sports did give them a leg up on the status ladder. In particular, established resident Hispanics with low socioeconomic status often benefited from participating on sports teams. By doing so, they were able to escape – at least for a while – their relatively marginal status in the community. At least during the time they were high profile athletes, some even enjoyed celebrity status.

There was usually a presumption that immigrants and refugees could also use sports to raise their status. In many respects, newcomer students started out with two strikes against them: they were minorities who often did not fit in linguistically and culturally; most were presumed to be lower class because of their association with the meatpacking industry. Not only could these students demonstrate their willingness to assimilate through sports, but they could also temporarily escape their relatively marginal class standing.

In most cases, however, sports did not democratize the student body but exacerbated the already established social pecking order. The GCHS research helped me understand the two most important flaws in the sports-as-democratizer argument. First, by their very nature, school sports only allow a limited number of participants. Although sports allowed students from lower class groups to gain a higher status at GCHS, the criteria for achieving this status were rather narrow and highly selective: athletic ability and a willingness to commit to the team. Using this narrow means to allow status transformation meant that the majority of students never achieved the high status associated with sports.

The other fundamental flaw in the democratization argument concerns the status of those who did not participate versus those who did. Most teachers and students may have expected that most Anglo students would not play sports, but different expectations were placed on immigrant, refugee and other minority students. Namely, sports were offered as an opportunity for these students to demonstrate their commitment to assimilation and their desire to become part of the mainstream. The message was clear: "If you want to be like us and have a higher status in the school, here is the one way you can do it." The student body could be democratized, but only under the conditions set by those who already had a relatively high status.

When most of the minority students did not accept this invitation, the usual response could have been summed up this way: "You had your chance. By not accepting our offer, you have condemned yourself to this lower status. You're getting what you deserve!"

Not only did the non-participation of these students in sports leave many of them isolated and marginalized, but the limited number of students who could participate in high profile sports necessarily led to the creation of a student elite. Instead of flattening the distribution of status among students by bringing the elite and low status groups closer together, an emphasis on sports actually made the differences between them worse. Instead of democratizing the student body, sports assured that many students could never fully enjoy a status equal to most of their peers and certainly not with the sports elite.

Conclusion

There was a great deal in this investigation that I never could have achieved without ethnographic research methods. Using traditional approaches such as surveys, I would have never heard people say what they really thought in the context of their experience. By becoming a part of the school environment, I was able to develop a good rapport with many students, teachers and administrators. With this rapport came a degree of comfort that gave me access to behind-the-scenes activities and the private thoughts of these people.

The relationship between the school and sports existed without much public opposition. So strong was this relationship – and the assumption that one cannot go on without the other – that even those who opposed the emphasis on sports usually had to say so behind closed doors. Some feared losing their jobs; others feared alienating friends and colleagues. But for most there was nothing special at all about sports. To them sports were as much a part of school as textbooks and homework, perhaps even more so.

Even critics had their limits though. They were often willing privately to criticize high expenditures for new football equipment or how much time was wasted at pep rallies. But when it came to sports and the status of refugees and immigrants, there were few who recognized or were willing to criticize how sports put these particular students in a double bind. Even for critics, these new students' non-interest in sports was often bewildering. This attitude, of course, pointed to exactly how sports could marginalize minority students. As long as people were unwilling to accept these students' different cultural understanding of sports, they would not be likely to appreciate how sports force newcomers to the bottom rung of the social ladder.

Reference

Grey, M. A. (1992) "Sports and immigrant, minority and Anglo relations in Garden City (Kansas) High School," *Sociology of Sport Journal* 9(3): 255–70.

4

LATE TO THE LINE

Starting sport competition as an adult

Kitty Porterfield

Unlike other authors in this book, I am not trained as a social scientist, but I have had a range of experiences related to sports and I am clearly aware that history and culture influence how we include sports in our lives. Jay and Peter asked me to write this chapter partly because my experiences as a competitive rower did not begin until I was 44 years old. My reasons for becoming an athlete are tied to a combination of history, culture, and personal experiences. This chapter is based on a careful retrospective look at my experiences over more than five decades.

The only success I had in sport growing up was playing volleyball in the sixth grade. That was probably because I was taller than the other girls on the team. In college, freshmen were required to take gym: I chose a semester of fencing (where did that come from?) and one of relaxation and stress management (the most practical course I ever took).

I came to rowing as a mom and volunteer. I chaired the local crew parent booster club and other support committees as my children made their way through high school and collegiate rowing. I was twice elected Vice President of the US Rowing Association, the national governing body for the sport. I retired from that post, sadly and quietly, when my son's national team coach made it clear to Michael and to me that he did not like women making decisions, and my position threatened Michael's place on the squad. That was the very darkest moment in my life in sport.

Today, I work out regularly – though not often enough – and have become a T'ai Chi enthusiast. Physical exercise is now as much a part of my life as my cereal bowl in the morning. As for the rest of it, I am presently the Director of Community Relations for the Fairfax County Public Schools, a large and complex public school system in northern Virginia. I have worked in education for the last twenty years, designing programs and managing school communications. Public education is another passion. My husband and I live in northern Virginia under the watchful eyes of our three grown kids.

I started rowing – never having trained or competed in any sport – when I was 44 years old. My first race was the Head of the Potomac, a three-mile race down the Potomac River in Washington, DC, starting at a point near where the river broadens and becomes navigable just below Three Sisters Rocks. The course winds past the Washington Canoe Club, the Potomac Boat Club, beyond Georgetown and Georgetown University, past Watergate and Foggy Bottom and ends where the river widens just beyond the Kennedy Center. Head races are run single file, rowers working against the clock. I was in a single scull feeling very much alone. I had been rowing less than a year, and this was my first organized competitive experience.

About a third of the way down the course – mercifully just out of sight of the cheering crowd on the boat club dock – I caught a crab (a bad stroke that throws the boat off balance) and flipped my shell. It was late September, and the water was cold. Some local fishermen on shore saved me that day – not because they plucked me out but because, when my head broke the surface and I drew a breath, I heard their laughter across the water. Enraged at their derision, I lifted myself back into the boat and finished the race. That race is not a bad metaphor for my entrance into sport as a master woman athlete: long, cold, wet, sometimes lonely, sometimes in hostile territory, but finally successful and enormously satisfying.

I grew up at a time when most young women were taught that sweating and head-to-head struggle was boy stuff. Physical exertion was not feminine, I was told, and not the way to attract a husband (which was, then, what growing up female seemed to be all about). As a teenager in the 1950s, I slept with my page-boy haircut wound around big wire curlers with prickly, pink brushes protruding from the core. Having made that painful commitment to beauty every night, I had little incentive to blemish my exterior by exercising in the morning. My role model was my petite classmate, Judy Buxton, who dressed in pastels and petticoats and whose long, blond corkscrew curls were never out of place.

Most of us who were girls in the 1940s and 1950s and went to public school never gave thought to being on the playing field. As a kid I rode my bicycle and played softball at Sunday school picnics. My prettier classmates who were athletically inclined became cheerleaders. The rest of us filled the stands at football games. Though I resented the perks that my father and brother had in other arenas, it never occurred to me that the masculine order of the sport world might be unfair.

Our only brush with sweat was gym class, which we girls universally hated. For fifty minutes, three times a week, beginning in junior high school, we "dressed out" in heavy cotton, royal blue uniforms with short skirts and bloomer pants. We played half-court basketball or, in the spring, two innings of dispirited softball, ran as little of our bodies through the shower as possible under the watchful eye of the gym teacher, and dressed again to go to math class.

In college, in order to earn a degree, I was required to take one year of physical education. I chose a semester introduction to fencing (which I actually quite enjoyed) and one of "relaxation techniques" (something akin to yoga).

So at the age of 44 I had never tested my physical limits. I had no idea how much stress my body would endure or if it would break under pressure. I had arrived at adulthood with no understanding of physical training and no experience in team sports. I had no appreciation of the physical high of pushing hard, the mental rush of a good race, or the sense of power and satisfaction that comes from conquering a skill or setting a personal best.

Furthermore, I froze at the thought of competition. As I grew up, our family mythology was that competition was motivated by an unhealthy desire to get the better of a rival. The notion that aggression was healthy and normal, that competition could be fun and friendly, that losing a race could be an opportunity to grow or a mile marker in the search for excellence, never crossed my screen. I had a lot to learn.

I came to sport and rowing because our three children – now adults – were rowers in high school and in college. All told, our family celebrated eighteen high school and collegiate rowing seasons, as well as four football seasons, five wrestling seasons, one track season, gymnastic training and three grade school soccer seasons (one per child).

Our eldest daughter, Karen, being first, came out on the short end of the sporting experience. She did not gravitate naturally to an available sport, and she received no encouragement from her parents. (I did not understand then how to coach.) She turned instead to theater and rowed only a year in college. In that year, however, she helped to organize her school's young crew team.

Our second daughter, Deb, in contrast, determined long before she entered eighth grade, a key time for deciding to play a sport, that she would row. Public school rowing in Alexandria was among the first secondary school programs established in the country (1947). The city's single high school, T.C. Williams High School, has one of the largest, best-equipped and fastest secondary crews in the country. It is also a program where young women get an equal shake. Indeed, the women's team has won far more championships in its twenty-five years of rowing than the young men's team has in fifty.

During Deb's first year in the sport we learned how to adjust family meals around practices, plan vacations around regattas, and unhook a young athlete's ego from a coach's temper tantrum. Two years later, her brother Michael joined the team. Unlike, Deb, Michael was not new to sport. By his eighth birthday he had learned to mark the passing of time by the recreation league seasons: football, basketball, baseball. Through high school Deb remained devoted to her one beloved sport. She trained off season only to row better. Michael quickly became a three-letter man: football in the fall, wrestling in the winter, rowing in the spring.

Dinner-table conversation in those years was filled with sport talk. By osmosis I learned from each season. Rowing demanded concentration, focus, patience, teamwork and the daily endurance of pain. Football cultivated toughness, aggressiveness, coordination and chutzpah. Wrestling – the sport that I could least bear to watch – perhaps taught me the most: personal courage, self-reliance, quickness, skill and the ability to pick yourself up off the mat over and over again.

In the spring their dad and I traveled every weekend, following our children's team – eventually up and down the Eastern seaboard – standing on the race course shore for hours, often in unrelenting snow, rain or heat. I was a busy crew mom and early on took an interest in the organization of the sport. I served as president of the local parents' booster club. Later, I served as Vice President and member of the board of directors of US Rowing, the national governing body of the sport. But I got tired of cooking spaghetti and brownies for the team, organizing car pools, planning regattas and raising money for equipment. I got tired of watching the fun from the shore. When Michael graduated from high school and left for college, I determined it was my turn. I resigned my local board duties and got into a boat.

I remember the day well – an open house at a local boat club. Experienced club members were taking guests out in eight-oared shells, four guests at a time, to give them a feel for the boat. I sat in the six seat, behind a classmate and former teammate of Michael's. I remember instinctively watching his back for cues. I remember calling up from somewhere inside the mental images of all the races I had watched and hearing all the coaching words that had flown around our dinner table over so many years. It worked. Of the novices in the boat that day I knew best what to do.

We rowed slowly down the tree-lined reservoir in the summer sun, four oars moving at a time, the other four keeping the boat balanced. The oar handle seemed huge in my hands, the shaft and blade a formidable ally. But the power of the stroke was unmistakable. It was awesome. I was hooked.

By this time Deb was rowing at Radcliffe College. The Radcliffe Boathouse, a turn-of-the-century stone and masonry building, sits at the corner of Memorial Drive and J.F. Kennedy Street, at the foot of the Larz Anderson Bridge in Cambridge, Massachusetts. On most afternoons during the collegiate year young women – strong, tall young women – are everywhere, finishing workouts, fixing rigging, launching boats. There is an air of good humor, purpose, intensity. It was a world I missed when I was young.

As I began training and learning to work my own body, the Radcliffe coaches extended an invitation to me to use the team's land training equipment when we visited Cambridge. I felt shy the first times I made my way to the locker room to change, but I loved being there. These women were so much larger than I. They were strong and beautiful and, by association, for the first time in my life I felt I must be too. I was bound to these young women by the pleasure and pride of taking charge of our physical selves. Some of them have become lifelong friends.

Michael rowed and studied at Northeastern University across the river. I felt equally welcome at the NU boathouse and sometimes worked out there on the ergometers (rowers' indoor training machines) and stretched out on the mats. One of Michael's teammates taught me how to throw a baseball "like a boy."

There were still few women of my age rowing so these younger women and men became my support system – even as I became part of theirs. I modeled for the women the adventure of breaking barriers, of being first. I taught them the organizational and fund-raising skills needed to support their program. I taught them how to use their political power. They taught me that it was fun to test your physical limits, to grow strong, to compete with friends and then to laugh together. They modeled teamwork on the water. I showed them the art of boardroom competition. We all learned valuable lessons.

Back home in Virginia the boat clubs were still full of men. My earliest and staunchest supporters were male athletes and coaches, some my age, some half my age, some nearly twice my age. They helped me rig my boat, coached me, taught me the course on a strange river, trained and raced as partners, and shared beer with me after the race.

It had not been long, however, since boathouses were solely a man's domain, and even in the 1990s there was a price to pay for invading the dock and the club room. One day, long after I had become a member of the Occoquan Boat Club, I rowed to the dock in my single to find a 35-year-old male with the shape of a lapsed rower looking out over the river. "Nice boat," he said, as I got out. "Whose is it?" It did not occur to him that it could be mine.

I was elected to the board of a regional association governing high school rowing, the second woman ever and the first in many years. At my first meeting an elder member of the group advised me that, though he was happy to have me come, I would not be allowed to vote.

In that still male world a major issue for me was one of images. I needed pictures in my head: pictures of women, strong women, women mastering the sport, leading the way. It was hard for me to see myself as an athlete, to use the word to describe me. (I still stumble. Not long ago I wrote a piece about working out in the gym – it was in the third person.)

Soon after I was elected to the USA Rowing board of directors, the women's crew team at the US Naval Academy in Annapolis asked me to speak at their annual awards dinner. I drove to the Academy early in the day to watch the women practice from the coach's launch before we dressed for dinner. That night I talked about the images we hold of ourselves as athletes.

I had gone back through ten years of rowing magazines to look for pictures of women rowers. What I found was that – even where there was parity in the numbers of men and women rowers – the men were photographed looking determined, sweaty, often in the midst of a race, while the women were posed standing by their boats, smiling, clowning, wearing the latest in brightly colored rowing gear. In the forty-seven magazines I had examined, I told the female cadets, there were fewer than ten photos of women whose bodies "make my body remember that moment in every race when I am sure I cannot finish." We need to celebrate in pictures women taking risks – women risking losing or winning – women pushing through the wall and dropping their oar into the water again. Our goals are not reinforced by what we see, I said. We are left only to imagine what we are striving for.

The climate has changed some in the years since then. Now women Olympians make the cover of the *New York Times Magazine*, a women's high school basketball team is the subject of a book, and even stories about women athletes over forty make the papers from time to time. In mainstream white America, at least, we are becoming more comfortable with the images of women's sweat.

The young women who came to college in the late 1980s and early 1990s had opportunities to participate never before so widely available to girls. But these women still arrived with little experience in organized sport. "Before I can teach these girls to be rowers," one coach said to me, "I have to teach them to be athletes. They've never learned. It is hard for them."

For my generation, the gap was even larger. My friends and I grew up in an era of little competitive sport for women. It was after the active generation of the 1920s and 1930s, and before the generation that benefited from Title IX (the federal anti-discrimination law that was passed in 1972). We were middle-aged before we began the journey.

On the Occoquan Reservoir, near my home, I trained with three other women and an unpaid coach in a boat built for men. We juggled work schedules, personalities and various degrees of commitment to the venture. One of us, a soccer player, understood the rules of game. The rest of us struggled to learn how to be coachable as well as how to rig a boat. Because of all those dinner-table conversations with my children, I knew to keep my mouth shut in the boat, not to complain about my boatmates, the length of the workout or about fatigue. I knew to focus on the practice one stroke at a time, to listen carefully. I understood that, over and over, I literally had to pull my own weight.

One problem we encountered was a lack of local racing opportunities for women. Our first race together was at the annual Masters' National Regatta on Mirror Lake at Lake Placid, New York. We traveled separately to New York, borrowed a boat and met over breakfast on the morning of the race. I was appalled to watch "the bow" and "two-seat" eat a huge meat and potato breakfast right before the race, a training error I had learned at home to avoid. Two hours later I was sitting at the start, scared and tense in the cold rain, wondering why in heaven's name I had chosen to come. Two-thirds of the way down the course I caught the crab that put our boat out of contention. (Was this a racing pattern?) I went home miserable.

Not long thereafter I bought my single – in part a gift from my mother who was delighted with my new passion – and determined to manage my own training. A male coach and friend became my double partner. We trained and raced together often in the masters' mixed double event.

One of my early supporters, Jerry Ulrich, was a member of the Cambridge Boat Club in Cambridge, Massachusetts. Jerry, then in his seventies and a veteran rower, arranged for me to borrow a sleek and finely crafted wooden shell from the club in Boston for my first (and so far only) run at the Head of the Charles.

Outside the Harvard–Yale race, the Head of the Charles is perhaps the best known and most prestigious of all American rowing races. It is rowed, like the Head of the Potomac, against the clock for three miles down the Charles River in Boston every year on the third Sunday in October. The competitors include high school novices, world champions, collegians, octogenarians, both men and women, classed by age and ability. In preceding years I had watched all three of our children row the course.

For Boston it is a community event – a day for picnics and reunions, for cheering friends and perfect strangers. The shores of the river are lined with tens of thousands of people, some watching the races, many partying, but all together creating a din akin to what one must hear on the line of scrimmage at the Super Bowl on fourth and goal to go.

Rowing to the start of the Head was one of the most frightening trips I have ever taken. The competitors in the master class gathered in the river basin near the MIT boathouse at 11.15am: 49 men and 10 women. The men would go first down the buoyed shoot to the starting line since they would move faster. The numbers on our bows set the order.

The day was grey and cold. There was a fair chop in the basin. From his launch the referee explained the rules of the start. As we proceeded in order down the chute, we were to increase our stroke rate. If we time it right, we would cross the line at racing speed.

The competitors eyed each other. Some of us were silent. Some were jovial – nervously loud. Everyone seemed dead serious. Only the real-life need to keep my boat upright and stay out of the chilly water kept my terror in check and my body parts moving. I tried to remember that in thirty minutes it would be over.

"You can endure anything for thirty minutes," I told myself, but I had the feeling I was lying. I had talked with other rowers, mostly men, about my fears of competition. No one seemed to understand. "Of course, " the answer came back. "Everyone is afraid." I never could make anyone understand how paralyzed I felt. Were my parents right after all, I wondered? Is competition a male gene?

I set out between the buoys, hoping the lines would keep my boat straight and my heart contained within my chest. The course led the boats under the Boston University Bridge and around a bend toward the first straightaway in the river. The deafening roar from the crowd enveloped me as I came out from under the bridge. Past Magazine Beach, I reached the Northeastern Boathouse where Michael and his teammates were waiting. "Go Kitty! Go Mom!" I heard them yell.

There were hundreds of strokes between Northeastern and the Radcliffe Boathouse where Deb and her classmates, my husband and my mom were also cheering. By then I was tired, and I took the turn under Anderson Bridge too wide. Exhausted, I passed the Cambridge Boat Club, where Jerry Ulrich and his friends were watching from the second-storey porch. I tried my best to look smart in the boat that they had lent me. My race time was not good that day. I did not steer the shortest course. I hit a buoy (loss of points). But I was wrapped in pride as I rowed back to the boathouse from the finish. That feeling has informed my life ever since.

In the last twelve years I have learned to love breaking a sweat. I look forward to that part of the workout when the kinks shake out, the muscles begin to move in concert and the stroke lengthens. I love turning at the top of the river and heading home. I look forward to coasting to the dock after a long row. I love planting my foot on the wooden strips and lifting my body out of the boat. I love reaching down, grabbing hold inside the shell, swinging it above my head and carrying it to its rack inside the boathouse.

If my body would stand the stress and I could make the time, I would work out every day, but I don't. Older bodies take longer to repair. Workouts too close together lead to injury. I have learned the hard way that injury can shut down a season.

Sport in grown-up life cannot always claim top priority. The demands of a new job, a long-term family illness and a family business overdue for attention have gotten between me and the water. Two seasons ago I was on the water twice; last season not at all. My boat was collecting dust. Recently, I loaned it to Deb.

My mother will be 80 in the fall. Eight years ago, after watching me awhile, she bought her own ergometer. Then she bought a boat. That year we gave her new oars for Christmas. She lives ten minutes from a boathouse and rows twice a week all summer. My mother grew up in the 1930s and was a fine athlete in high school. She attended a girls' boarding school where sports were honored. She was a star tennis player and a forward on the field hockey team. When she married and became a young mother, however, she put her athletic ability away. I never saw it until one day, when I was grown, we coaxed her onto the tennis court. Her backhand blew me away.

Two years ago, I returned with her to her fiftieth high school reunion. There, in an exhibit in the school library, was a picture of her lacrosse team in play. Mother was in the middle of the battle. Had I known, she could have been my model. Before she bought her boat, my mother and I and daughter Deb decided to take a week at Craftsbury rowing camp on the edge of little Lake Hosmer in Vermont. Each week all summer twenty-five men and women from seventeen to seventy years spend six days under the tutelage of coaches from clubs and colleges across the East. That week we took great pleasure in being three generations of women in sport.

A Craftsbury week always ends with a two-mile head race. Mother was the oldest camper that session – and the only woman over fifty – but she was not the last person to cross the finish line. She beat two men.

Last month I watched Deb, now a doctor, row two master races on the Potomac River. We stood at Thompson's Boathouse in Washington – her father, her beau and I – in the summer rain. Her first race was in a four, her second in an eight. Both boats came in second. Neither boat rowed with the precision of her collegiate team, nor the power, but the athletes were all smiles as they came back to the dock, lifted their long bodies out and opened the oarlocks to free the blades. There were none of the tears or regrets that there might have been years ago. These master women athletes had had fun. They would be back another day. I understood.

In racing there are penalties for being late to the line. Usually, you are assessed one false start. Two false starts eliminate the boat. Sometimes when you are late, the race has left without you. Coming to sport late in life has penalties too. You know from the beginning that you will never make it to the Olympics. It is easy to regret the years lost, the skill and speed that you will never attain. It is easy to mourn the opportunities missed, the friends you did not meet, the lessons that you could have learned much younger, the games from which you were shut out.

But there are consolations. There is a sparkle, a sheer delight, that master women athletes of my generation have that our aging male collegiate rowers miss. For us it is all new. For us it can only get better. We do not watch our records fading in the distant past. We have no time to sit around and tell old war stories. We cannot wait to get out on the water to write new history. We have so much to learn. We feel the press of time. We want to get on with it. We want to have fun. Our bodies are our new toys. We have let loose. We glory in the challenge.

With time out for injury, I figure I have twenty seasons left: rowers compete well into their eighties. I continue my workouts at the gym. I look at my present distance from the water as a leave of absence. I have promised myself I will be back. In the meantime, I take my rowing with me every day. The lessons I have learned – the focus, the team-work, the patience – stay with me. I hold the images and the messages in my head:

"Don't worry about the finish. Just get as many starts under your belt as you can."
"Races are won one stroke at a time."
"It's the last five hundred. Just suck it up and pull."
"You learn more from your losses than your wins."

Over the course of his post-collegiate career as an athlete my son Michael has rowed in five world championships. We have traveled to England, Austria, Yugoslavia and even Australia to see him compete. We celebrated a silver medal finish. We nursed him through injury. We shared the disappointment of back surgery in what should have been an Olympic season. Now we mark with him the transition from elite athlete to businessman and coach. There are still new lessons to be learned.

Once I raced with Michael in a parent–child race. Our opponents were fathers and sons. I felt very tall that day. Our medal hangs above my desk among my treasures. From the beginning Michael tutored me, gave me athletic sox for Christmas and sent me encouraging postcards from around the world. He made me a valentine with a photo of me in a race for which he was my coach.

I hold a different image of Deb, one from the MIT gym in Cambridge. I was competing in the CRASH-B Sprints, a grueling, insane indoor competition on rowing ergometers, conceived by athletes boared by winter training. Rowers come from all across the country each February to compete. My race that day was close. Michael was sitting by my side, coaching. Through the pain and sweat running in my eyes, I saw Deb with her friends sitting in front of me in the first row of bleachers. Her body was twisted and her face contorted with nervousness as she screamed encouragement.

We had switched roles. The fact that she was so invested in my victory gave me energy. I finished first.

In the end sport for me is irrevocably linked with family, with relationships, with teaching and learning, with facing challenge and having fun together. Without my kids I never would have known.

5

LITTLE LEAGUE MOTHERS AND THE REPRODUCTION OF GENDER

Janet Saltzman Chafetz and Joseph A. Kotarba

Janet Chafetz and Joseph Kotarba, whose offices are next door to one another, have been colleagues for 18 years. Nonetheless, they could scarcely be more different in their general theoretical and methodological approaches to sociology, which made this chapter, their first collaborative scholarly project, so interesting and so much fun. What they share, besides long years of friendship and collegial cooperation, is residence in similar, nearby neighborhoods and the fact that they have sons only a year and a half apart in age, both of whom were once deeply involved in Little League baseball (Joe's younger son is currently similarly involved). As the chapter demonstrates, when children get involved in Little League, it typically entails considerable parental commitment as well.

Janet and Joe combined different research interests to accomplish this study. Janet's specialties are gender inequality and sociological theory. Joe's are qualitative methods, medical sociology and popular culture. He had conducted research on the ways in which team physicians and trainers manage athletic injuries, so he was acquainted with the literature on the sociology of sport. Nevertheless, this study originated for non-theoretical reasons: Janet's efforts to maintain her sanity while living the experiences reported here and attempting, in what she thought to be the interests of her son, to bite back her feminist-inspired horror at the expectations attached to the role of tournament team mom.

Janet did what was expected of her by the other mothers and then ran home each night to record everything she could remember, guided in her note-taking by her sociological understanding of how gender, especially femininity, is structured in white, middle-class America. Later in the summer, weeks after the experience ended, she wrote a detailed narrative from those notes, which she showed to Joe. Never having conducted an ethnographic study, that version of the paper was far from being publishable, as Joe gently pointed out. The solution was immediately apparent. As a trained ethnographer, as well as another "informed observer" of the middle-class, Houston Little League scene, Joe would make the perfect co-author.

The detailed description of Janet's experiences was not yet a sociological analysis. The next step was to take this autobiographical and anecdotal account and to conceptualize it, which in sociology means to write about social activities and experiences in a way that reveals their broader meanings. In adding his everyday life theoretical perspective, Joe was able to show how the ongoing interaction "work" that these moms did enabled them to construct a sense of gender for self, others and the community. He also used his insights as a Little League dad and coach in focusing and giving form to the chapter. Copies sped back and forth between us as we revised each other's words and ideas. Finally, we submitted it to a scholarly journal whose editor of which suggested that, while it was too long for the journal, he preferred to publish it in an annual, *Studies in Symbolic Interaction*, which he also edits. By then, Little League baseball was long over for Janet and she returned to her other interests (women's labor force participation and its effects on family structure). Joe, whose younger son now plays on a Little League tournament team, will probably revisit the sociology of kids' sport soon, and is threatening to bring Janet to the plate with him to update this study.

According to many observers of the American scene, baseball is central to US culture. The game highlights widely accepted values that influence competition, leisure, work, patriotism, and many other everyday life issues. A common theme in the depictions of baseball in fiction (e.g., *The Boys of Summer*), film (e.g., *The Babe*), and sports journalism is the way the sport defines what it means to be a man. Similarly, studies by sociologists focus on the process by which baseball, especially Little League, teaches boys how to be men. Only rarely have authors in the mass media or sociology given attention to the impact of baseball on what it means to be a woman. This omission is understandable, given that most players, coaches and ancillary personnel at all levels of baseball are men.

Our purpose in this chapter is to complement other depictions and analyses of baseball by focusing on a particular collection of Little League mothers. We will describe how an organized Little League baseball program provides the occasion for these key women in the setting to recreate and reinforce dominant ideas about gender and the prevailing gender order for themselves, their sons and the community at large.

"Doing gender": the focus of our study

We use data from a case study to illustrate how everyday tasks, accomplished by a group of Little League mothers, create and reproduce gender at several different levels of social life. The data we use were collected in connection with the activities associated with an all-star tournament team that competes with similar teams representing other leagues. The teams that win regional tournaments then participate in the national tournament that culminates in the Little League World Series. The events described in this chapter occurred during a three-and-a-half-week period between the announcement of the boys selected for the team and the team's final elimination from the tournament. Our analysis focuses on the activities that revolve around and support the actual practicing and playing of organized youth baseball. Parents, especially the mothers of the players, defined and carried out the majority of these activities.

We have chosen "community" as the main focus of our analysis. We will show how parents and players identify, define, and in general make sense of the boys' team in terms of the particular community in which the players and facilities are located. The social dynamics of this team served to recreate and reaffirm a particular style of gender relations found in the upper-middle-class, "yuppie" ("young, urban professional") community that sustains the team. Our data enable us to describe how a few key actors provided the team parents, especially the mothers, with a very specific, gender-based definition of the tournament team experience. The legitimacy of this definition was grounded in claims about community traditions related to Little League. The underlying effect of this complex gender work, done primarily by mothers, was the recreation and strengthening of the community's collective identity as a place where, among other things, women are primarily mothers to their sons.

Texasville and baseball: a community profile

Texasville Little League (TLL) is located on the grounds of a public elementary school that serves a small incorporated community (population: approximately 14,000). This community is surrounded by the city of Houston, Texas. The league also services two other nearby neighborhoods, but about 80 percent of the children who play on TLL teams live in Texasville. All three communities are predominantly middle to upper middle class. They are composed of mostly single-family houses, and they contain very few people of color. The particular culture of TLL reflects the rather distinctive way of life in Texasville as a whole.

Texasville has an unusually tradition bound personality for an upscale community in the 1990s. Many of the changes in the status of women and in the nature of gender relations that have occurred in much of US culture over the past three decades have, to a significant degree, bypassed Texasville.

Apart from regular church attendance, Little League baseball represents perhaps the single most important, community-wide, cultural activity in Texasville. Texasville is crazy about Little League. The overall Little League program consists of six age-specific leagues, beginning at age 6 and ending at 15. Over 800 children played during the 1992 season. The annual program budget, excluding contributions by team sponsors, is over $100,000. Even the concession stand generates about $30,000 profit for the league annually. On any given night during the regular season, 100 to 200 people attend games at the field. Eating dinner at the concession stand is a "tradition." League parents add to the normal concession stand menu by bringing quiche, fancy pasta salads, and other homemade and purchased dishes. From March through June, much of the social life of younger Texasville families, including all family members, revolves around the Little League field. Of particular interest to us as sociologists was that the commitment to Little League, with teams overwhelmingly composed of boys, starkly contrasted to the almost total lack of community support for the Texasville's girls' softball league.

The primary focal point of most of this family and community interest in Little League is the major league. This is the ten-team league composed of 120 children aged 11 and 12. The major league is the most competitive, and the success of the major league season is often measured by the success of its tournament team.

Tournament team Little League baseball is a highly crystallized expression of regular season Little League ball. The processes that Janet observed both on and off the field in connection with the tournament team are extreme relative to what went on during the regular season. These processes are also relatively intense compared to other leagues. Nonetheless, the very intensity and excess of tournament activities serve to highlight the importance of these activities in the overall process of reproducing gender in the community as a whole.

The team mothers: women's culture in Texasville

The team mothers reflected the traditional flavor of Texasville culture. Virtually all had college degrees, and their husbands worked as physicians, lawyers, corporate and public administrators, and so forth. However, Janet was the only mother employed in a professional career. In an era when the majority of American women between 35 and 45 years old, including mothers, are employed, 15 of the 20 team mothers were full-time homemakers.

Women's culture in Texasville revolves primarily around consumption. The family is the key social unit in the community, and a traditional family division of labor prevails. Husbands provide financial support for the families, while the mothers locate and allocate relevant goods and services to the families. This division of labor and the community system in which it exists is ideologically supported by the Southern Baptist and Calvinistic ethic permeating the community. In other words, a family's apparent goodness, viability and solidarity is demonstrated and proven by its material success.

The woman's role in this community system is mainly to provide her children with the best of everything within a family framework. Women, especially mothers, are expected to support Texasville's version of the cult of the child. In this context, Little League provides the ideal leisure-time vehicle for displaying one's competence as a mother.

The reproduction of gender: an insider's account

Our research story begins with the selection of the boys who would play on the tournament team. When selections were announced the parents of the boys on the team were called to a meeting. At the meeting everyone received a two-page, single-spaced handout. It outlined how the boys would be treated and judged, how they should behave, and other information about how coaching and practices would be conducted. It was explained that on each night for two weeks until the real games began there would be a black vs. gold (the team colors) practice game. These games would be played as if they were the real thing. They would begin with the boys being individually introduced, the Little League Pledge recited, and the Star Spangled Banner played. The games would be officiated by hired umpires, official statistics would be kept, the concession stand would be open, and "We should all be there so the stands are as full as possible." According to one of the parents, the purpose of this complex ritual was to help the boys adjust to the exceptional fanfare associated with real tournament competition.

One of the announcements made at the initial meeting was very relevant to the focus of this analysis. The fathers were told that they would not be involved in the coaching except when officially invited. In fact few fathers were asked to participate in any way, although one kept player statistics and another served as the scorekeeper and announcer at practice games. One father was responsible for field maintenance and a handful of others were invited to do baseball-related tasks during practices, but most of this involvement occurred during the first week only. Significantly, virtually all other activities were explicitly and exclusively reserved for the mothers. As a result, most fathers had no role to play other than as spectator for the entire three and a half weeks.

Midway through the initial meeting two women assumed leadership for the group as a whole. They announced that the remainder of the meeting was for mothers only, and that the fathers should leave. These women then told the other mothers about the many tasks that had to be done and the committees that had to be staffed. The mothers were asked to volunteer for these roles. The key mothers in the group made it clear that these tasks and committees were traditional for TLL major league tournament teams, and they implied that it was traditional for mothers to do these things.

This list of tasks was overwhelming. There was a committee whose job was to schedule two to three non-strenuous activities for the boys each week (e.g., bowling, movies, picnics, and miniature golf), chauffeur the boys to and from the activities, and supervise them while they participated. There was a committee whose job was to create an individualized scrapbook to be given to each boy after the tournament was over. Some of the fathers had volunteered to be photographers, along with several of the mothers, but the scrapbook assembly was the job of a committee of women. T-shirts silk-screened with "Tournament Team Mom" in team colors had to be designed and ordered. Someone suggested that the men might want similar "Father" shirts, and everyone agreed. Commemorative T-shirts, listing all twenty of the boys' names, also needed to be bought for team members. Pins with a picture of her son, and ribbons had to be made for each mother, along with sun visors in the team colors labeled with the boy's name and "Mom."

All mothers were told that they were expected to wear three items that identified them as team moms. Their identity was through their son's name or status. For the practice games, one of the mothers was expected to get ten black shirts and then collect and launder them nightly. A team roster with addresses and phone numbers had to be made and distributed. Then there was the "spirit committee" to decorate the field with balloons (in team colors), pennants, and other objects for each tournament game and plan the traditional pep rally before the first game.

The key job for the mothers was making, hanging, and maintaining door decorations indicating their sons' membership on the tournament team. A two-foot high star was the primary decoration to be placed on the front door of each boy's house. It had the player's name in huge letters, the league name and "Tournament Team" written on it, the name of all other team members, and four paper baseballs. The star was bedecked with ribbons and glitter, all in team colors. Later, the mothers were to make other things to add to the door decoration before each tournament game. Before the meeting ended, everyone wrote a $50 check to defray these expenses, excluding the adults' T-shirts and the costs of the boys' leisure activities.

The main message in this meeting was that throughout the tournament it was the mothers' job to convey to the boys how special they were for making the team, and how special the entire experience was. The division of labor outlined at the meeting was based on a highly gendered definition of the kinds of activities appropriate (and inappropriate) to each sex. Cutting, pasting, lettering, and other arts and crafts were defined as women's work. Men (as well as women) could take photos, but women would assemble them or, in the case of the pins, arrange and pay to have them made into appropriate mementos. Buying things such as T-shirts, balloons, and art supplies was defined as a woman's task, as was organizing and supervising leisure activities for 12-year-old boys. It never occurred to the two official team mothers, or to any of the other outspoken and active women that men could or should participate in any of this work. Except for driving and supervising the boys during the weekdays, the rest was done exclusively by women over the weekends and/or at night.

The division of labor set at the meeting and carried on during the tournament meant that mothers spent considerable time doing, often collectively, traditional gender-specific tasks. In performing these tasks competently, the mothers were "doing gender." In sociological terms, they were reproducing and validating for one another traditional definitions of femininity. They also reproduced and validated the community's sense of gender because their performance took place in a widely supported and publicized community activity. In this way, the tournament team came to be something much more than a collection of children playing baseball. This point is further supported by other examples of "doing gender" that occurred during the tournament.

"Doing gender": more examples

Eating and drinking as a group was central to the tournament team experience, and mothers were expected to organize things around food and drink. This served two important functions related to gender. First, in preparing and serving food, traditionally defined as tasks for women, the women "did gender" for each other and for the men and boys. Given the number of people for whom food was prepared, the women spent much time, effort and money in demonstrating their commitment to, and competence in a nurturant role. Second, because there was so much emphasis placed on collective eating (whether prepared by the women or in a restaurant), the mothers apparently believed that coming together around food would enhance social cohesiveness among team members and team parents. Eating and drinking together also created the image of social solidarity as an objective feature of the Texasville Little League, and this enhanced Texasville's status among other Little League organizations in the area.

Another way that women "did gender" was through collective arts and crafts activities in which no men participated in any capacity. Such female involvement in these arts and crafts is reminiscent of old-fashioned quilting bees. The women worked collectively, competently, and efficiently on a gendered task, all the while enjoying friendly social interaction. "Doing gender" with one another in this way served to build among the women a sense of their sisterhood as mothers of very special boys. This ritual also provided a visual display to other leagues and to non-Texasville neighbors of the community's strong commitment to its children.

Finally, after the mothers had learned that it was TLL tradition to have a pep rally the night before the first game, a few of them started talking about rounding up some girls to be cheerleaders. Although several parents objected to this, one mother recruited a group of 11-year-old girls (one of whom the mother proudly described as her son's "steady girlfriend") and worked with them on their "routines." The girls were given their own hand-decorated T-shirts and then performed at the pep rally. However, they never performed at any of the tournament games. As one of the team members explained, most of the boys did not like the idea of cheerleaders. About half were not interested in girls and thought that cheerleaders were silly. The other half complained that the cheerleaders were too young (the girls were about to be sixth graders and the boys were a year ahead of them in school).

Parental and community support: money and time

The resources (time, energy and money) committed to the major league tournament team by both the parents and by the community were substantial. Each family spent at least $200 of its own money. Most mothers devoted an average of 60–85 hours of their time (much more by the two team mothers and some other core mothers) during the three and a half weeks. On average, most mothers spent about four hours in collective meetings, mostly devoted to arts and crafts. Some spent several more hours planning meetings, shopping for art supplies, T-shirts, and so forth. Programs containing the boys' pictures were distributed at the games, and each team mother received a pin with her son's picture before the first game. The team mothers and/or a few core mothers produced the programs. In addition, on three occasions, parents were given printed schedules of activities for the boys and schedules of work to be done by the women. Those half dozen women who were involved in the boys' free-time activities devoted up to twenty-five more hours. A small committee put time into making individualized scrapbooks for each of the twenty boys. Of course, there was also time devoted to cooking collective meals, doing laundry, and organizing and hosting the end-of-season party.

Most mothers and fathers spent about forty hours at the field observing practice games during the first two weeks. The four tournament games consumed ten to twelve hours of field time, and the two post-game parties another three hours. Men and women rarely sat together during practice or real games. Only at the parties did most husbands and wives sit near each other. Almost all other activities off the field were conducted by the women in the total absence of men, while activities on the field were conducted by men and boys in the absence of women. (Meanwhile, the girls' softball tournament team often practiced at the same time and had no spectators.)

Team members: the son gods

Were the boys aware of all this expenditure of work, time and money? How did they react to the experience? In general, the boys did not define the caring and attention showered upon them in any distinctively moralistic or sociological terms, which is not surprising. Clearly, the boys expected and took for granted the door decorations, the pep rally, and all the carefully planned leisure activities. They knew that these things were traditional for TLL Major League tournament teams because their older brothers and many of their older acquaintances had played on them in past years. The boys' behavior indicated a taken for granted attitude that the adults would serve them.

It is interesting that the only woman who worked actively to prevent the boys from behaving like "son gods" had no son on the team. Some of the fathers joined her efforts. The only people who explicitly recognized the work being done by the mothers, and expressed that the boys should not take for granted the service provided by the adults generally, and mothers specifically, were some of the men. The team mothers behaved like proverbial martyrs. They did everything for their son gods while seemingly expecting nothing in return except that their sons work hard at baseball and enjoy the tournament team experience.

Conclusion: "doing gender" isn't easy

People do not accomplish gender work in a social vacuum. The meanings of masculinity and femininity do not simply appear at various points in our lives either to haunt us or empower us. These meanings are not part of a free-floating culture that exists outside our everyday experience. Instead, we create and reproduce gender in real, concrete situations for real, particular audiences. These audiences include the self, significant others, and the general community.

The Little League mothers in our study created and reproduced gender for *the self* by doing tasks that established for them a sense of significance and competence. The demands of the mothers' activities, the amount of energy required to do them, and the level of commitment all rivaled and often exceeded the efforts of the sons on the field. Playing baseball was easy compared to being a Little League mother. The mothers "won" when they felt like "good mothers." An integral part of being a good mother was doing all this work without expecting reward or gratitude.

Little League mothers created and reproduced gender for two *significant others*: husbands and sons. Although research on gender relations reminds us that women in our culture are ordinarily expected to care for and nurture their husbands, the women in this study were good wives because they took good care of their husbands' sons. The fathers were not so much excluded from direct participation in the tournament as they were freed from support work so they could enjoy the tournament at leisure as fans. Because the mothers' primary devotion was to their sons directly, the boys received a number of strong messages about being a woman. The boys saw that women not only take care of males, but they put those activities first in importance. They saw that women organize their activities to enhance the success and value of male activities. They saw that women work while males play, and that women organize integrated family activities around the needs of males. They saw that women care for their males without complaining or expecting males to appreciate the costs to women of caring for them. They saw women cheer on their efforts, and they saw young girls organize many of their everyday activities around those of young boys.

Little League mothers also created and reproduced gender for *the community at large*. They upheld widely accepted values concerning how to act as competent mothers in their particular community. These values were grounded in the notion of tradition. The team mothers did not want to deprive their sons of the rich tournament team experience enjoyed by older brothers, neighbors, and acquaintances – a set of experiences which their sons had long since come to expect if they made the team. The women performed all the work needed to sustain these traditions, and they did so in an organized, intentional, ritualized manner.

The intentional enactment of these rituals helped mold the mothers into a special social group, and served to reinforce the continuing sense that Texasville is indeed a "special" community. Of course, all this physical labor was added to their normal work as wives and mothers. In this real-life context, creating and reproducing gender is not only a set of cultural practices studied by sociologists, it is also a set of exhausting activities. In fact, it is so exhausting that we must end with a question: Is it more exhausting to reproduce gender than it is to challenge and change traditional gender definitions and gender relations?

Note

The paper on which this chapter is based was published in 1995 as "Son worshippers: the role of Little League mothers in recreating gender," *Studies in Symbolic Interaction* 18: 217–41.

LEARNING EXERCISES AND RESOURCES

Projects and discussion topics

1   The chapters in Part 1 deal with early experiences with sports. Think back to your own early experiences and describe them in terms of when they occurred, the context in which they occurred, and what was going on in your life as they occurred. How were those early experiences related to your age, social class, race or ethnicity, family, and neighborhood or community? Use the articles to inform your discussion.

2   When children first play sports, they bring with them ideas about themselves, their bodies, and the meaning of sport participation. Where do these ideas come from, and how might they influence how the children play and what they learn in connection with those experiences? If it is possible to observe 6–8-year-old children at a school playground during recess, watch for a while and record what you see. You could also do this at a youth sport team practice in a local neighborhood. Use your observations to help answer the questions above.

3   Talk with your mother and grandmothers (or other women who went to high school or college before 1972) and ask them about their involvement in physical activities and sports. What factors in their lives encouraged, limited, or prevented their participation? Talk with your father and grandfathers (or other men about the same age as the women you talk with) and ask them the same questions. Were their experiences different or similar? Explain why they were either different or similar? Use the chapters, especially Chapter 4 by Kitty Porterfield, to help you formulate the questions you will ask in your conversations.

4   After talking with the women you talked with in connection with question 3, talk to two women your age and ask them similar questions about their participation in physical activities and sports. If their experiences are different from the experiences of the older women, why is this the case? What social changes have occurred over the past two generations that have made early sport experiences for young women today and in the recent past different from the experiences of women who went to school before the early 1970s?

5   Early sport experiences are often different for children from different racial or ethnic groups, and for children from different social class backgrounds. Use your own experiences and the material in the articles to develop an outline of possible ethnic and class differences in participation experiences, and then explain why those differences might exist and what impact they might have on the meanings that the children give to their sport experiences.

6 Many athletes say that without their parents they never would have had the opportunity to play sports as a child. Use your own experiences or the experiences of one or two of your friends who played sports early in life and outline the ways that parents encouraged or facilitated sport participation. If you cannot remember what your parents did, ask them, or have your friends ask their parents. Are there differences between the support provided by mothers and the support provided by fathers? (This question could also be discussed in small groups of class members. A group list of examples of parent support could be developed and then shared with the class as a whole. What does the list tell you about the social dynamics and implications of this support? Use Chapter 5 by Janet Chafetz and Joe Kotarba as a guide for your analysis.)

Films and videos

Film and video annotations are provided by Steve Mosher, Department of Exercise and Sport Science, Ithaca College, Ithaca, NY 14850, USA.

Feature-length film

- *The Bad News Bears* (1976), 102 mins, Paramount Home Video.
  Simply put, *The Bad News Bears* is the best feature-length film ever to explore the subculture of youth sports. Clearly, the writers of the screenplay know children. The story of Mr Buttermaker (Walter Matthau), the beer-drinking, sloppy, ex-professional pitcher trying to manage a group of misfit 12 year olds in a highly competitive Little League makes for entertainment as well as social science. Buttermaker soon discovers his Bears have no talent and quickly become the laughing stock of the league. The addition of Amanda, a girl phenom pitcher with ties to Buttermaker's past, and Kelly Leak, the motorcycle riding rebel who happens to be the best athlete in town, turn the Bears around and point them toward the championship game. What is of interest to the student of sport is the moral behavior of the children and the politics of Little League. The moment of truth for Buttermaker and the Bears comes when he discovers, just in time for moral redemption, that winning is not what matters most to 12 year olds. Should be seen in tandem with the film *Two Ball Games* (1975) and Gary A. Fine's book, *With the Boys* (1986). The issues of sport involvement and identity construction are clearly outlined here.

Shorter films and educational programs

- *Two Ball Games* (1976), 30 mins, Consortium of University Films Center or Cornell University, Ithaca, NY.
  A cinema verité study that contrasts an informal, neighborhood softball game with a championship Little League game, *Two Ball Games* is far more than first meets the eye. On the surface, the film lets the viewer compare and contrast the ways in which children of the same age play games in pick-up as well as highly institutionalized settings. Looking deeper, however, there seems to be a strong message

coming from the filmmakers that the harm caused by overbearing managers in Little League cannot be overcome by the increased mastery of skill; and that the benefit of friendship and cooperation found in the informal setting is preferable. The study guide that accompanies it seems to soften the propagandizing found in the film. The Little League game in *Two Ball Games,* while absent the blatant vulgarity, is virtually identical to the games in *The Bad News Bears,* thereby confirming the latter's brilliance. These two films and the following video highlight the "social side" of becoming involved in sports.

- *The Playing Fields of Scarborough* (1990), 60 mins, Canadian Broadcasting Corporation.
  Part Two in Ken Dryden's six-hour made for Canadian television series *Home Game, The Playing Fields of Scarborough* explores the process by which Canadian children (especially boys) are socialized into the national sport of ice hockey. This episode, as well as the entire series, vividly demonstrates the differences in Canadian and American sport (e.g. ice hockey in Canada is a working-class and middle-class sport), while demonstrating universal features of children's and youth sport.

Editors' note: Special television shows are sometimes devoted to the topic of early experiences in sports. When they are, they focus most often on physical and psychological issues rather than the social issues raised in the chapters in Part 1. Issues related to access to participation opportunities, decision-making processes related to becoming involved in sports, and the connections between early experiences and gender, age, and racial and ethnic relations are seldom, if ever, mentioned. If these issues are discussed, it is important to call the attention of others to the programs.

Additional books and articles

- Adler, Patricia and Adler, Peter (1994)" Social reproduction and the corporate other: the institutionalization of afterschool activities," *The Sociological Quarterly* 35(2): 309–28.

Sociologists Patti and Peter Adler (authors of Chapter 16) have spent their lives doing notable qualitative research. To write this paper (and *Peer Power: Preadolescent Culture and Identity,* Rutgers University Press, 1998) they spent six years gathering data through participant–observation with students in elementary and junior high schools in a predominantly white middle and upper-middle-class community. They focused on a range of afterschool activities, including spontaneous play, organized recreational activities, and competitive sport activities, including some elite competitive sport teams and clubs. They analyzed each of these activities in terms of their emphasis on democracy or meritocracy. They found that early sport experiences become increasingly organized, competitive, and professionalized as children get older and as their skills improve. They note that afterschool activities are becoming increasingly organized and supervised by adults who use the activities not only to reproduce the existing social structure, but also to introduce children to work values emphasized in corporate America. (Note: Chapter 5, "After-School Activities," pp. 98–114 in *Peer Power,* is very similar to this article.)

- Coakley, J. (1983) "Play, games, and sport: developmental implications for young people," Chapter 18 (pp. 431–50) in J.C. Harris and R.J. Park (eds) *Play, Games and Sports in Cultural Contexts*, Champaign, IL: Human Kinetics.

This comparison of children's experiences in spontaneous play, informal games, and organized competitive sports is based on observations and semi-structured interviews with children younger than 13 years old. Sociology of sport students conducted the interviews and observations under Coakley's supervision. Analysis focused on the characteristics of the social contexts in which the play, games, or sports occurred, the meanings that children gave to their experiences, and the dynamics of the events and relationships involved in each observation setting. The findings indicate that experiences varied in each of these settings, and the differences had implications for what we might expect children to learn through participation in each of these three types of physical activity.

- Fine, Gary Alan (1987) *With the Boys: Little League Baseball and Preadolescent Culture*, Chicago: University of Chicago Press.

Sociologist Gary Fine spent three years gathering data through participant observation, interviews, and informal conversations with 10- to 12-year-old boys on ten different Little League baseball teams in five communities in the northeastern USA. This is a classic study covering a wide range of issues related to early sport experiences. Fine discusses issues related to adult organization of child's play, the organization of Little League, adult concerns versus peer concerns about moral lessons to be learned while playing youth sports, and how sport participation cannot be understood without considering preadolescent peer culture in the society as a whole. One of his many findings was that the boys on these teams played an active role in their own socialization. They did not internalize the moral lessons of their parents and coaches as much as they revised them and used them to meet their needs as 10–12-year-old boys dealing with issues of gender, identity and social acceptance among peers in US society in the 1980s.

- Landers, Melissa A. and Fine, Gary Alan (1996) "Learning life's lessons in tee-ball: the reinforcement of gender and status in kindergarten sport," *Sociology of Sport Journal* 13(1): 87–93.

This is a good example of the type of study that one or more students could do during a semester. Melissa Landers, with the help of Gary Fine, observed a YMCA tee-ball group in a southeastern US city. Field notes were taken in connection with 22 hours of observation. Field notes were supplemented with data from informal interaction and conversations with the children and with data from a formal, tape-recorded interview with the two coaches in the program. Eighteen boys and six girls were involved (13 Euro-American boys, 6 African-American boys, 1 Asian American boy, and 6 Euro-American girls). They were mostly from middle- and working-class families. The coaches emphasized skills and competition, and gave more attention to highly skilled children than to the others. The girls were less often "coached" than the boys, but were scolded more often and more severely than the boys. The boys teased the girls when they did something wrong or demonstrated poor skills. Coaches allowed this to occur. Overall, the 5- and 6-year olds learned to rank each other on the basis of skills and differentiate each other on the basis of gender, with girls often being taken less seriously as athletes.

- Messner, M. (1992) "Boyhood: the promise of sport," Chapter 2 in *Power at Play: Sports and the Problem of Masculinity*, Beacon Press: Boston.

Mike Messner (the author of Chapter 10), conducted open-ended, in-depth interviews with thirty former professional athletes. He selected athletes from different racial and social class backgrounds, and asked them about their sport experiences from the first things they could remember until the present day. He found that these men had brought with them already gendered identities to their early sport experiences. Messner discusses the relationships the boys had with their fathers when they started playing sports. He also outlines how masculinity and class differences were related to their early experience, and how the hierarchy and homophobia in the sports they played had a negative impact on their willingness as boys to develop intimate friendships with other male athletes.

- Nixon, Howard II (1989) "Integration of disabled people in mainstream sports: case study of a partially sighted child," *Adapted Physical Education Quarterly* 6(1), 17–31.

Howard Nixon has a long-term interest in sport participation issues for young people with disabilities. In the early 1980s when laws mandated that students with disabilities be integrated into US public school physical education and athletic programs, Nixon began studying the conditions under which integration might succeed or fail. He studied the law itself. Then he did in-depth interviews with parents of eighteen partially sighted and totally blind children who attended public schools in a northwestern state. After analyzing these data, he undertook a three-year case study in which he periodically observed a partially sighted boy play different sports starting when the boy was 7 years old and ending when he was 10. This case study enabled Nixon to develop hypotheses about the conditions under which young people with disabilities might be success-fully "mainstreamed" into community or school sport programs. According to these hypotheses, the success of mainstreaming depended on a careful matching of two sets of factors:

- the structural aspects of a sport (type of sport, amount of adaptation needed to accommodate the disability, and the intensity of competition);
- the actual level of ability and disability of the young people involved in the sport.

Nixon suggests that the challenge of mainstreaming is to determine clearly the actual degree of limitation among athletes with disabilities and the implications of those limitations in specific roles and situations in particular sport programs. His research shows that the first sport experiences of children with disabilities depend on the awareness and flexibility of everyone involved.

Part 2

EXPERIENCE AND IDENTITY
Becoming an athlete

Most people participate in sport relatively early in their lives. They are involved in family or community pick-up games, their parents enroll them in organized sport programs in their communities, or they experience participation through mandatory physical education programs in their schools. However, the number who go on to become regular participants, and begin to identify themselves – and be identified by others – as athletes, is significantly less. The readings in Part 2 are concerned with individuals beginning to play the role of athlete, and experiencing the process of becoming an athlete at various levels of sport participation.

Erikson's (1950) classic work on *Childhood and Society* shows how most adolescents undergo a crisis of identity. Their social interactions serve as a context for trying out different identities before they establish a more stable sense of self. For athletes, their sense of self is grounded partly in the role of athlete, a position that figures to a greater or lesser extent in the formation of their identities. The extent to which this role becomes a basis for the identities of different individuals depends on such things as their talent, their social relationships and whether those relationships continue to reaffirm their athletic identities, and the stage in their athletic careers. Of course, other roles such as student, employee, girlfriend, daughter, etc. also serve as a basis for identities among those who play sports.

Because sport participation often occurs at various levels of competitive intensity, and because individuals change the sports in which they participate, the process of becoming an athlete is ongoing. For example, an individual who is a star athlete in high school will have to try for a university team, even if he or she has been recruited. So, even if the individual identifies him or herself as a volleyball player, the identity status of varsity volleyball player in college has not been achieved or confirmed by other intercollegiate volleyball players and coaches. Furthermore, decisions about sport participation are made continually, not once and for all time. As social conditions change, so do people's decisions about sport participation. As a person stays involved in sport, the reasons for participating on one day may be different from the reasons for participating the next day or the next; and when there is no reason, sport participation may be discontinued or changed.

When individuals begin participation in a particular sport during childhood, it is difficult to distinguish the specific development of their identity as an athlete from their overall identity development. This means that the process of becoming an athlete is much more evident when individuals begin to participate in a specific sport during their late teens or young adulthood. In Chapter 6 Peter Donnelly and Kevin Young have focused on the sports of rock climbing and rugby precisely because the novices who were becoming involved in these sports were well past their childhood. Peter and Kevin guessed that the process of becoming an athlete would be relatively clear in the case of these "older" individuals.

Peter (rock climbing) and Kevin (rugby) had both been involved in extensive ethnographic research – involving participant observation and interviewing – in these sports while they were graduate students. As they discussed their data with each other they began to realize that there were striking similarities in their observations of novices who were becoming involved in the two sports. They noted that novices made mistakes, but that these went well beyond those involving the rules and techniques of the sports. The mistakes involved various aspects of the culture of the sports, such as how to behave in informal interaction with other participants, what attitudes to take, how to dress, what to talk about, and when to do certain things.

It was rare for individuals in either sport to begin participation with absolutely no prior knowledge of it, but that prior knowledge was often faulty because it was based on caricatured and incomplete information. Both Donnelly and Young had watched novices actively attempting to construct their identities as rock climbers and rugby players, but because they made mistakes those identities were not confirmed without question by veteran participants in the sport. It was only when the novices became more experienced and began to demonstrate appropriate sporting and cultural behavior that their identity as a "rock climber" or "rugby player" was confirmed by established climbers and rugby players. Donnelly and Young outline a model of the stages of identity construction and confirmation, giving examples from their respective sports.

In Chapter 7 Jay Coakley and Anita White show quite clearly how the structural contexts of young people's lives, whether they are male or female, from working-class or middle-class families, influence the decisions they make about becoming athletes. Jay and Anita interviewed 59 young people, 13–20 years old, in England. Of the 26 females and 33 males, approximately half were involved in sport while the other half were identified by adult informants as "non-participants" or "dropouts."

The interview data indicated that the decisions these young people continually made about playing sports were strongly associated with their stage in life and their previous experiences with sport and physical activity. The decisions were influenced by their social class and especially by their gender. Conscious decisions were made about whether participation would enhance their transition to adulthood, and their images of themselves as adult males or females – decisions that were often resolved in favor of participation by the males, and against it by the females. They were made on the basis of their feelings of competence in particular sports, and these were often related to their experiences in school physical education and sport programs.

The young people's social relations, with their families and with friends, also had a strong influence on their decisions about sport participation. Those from working-class families, where gender relations can be more traditional than in middle-class families, tended to follow the pattern of males continuing to participate into early adulthood while females ceased participation in their early teens. This pattern was enhanced by parental expectations about daughters being involved in chores and looking after younger siblings, and by concern about daughters being out after dark. When combined with financial constraints in some families, these conditions tended to restrict female participation. Relations with boyfriends and girlfriends also seemed to follow traditional patterns with boys assuming continued participation in their sport even when they had a girlfriend, and girls investing more in the relationship than their sport participation when they had a boyfriend. Coakley and White conclude that campaigns which seek to increase participation in sport by young people must take into account the whole circumstances of young people's lives.

Coakley and White show clearly that developing, or failing to develop, an identity as an athlete is not a simple matter of interest and talent. Christopher Stevenson reinforces this point in Chapter 8 by looking at the very highest levels of participation. He interviewed national team athletes in Britain and Canada (10 male water polo players, 8 female field hockey players, and 11 male rugby players). His findings demonstrate that reaching the national team level requires talent, but it also requires a series of conditions such as parental interest, working with a particular coach, and being in the right place at the right time. Chris found that reaching the top levels of a sport often involves complex decisions on the part of the athlete. Only eleven of his twenty-nine subjects reached the national team in their preferred sport, that is, the one in which they had invested the most time and interest. Of the other eighteen, twelve said they had to choose one of several sports in which they were talented, and six had shifted from a sport that they liked to one in which they felt they had a better chance of success.

Stevenson uses an economic model to interpret his findings, proposing that athletes make decisions on the basis of maximizing potential rewards and minimizing potential costs before they commit to a sport. As he points out, we have a tendency to assume that the journey taken to become a star athlete is somehow preordained; that it occurs automatically as an individual shows remarkable talent and has the psychological make-up to exploit that talent and become successful.

Coakley and White, and Stevenson, show that the journey is often much more problematic. Becoming an athlete, and developing the identity of an athlete in a specific sport, involves social conditions and personal decisions that often are rooted deeply in those social conditions.

In Chapter 9 Alan M. Klein takes us out of the developed world to examine the process of becoming an athlete in one country in order to participate in another. He helps us understand the process of identity change that occurs as skills are developed and recognized, and as the athlete experiences life in a new and different culture. Players from the Dominican Republic have been a force in North American baseball for some time. Major League teams such as the Los Angeles Dodgers and the Toronto Blue Jays have been particularly effective in exploiting and developing this pool of Dominican talent. Klein made seven trips in four years to study baseball in the Dominican Republic, and his analysis focuses on the baseball academy funded and operated by the Los Angeles Dodgers.

Baseball academies in the Dominican Republic and other Latin American countries were established by Major League organizations in an effort to develop the skills of talented young players. Part of the training received at the academies was intended to prepare players for the transition to playing in Canada and the USA in the minor league and eventually the Major League systems. In addition to teaching the North American style of baseball, the academies have also attempted, less successfully, to prepare the players to overcome the culture shock of going from the poverty of a developing nation to the affluence of the developed world. Klein gained access to the academy when he offered to help with the cultural transition training. This enabled him to meet everyone in the academy and collect his data. Through these data he clearly documents the problems of socializing players into the Dodger system, and the problems faced by these players once they begin their careers in North America.

Although research done by other sociologists has begun to document and enumerate the migration of athletic talent around the globe (such as scholarship athletes from all over the world on US university teams, and North American ice hockey and basketball players on European professional teams), Klein's study is one of the few that attempts to outline the cultural conflicts that result from this migration. His findings show that even though an individual may have developed an identity as a baseball player in the Dominican Republic, Cuba or Japan, that identity has to be reconstructed and reconfirmed when he begins a playing career in North America.

Michael A. Messner expands on the idea of identity to explore the notion that, for males, developing an athletic identity goes along with developing a gender and sexual identity. He introduces new methodology in Chapter 10. He goes beyond interviewing to a new form of biographical/autobiographical analysis called life history, or in his case, memory work. He juxtaposes a story about his own experiences as a teen with the story of Tom Waddell, a well-known gay athlete, to examine the way in which, for male adolescents, the development of an athletic identity often includes the development of a very narrow masculine identity. That identity combines a kind of domineering aggression with compulsory heterosexuality, and denigrates any forms of masculinity that fall outside of those parameters. When Messner interprets his own story in terms of shifting sexuality, he shows the cruelty that results from a heterosexual male rejecting typical adolescent homosexual feelings in order to establish his athletic and masculine identity. Waddell's story shows how the sport of distance running became his closet, and that if you behaved like an athlete no one would suspect that you were gay. Even today, despite the fact that a few well-known male athletes have come out, many people assume that male athletes in most sports must be heterosexual. In the rather simple-minded world of athletic masculinity, the admission of homosexuality evokes cruelty and has career-ending potential. This, of course, continues to keep many athletes closeted.

Finally, in Chapter 11, Shona Thompson summarizes a study that neatly follows the chapter by Chafetz and Kotarba on Little League mothers. Shona describes how women's work continues to facilitate the sport participation of their husbands, partners and children. She became sensitized to the extent of women's assistance in sports when she helped to organize a boycott of such work to protest the visit of the South African rugby team to New Zealand in 1981. After moving to Western Australia in 1990, she began to document this work more systematically in the locally popular sport of tennis. Her sample consisted of 46 women – 16 mothers of elite junior players, 15 wives/partners of men who played competitive tennis, and 15 women who played tennis. As she did her in-depth interviews it became apparent that the entire economy of amateur tennis was built on the free labor provided by women. Mothers drove "Mom's taxi," laundered clothes, prepared meals at convenient times, and helped to supervise, chaperone, and raise funds for the various teams and tournaments in which their children were involved.

Women who were wives or partners noticed that the men in their lives started to play more tennis after they began to live together as a couple. As this occurred, the women were expected to take responsibility for tasks that the men previously had to do for themselves. Even the women who played tennis found that most of the menial and time-consuming tasks involved in running clubs and hosting tournaments fell to them. Thompson's study shows clearly that becoming an athlete, and continuing to be an athlete, often depends on a hidden pool of labor primarily provided by women.

In summary, these six chapters take us beyond the idea of participation in sport to the concept of becoming an athlete – that is, taking on the role of athlete as a part of our identity. The construction and reconstruction of an athletic identity may be seen at many different levels of sport participation. It occurs both at the level of complete novice, and at the level of experienced athlete who is making the transition to a higher level of participation. This identity formation process not only involves demonstrating appropriate athletic skills, but also social and cultural skills that lead a person to be accepted by fellow athletes in the sport or at a new level of the sport.

6

ROCK CLIMBERS AND RUGBY PLAYERS

Identity construction and confirmation

Peter Donnelly and Kevin Young

Both of us were involved in the respective activities at the time we conducted the research. KY played rugby at high school and university in England, and joined a Canadian university team while he was working on his Master's degree. PD began climbing during his last year at high school in England, and still manages to complete the occasional easy route. As participant observers we were very close to the activities, a closeness that sometimes leads to a situation where it is difficult to be detached and recognize the importance of everyday and familiar behaviors in the environment under study.

One day we were having coffee, and discussing some of the bizarre and stupid things that we had seen rookies do, and heard them say, in our respective sports – both when we were participants, and when we were engaged in participant observation and interviewing as part of our research. As we were talking, we became aware that our knowledge of "rookie mistakes" was very revealing. An important question to ask in this type of research is, "How do you know what you know?" We slowly began to realize that we knew a great deal more than we thought, that being able to distinguish "rookie mistakes" meant several things: we knew what was appropriate behavior – insider rather than stereotypical or outsider knowledge; we could see how and why the mistakes were being made; and we were observing the processes of becoming a rock climber or rugby player. Also, our judgement of the mistakes revealed to us the process of identity confirmation – we would not accept, as fellow participants, people who could do or say such stupid things.

So, this chapter grew out of two larger studies as it began to focus on two potentially different points during a participant's career:

- the point at which an individual begins to say to him/herself, "I am now a [rock climber/rugby player];"
- the point at which veterans begin to accept the rookie as a fellow participant, a member of the subculture.

As we began to talk to people about our research, we realized that the model we were developing applied to a wide range of work and sport situations. People began to tell us about "rookie mistakes" from jobs they had held, and in various sports in which they had participated.

The original study (Donnelly and Young 1988) has been used in a variety of ways since that time. In particular, it has become a part of the new focus of research on socialization into sport – research concerned less with the demographic characteristics of the individuals who become involved in a particular sport, and more with the actual processes by which those individuals become involved. However, we have also found the research to be particularly useful in our teaching, since it provides an easy model to outline those processes. Many students find that they are able to identify with (and give their own examples of) "rookie mistakes" during the socialization process.

Our research focused on two questions:

1   At what point in your involvement in a sport do you actually begin to think of yourself as a rugby player, rock climber, scuba diver, or whatever?
2   At what point in your involvement in a sport do veterans begin to relate to you as a fellow participant?

Also, as sociologists, we were interested in the process(es) by which people arrive at their answers to these questions.

Any new "role" that we take on, a new job or a new sport, involves changes to our identity – to who we are and how we think of ourselves. Sociologists have described this process as "identity formation." But we found that, in the case of becoming a participant in a new sport, this process actually involves a much more deliberate process of identity construction. We also found that the point at which a novice begins to think of him/ herself as a rock climber or rugby player might actually occur well *before* the veterans began to think of him/her as a fellow participant. In order for the new identity to be accepted, the new peers must confirm it. Thus, in becoming a member of a new group such as a sports team, two complementary processes must occur – identity construction and identity confirmation. One cannot become a full participant in a new sport without both. It should be noted that these processes seem to take place without much notice when sports are started at a young age. However, they occur in a much more obvious way when sports are taken up during the teens and young adulthood.

We identified three stages of identity construction:

*   presocialization (involving all of the information an individual acquires before his/ her first participation);
*   selection/recruitment (the first participation);
*   socialization (an initially active but ongoing stage where an individual receives training in both the skills and the lifestyle characteristics – the culture – of the activity).

In identity confirmation, the rookie is either accepted or ostracized by veterans.

Before considering how these stages are experienced by rock climbers and rugby players we should point out that these ethnographies were conducted during previous "incarnations" of the sport. The climbing research was carried out in the 1970s and early 1980s, before innovations like indoor climbing walls and sport climbing revolutionized the sport. The rugby research was undertaken in the early 1980s, toward the end of the first generation of modern rugby in North America. Rugby is far more professionalized now, and a great deal less playful. So, although the data may seem to present rather romanticized and old-fashioned versions of the two sports – versions that have now almost disappeared – the study should be read in the context of its time. Despite the enormous changes that have occurred in the sports, including the fact that a great many more women[1] are now participating, the processes of identity construction and confirmation are still relevant to membership and participation in these and other activities.

Identity construction

It is impossible to study presocialization in a complete way, and we were forced to use subjects' memories for this stage. We were able to see some aspects of selection/recruitment, but the most significant stage is socialization, and that is where we obtained most of our data.

Presocialization

Non-participants learn about specific sport subcultures from a variety of sources including their families and peer groups, and direct or indirect contact with participants. However, the media may be the most consistent source of information with reports, games and documentaries, fictional and artistic accounts, and even humorous references to the participants (e.g., comics showing climbers hanging from a rope, or fiercely aggressive rugby players). This information frequently involves caricatured and stereotypical images of participants, and the potential participant may develop misconceptions about appropriate behavior.

Selection and recruitment

Presocialization is an ephemeral stage that ends when an individual makes direct contact in order to become a participant. Whether an individual selects and seeks out membership or is actually recruited by a veteran, it is important to consider issues such as proximity (there are more climbers in Colorado than Illinois), life circumstances, and even chance.

Socialization

After the preconceptions and frequent misconceptions of presocialization, accurate identity construction begins during this stage. However, as already noted, most of our insights into this stage resulted from recognizing 'rookie errors'. We examine these in terms of:

- accuracy of presocialization;
- impression management;
- anticipatory socialization;
- resolving contradictions.

Accuracy of presocialization

During a rookie's first exposure to established participants, any aspects of identity formed during presocialization are put on view. If the presocialization experiences are accurate the rookie will have few problems. One rugby player gained his prior knowledge from an established player and was attracted to the sport's reputation for a boisterous social life, but even he found a few surprises:

> I had heard from a friend some of the things that happened after games but had never really bothered to find out for myself. Then this guy told me a story about the players at his club playing a trick on a stripper that made her run off stage. Apparently one guy made out he was really interested in her while his friend knelt down behind her and bit her ass so bad that it bled. Now I've started hanging around with those guys I've never seen so much butt-biting in my life!

However, one ex-football player who misunderstood the nonprofessional approach of rugby and thought that the stories he had heard about rugby behavior were exaggerated, found certain aspects of the sport rather alarming:

> It was my first night and people had warned me that Rookie Night was a bit of an ordeal, but I'd just shrugged it off. Well we [rookies] were forced to chug three full beers right at the start. After that things slowed down for a while and I thought it wasn't going to be so bad. Then they [veterans] lined us up and brought out the goldfish. Live goldfish! We had to bite each fish in half with our teeth, chew them, and pass them mouth to mouth among each other. I couldn't believe it. And it got worse!

Another said:

> I didn't expect anything like it. We'd train real hard for two hours a day and then go down to the bar and get hammered; and [post-game] beer-ups . . . well, they're twice as bad. I was surprised because I thought the coach would be angry if we didn't try to keep in shape. In actual fact, he condones it as much as the rest of us. If we were on the football or hockey team we'd have been benched by now.

Another ex-football player who was angry at being cut from the [football] team, started rugby with an attitude and took pleasure in injuring several players:

> Then all of a sudden, you know, after all those games and going to parties afterwards and meeting all of the other players, I lost this attitude completely.

70

I was starting to feel really ashamed of myself because this just isn't the rugby spirit. If you're playing football that's something else. But in rugby as long as it's a good game you don't really mind if you win or not. I don't hold any animosity to anybody now.

(Thomson 1976: 113)

Though accuracy of presocialization also affects climbers, nothing can really prepare them for their first climb – something they have to experience personally.

Impression management

Impression management involves controlling the expression of your true feelings. Novice climbers learn quickly about hiding obvious symptoms of fear, and about never avoiding an opportunity to climb. While it is perfectly acceptable for an established climber to waste a day by being off form, hungover, or just too lazy to do any climbing, a rookie can never appear to be unenthusiastic or s/he may develop a reputation as a "groupie," or a "pseudo" (seeking the glory without the risk). One climber had heard about "pseudos" hanging out below cliffs without doing any climbing, and one day he saw two:

> It was quite obvious that they weren't climbers because they had a complete rack [of equipment] each and all of the chocks were threaded upside down! I watched them for a while and they just walked up and down, stopped and had a drink, and every now and again they would put the rope down and chalk up [their hands] as if they were going to do a climb. Then they would pick up their gear and move on. Unbelievable!

Rookies must accept all invitations to climb because the offer may not be repeated. Earning a negative reputation as a rookie may have consequences for identity confirmation. Rookies may be tested by being taken on climbs that are difficult and scary. While there may be little objective danger for rookies not leading a climb, the experience can be intimidating. Precocious or boastful novices are sometimes given "the treatment" ("Let's take X on a climb and scare the shit out of him!"). In order to pass this test, rookies must be game to try anything, and be composed enough not to show fear.

Overt displays of fear might destroy an individual's potential career (presuming that s/he would wish to continue) because it would be difficult to rely on such a person in genuinely dangerous circumstances. In one situation a novice "froze" on a climb, and burst into tears after being brought to safety. None of his friends/rescuers (including PD) could bring themselves to comfort him; by freezing he had jeopardized the safety of the party. In the harsh and somewhat unfeeling social world of male climbers (an often macho world where emotions are silent/silenced) he could not be forgiven. The incident was never discussed, the individual never climbed again, and the resulting awkwardness led him to drop out of the circle of friends.

Under less extreme circumstances, novices develop a variety of techniques to give the *impression* of composure when they are scared. One often modeled for them by more experienced climbers is purposely to overstate the degree of one's fear. To say that one was "scared shitless" or "sweating bullets" is to use the humor of exaggeration in order to rationalize or diminish the fear that one actually feels, or to indicate no real fear in a situation where it should exist. In one sense it is a confessional act, but in another it conveys the message, "If I really felt that scared would I be telling you?" Thus, emotions are managed in order to conform to the often macho dynamics of this world.

Forms of impression management also occur in rugby. One player commented:

> Sometimes I just don't feel like partying or singing and drinking my brains out at all but feel I should. It's like, I don't want to be seen as not being one of the guys. So I go with the flow usually . . . I do feel like there's an element of pressure to do all these things that, to be honest with you, really aren't my style. But when all the other guys are watching you, it's really hard to avoid joining in, you know.

This player had a respectable professional career, and participated in rugby on game days only. In a sense, he was a peripheral member of the subculture who did not identify with or derive as significant a part of his identity from the rugby subculture as did the more central members.

Anticipatory socialization

This involves rookies making mistakes by spontaneously performing roles they assume are expected of them. For example, novice climbers typically want to show climbers and non-climbers that they are now climbers. This stage of identity construction involves wearing climbing clothes and shoes in non-climbing settings, conspicuously carrying equipment, and books and magazines about climbing, and turning the conversation to climbing whenever possible. Novices have been seen wearing tight-fitting climbing shoes (designed specifically for rock climbing and removed as soon as possible after a climb by veterans) in several non-climbing situations such as in class or in a bar. If confronted, they may claim to be breaking in the shoes. But rookies are invariably pleased that their shoes have been recognized, thereby identifying them as fellow climbers. Thus, the purpose of display is to indicate to non-climbers that one is now different, and to signal to other climbers that one is now a fellow member and may be approached as such.

Of course, what display actually does is to indicate to climbers that one is a novice. Experienced climbers have been known to take advantage of the novice's tendency to display by allowing him/her to carry all of the equipment, particularly if the approach to a cliff involves a long, uphill walk. What appears to be a parasitic or exploitive act is actually symbiotic – the novice is allowed to indulge his/her need for display and may even fantasize (often accurately) that non-climbers who see the group may think that the novice is actually the leader because s/he is carrying the ropes and other equipment. As novices become more secure in their identity as climbers, their tendency to display decreases and they gradually become conscious that such behavior is not "cool."

Anticipatory socialization takes other forms in rugby. Novices may pick up on what they believe to be symbolic cues and act out anticipated roles. One novice performed the requisite "Zulu Warrior" (striptease) on Rookie Night without any of the usual coercion from veterans:

> I knew I was going to have to strip, but I didn't know when or how. I was feeling pretty hammered and I wanted to show the rest of the team that I could party as well as anyone, so away I went. I guess I was a little over-eager in retrospect!

Aproximately three weeks into the Canadian University rugby season another novice, who was as talented as any of his teammates, found himself cut to the second team after a series of disappointing performances. Modeling his behavior on that of several veterans, he had started to stay up late at night and drink before games:

> I don't understand it. All those guys get away with it but I don't seem to be able to. Maybe it's because they've been doing it for so long they're used to it and I'm not. All I know is that when I stay up with those guys I play real lousy the next day . . . I think I'm playing "seconds" rugby right now. So I'm going to have to make a choice here.

Novices are aware from the presocialization stage that certain behaviors are expected of them. In trying to bolster their subcultural identities, they make deliberate efforts to demonstrate "typical" rugby behaviors, often before they are expected.

Resolving contradictions

This is the final and most important stage in identity construction. These contradictions lie between the expected or apparent values and behaviors, and the true values and behaviors which are acted out for novices, or told to them as subcultural folklore. The core values of rugby were truly mystifying for the average North American player who grew up believing in success at all costs, ascetic training regimens, and high levels of fitness. The amateuristic aspects of the sport were demonstrated in a variety of ways including the mandatory heavy drinking, in stories about players who left their cigarettes by the goalposts to be retrieved at half time, in legends about players who started a game drunk, and in gossip about who was playing with a massive hangover.

Other stories concern aspects of fair play: for example, players are willingly loaned to an opposing team in order to equalize the numbers for a game; actions are taken to assist referees (e.g., substitute players acting as linespersons); and players fraternize with opponents following hard-fought games. As one San Diego State player reported:

> Rugby is the only sport I know where you can go out drinking with your opponent before the game, try to kill them during the game and then have a party afterwards. If you play any team anywhere, then the host team provides a party for the opposing team. This is a tradition. We also provide two kegs of beer for our opponents after every single game, and we would expect them to do the same.
>
> (Cited by Orloff 1974: 45)

Similar views were expressed by a young Canadian university player: "Whether we win or lose it's important to us all that we enjoy the game and that both teams get together afterwards and party." In this sense, the way rugby has been played in North America has been quite different from most other organized team sports.

It became clear to rookies that these were the standards they were expected to live up to. The contradictions lie in playing a vigorous game where victory is important but how one played the game was even more important: in tackling opponents with abandon while knowing that one would be drinking with those same individuals after the game; and in practicing social habits that rendered one almost incapable of meeting the physical requirements of the game. The construction of an identity as a rugby player proved to be an interesting balancing act for most individuals.

The contradictions in climbing were mainly acted out between the public and private voices of climbers. As with most high risk sports, climbing is subject to public criticism whenever there is a well-publicized accident or expensive rescue. Climbers have tended to develop an entire mythology that is primarily for public consumption around issues such as safety (for experienced climbers, climbing is not really dangerous if you know what you are doing), character building, non-competitiveness, and comradeship (the so-called kinship of the rope). The reality presented to novices, in both actions and stories, is quite different.

It soon becomes apparent that real risks are frequently taken, character and friendship are by no means an automatic consequence of participation, and competition between climbers is rampant. The major theme of climbing lore concerns risk and accidents, the significance of which may be determined by the number of different expressions used to describe these conditions. Accidents and "epics" (situations that could have resulted in injuries or death) provide a major source of conversation among climbers. Narrow escape stories indicate to climbers that there is always hope of survival, even in the most impossible circumstances (e.g., Simpson's 1989 classic story of survival).

The construction of normal identities as rugby players or climbers therefore involves a complete turnaround from the preconceptions that may have been acquired during the presocialization stage. While many subcultures are able to accommodate a wide range of internal differentiation, some individuals are unable to adjust during the active stage of socialization to a set of values that may be diametrically opposed to the public image of the sport. (See also, Klein 1986 for the contradictions in bodybuilding.)

Identity confirmation

Under normal circumstances, identity confirmation is a relatively straightforward process during which a novice begins to accept the actual values of the subculture and leave behind any misconceptions. Confirmation may occur gradually in rugby, for example, in the process of making the team, undergoing the rigors of Rookie Night, and becoming increasingly involved with established players both on and off the field. It is the process of establishing a reputation as a reliable individual whose values and behavior apparently conform to subcultural expectations. It is not necessary to do something crazy, either on or off the field, but in the rugby subculture reckless acts may speed up and enhance the development of a reputation. In climbing, confirmation may be more immediate; for example, being asked to lead a section of a climb by a veteran climber.

In each case one's reputation is made, and one's identity as a fellow member has been confirmed. But reputations are such that they must constantly be remade, and it is this aspect of identity confirmation that is most interesting. Thus, novices, rookies on a new team, geographically mobile participants, and participants who are attempting to have claimed achievements accepted (e.g., "I played for [a well-known team] in New Zealand;" "I climbed [a very difficult route] in Utah") may need to have their identities (re)confirmed. Members of the subculture need to be able to trust such individuals, and to determine the truth of their claimed achievements. Again, this is usually straightforward. Most individuals joining a team or club are rookies who need to establish a reputation, or they arrive with a documented reputation. It is the exceptions that are of most interest.

On the rare occasions in climbing when an individual is unknown to a particular group (either personally or by reputation), or when an unobserved solo ascent is being claimed, it is necessary for the safety of other climbers and the integrity of the subculture to determine his/her legitimacy. For example, the "pseudo" climbers mentioned above were certainly making unspoken claims about their identities as climbers, but were easily revealed by veterans because of an equipment error. Poor climbers, or those who have a tendency to panic, could prove to be a real hazard to those who climb with them. Climbers need to know, with some degree of accuracy, if an ascent has been made previously (both for safety, and for reasons of accurate record keeping in the sport). If it seems possible for the climber to have done what is being claimed (given such variables as weather, ice and snow conditions, time available, and his/her ability, equipment, and physical condition), and if the claimed achievement is in keeping with the individual's known ability, past experience, and previous reliability, the claim is usually accepted. If there are apparent reasons to dispute the claim, judgement is withheld, and an individual may suffer a loss of reputation, a disconfirmation of identity, and even ostracism (see Donnelly 1994).

A common problem of reconfirmation in rugby concerns players coming from countries where there is a long tradition and reputation in the game. Such players arrive in North America with an aura of excellence that is sometimes undeserved, or with claims to knowledge about the game that they may not possess. Because North American players, many of whom are new to the game, are primed to accept claims of excellence and knowledge from these players, it is not unusual for the new arrivals to take advantage of the situation. They may be awarded a place on a team, or a coaching position, over a more deserving North American player. The Canadian players interviewed were all aware of such possibilities, and suggested that, in the case of players (rather than coaches), they would be resolved in the long term purely on playing ability, particularly if there were no other ways (e.g., well-known reputation) to confirm or deny the claimed identity.

In all of these cases, when there are genuine suspicions, or when an individual is being particularly tiresome by making obviously invalid claims, a number of sanctions are available. In climbing, some form of public and deliberate embarrassment (by exposing the individual's lack of knowledge, or by coercing the individual onto a particularly terrifying or difficult route), may be used. But it is more likely that the individual will be shunned and that his/her lack of reputation will become a part of local gossip. In rugby, players noted that liberal applications of alcohol may be used to loosen tongues and discover truths, and that culprits could be "punished" in practice games. In both of these sport subcultures it is entirely possible to construct an identity that will convince non-members and even rookie members that one has a reputation and a valid claim to membership. But the ongoing process of identity confirmation ensures that such individuals cannot do too much damage to the subculture itself, or to individual members. Participants are both the judges and the judged, and learning to become a rock climber or rugby player is partly a process of learning the signs of invalidity (i.e., who you can trust). Rookies might be "conned," but successful *socialization* eventually makes that much less likely.

Conclusion

The roles and identities of rock climbers and rugby players should not be thought of as static. They are constantly undergoing revision and change due to a variety of processes both within and outside the subcultures. Thus, socialization is an ongoing stage, and acceptance/ostracism is likely to be a repeated stage. In the model we have presented here, then, the key steps are the construction/reconstruction of an appropriate subcultural identity and the confirmation/reconfirmation of that identity by other members of the subculture. Similar steps may also be seen in recent versions of rugby and climbing, and in a variety of sport and occupational subcultures where individuals become participants after childhood.

Note

1 The relative absence of women during the time when we were doing the fieldwork for these ethnographies tended to blind us to the masculinist assumptions and styles prevalent in both sports. We have tried to rectify this in the present analysis.

References

Donnelly, P. (1994) "Take my word for it: trust in the context of birding and mountaineering," *Qualitative Sociology* 17(3): 215–41.

Donnelly, P. and Young, K. (1988) "The construction and confirmation of identity in sport subcultures," *Sociology of Sport Journal* 5(3): 223–40.

Klein, A. M. (1986) "Pumping irony: crisis and contradiction in bodybuilding," *Sociology of Sport Journal* 3(2): 112–33.

Orloff, K. (1974) "*Playgirl* presents the San Diego State rugby team," *Playgirl* 11(1): 44–6.

Simpson, J. (1989) *Touching the Void*, London: Pan.

Thomson, R. (1976) "Sport and deviance: a subcultural analysis," unpublished doctoral thesis, University of Alberta.

7

MAKING DECISIONS

How young people become involved and stay involved in sports

Jay Coakley and Anita White

We met when Anita took a leave from a teaching position in England to collect data in Colorado Springs for her doctoral dissertation. As we talked about the sociology of sport we both noted that research (in 1983) did not tell us much about how sport participation was integrated into the lives of young people in either the USA or England. Over the next two years we talked about putting our different cultural perspectives together and doing a study of how young people made decisions about playing sports and how they integrated sport participation into their lives.

While Jay was on a sabbatical leave in England we sought funding for a qualitative research project on sport participation among young people. By chance, we were looking for research funds at the same time that the British Sports Council was running a media campaign to encourage young people to participate in selected organized sport programs. Although the Sports Council was interested in slightly different issues from those we wanted to study, we negotiated with them and came up with a project that met their interests and ours.

This chapter represents a portion of the total project, a project that was an enjoyable learning experience for both of us. We worked as a pair when we did most of the interviews. It was useful to have a woman and a man do the interviews together, since this allowed us to ask questions from two gender perspectives. Also, Jay could rightfully act as if he did not have the cultural background to understand some of what the young people were saying during the interviews, so we were able to ask good follow-up questions in ways that didn't seem to bother the young people. They were happy to explain to a naive "foreigner" what was going on in their lives.

Our final research report was distributed to many people who worked at the Sports Council, and was used with other information as they formulated national policies (see White and Coakley 1986). We were pleased that some of our information influenced the Council's policy emphasis on youth sport participation. Our findings on how gender and gender relations influenced young people's decisions about sport participation were also reflected in the Council's new policies on girls and women in sports. When Anita left her position as director of a college sport science program to become Director of Development for the British Sports Council, she used our project as a starting point as she helped to formulate other national sport policies and programs for young people and for girls and women in Britain.

Partly in response to public concern about unemployment and crime among young people, the British Sports Council, the government agency that oversees and funds sport programs in the UK, sponsored a national media marketing campaign designed to "sell" sport participation to young people. The main target population for the campaign was 14–18 year olds who were not involved in organized sport programs.

The campaign slogan "Ever Thought of Sport?" was used with promotional materials which included three waves of poster blitzes (on buses, in underground train stations, etc.), a series of radio commercials featuring a popular comedian promoting organized sports, six national half-hour TV programs, colorful leaflets highlighting promotional images from the TV programs, and a phone-in service to provide information on available sport programs. The general goal was to encourage young people to be "switched on" to sports because government officials defined organized sports as constructive and healthy free-time activities.

The success of the campaign did not meet expectations, and the Sports Council wanted to know why. We knew this, so we proposed a national study involving in-depth interviews with young people about their lives and how they made decisions about participation in sports. Our proposal was rejected since the Sports Council wanted a quantitative evaluation survey that would give them nationwide statistics on participation. However, one of the regional offices of the Sports Council decided that our qualitative study might tell them things that would not be included in the national statistical survey. So they gave us a grant to do in-depth interviews with a sample of young people living in their region.

Our study

Instead of focusing on the media campaign, our study focused on young people's lives and how sport participation either fitted or did not fit into their lives. We interviewed 26 young women and 33 young men aged from 13 to 20. Half were chosen because they were participants in one of the sport programs promoted in the "Ever Thought of Sport?" campaign, while the other half were identified by teachers or program organizers as "drop-outs" or "non-participants." Our goal was to select a sample consisting of equal numbers of males and females from different class and ethnic backgrounds. About 85 percent of the young people we interviewed were white Britons, 15 percent had other racial or ethnic backgrounds (blacks with African or West Indian heritage, Indians, and other Asians). About 75 percent were from working-class families, and 25 percent were from moderately successful middle-class families. All interviews, lasting an average of about 45 minutes, were tape recorded (Coakley and White 1992).

Generally, our interviews were conducted as semi-structured conversations about how each young person in our sample went about making choices about what to do with free time. We talked about what activities they did and did not like, what they did with friends or by themselves, what they thought about as they made decisions about what to do, and how their activities were connected with their identities, their lives, and their relationships with others.

During the interviews we avoided asking "why?" questions (such as, "Why did you do this or that?"). These questions usually encourage answers in the form of clichés because people often find it difficult to explain their motives. When they try, they construct answers to justify their behaviors in terms they think will be accepted by the interviewers. So we asked questions about what, when, and how things happened in the young people's lives. This allowed us to request information and clarifications in an unthreatening manner. We never wanted the young people to think we were challenging their decisions or demanding justifications for "why" they did certain things, or "why" they chose some activities over others. We were looking for detailed descriptions of what happened in their lives. We assumed these descriptions would enable us to determine why certain choices were made. We were pleased with the dynamics of the interviews. The respondents generally enjoyed talking about themselves and even the shy or defiant ones seemed to warm up after conversations started. Only once did we seriously doubt the honesty of the information disclosed by a respondent. In this case, the young person seemed bothered by a parent who was often in a position to hear what she said.

Major findings

Our analysis involved listening to each of the interview tapes at least three times. We identified important points and patterns as we took notes and transcribed key statements made by the young people.

Our interviews indicated that sport participation was not a separate experience in the lives of young people. In fact, decisions about playing sports were closely tied with four factors:

- the concerns that the young people had about growing up and being seen as competent;
- the young people's sense of who they were and what was important in their lives;
- constraints associated with a lack of money, the rules and wishes of parents, and the expectations of girlfriends or boyfriends;
- vivid memories of past experiences in school sports and physical education.

Although our interviews were not designed to ask how gender was connected with decisions to play sports, we found that gender exerted a pervasive and powerful influence in the lives of the young people. In fact, each of these four factors played out differently in the lives of the young men than they did in the lives of the young women. Although gender and social class often were interrelated as the young people made choices about sport participation, we will focus primarily on gender in this chapter.

Sport participation decisions tied to concerns about "growing up" and being competent

Our interviewees were very sensitive to the issue of growing up. They wanted to be independent and in control of their lives. Therefore, they often chose leisure activities that were not tightly controlled by adults. They preferred activities that would prepare

them for adulthood or enable them to do adult things. When sport activities and programs were in any way associated with childhood, the young people, especially the young
women, generally decided not to participate. For example, a 15 year old told us that she
and her friends quit playing netball at school because they thought it was "babyish" and
that boys would see them as immature if they played.

This orientation was especially noticeable among girls who had just entered secondary
school. They assumed that at this point in their lives (age 13–14) they were supposed to be
"grown up," and that being "grown up" did not involve playing "kids games." Many of
our interviewees defined being an adult in terms of having a job and money of their own,
and being independent. A few 17 and 18 year olds spoke about being married and starting
a family. None of the young women saw sport participation as being important in their
transition to adulthood. For them, playing sports was perceived as a step backward in
their development. More relevant to becoming a woman were activities and relationships
through which their "femininity" could be reaffirmed. Playing sports, in their minds, did
not serve this purpose.

The young men, however, saw sport participation as compatible with their transition
to adulthood, even when it had no direct connection with jobs or future careers. Sport
participation, in the minds of the young men, was clearly associated with becoming a man.

Young people also chose to play sports when they thought they could use them to
extend and display their competence. For example, a 13-year-old dancer explained that
she liked dancing "because I know myself I can do it." A thoughtful, unemployed 20 year
old said that without certain skills a person could not experience the challenges provided
by sports. He played chess and board games because he was good enough at them to
experience the challenges they offered. He said he avoided soccer because he did not have
the physical skills needed to play the game at a level that involved exciting challenges. A
16-year-old member of a cycling touring club told us he would not join a racing club until
he knew he was "good enough." A 14 year old who enjoyed basketball at her school said
she would not join a basketball club because "I'm not very good . . . If you're not good,
you get shown up, don't you? You feel stupid – if you do something wrong you feel
stupid." A 17 year old explained that "if I did something that I didn't feel so useless at, I'd
keep at it . . . But when you're useless at something, you're not so enthusiastic."

Young women generally assumed that sports were not good vehicles through which
they could demonstrate their competence, but there were exceptions to this. Three young
women used sports to prove they deserved respect among men. A 17 year old who did
weight training explained this in the following way:

> I think mainly I want to be able to be equal with the blokes because I think too
> many girls get pushed around by blokes. They get called names and things.
> I think that's wrong. They say "a girl can't do this, a girl can't do that," and I
> don't like it at all. I'd rather be, you know, equal.

A second young woman, 15 years old, indicated that sports were important to her because
"if you . . . excel at sport as a girl at least you get the respect of the boys rather than
hearing 'oh, she's a sissy little girl.'" An 18 year old, who had taken a sport leadership
training course and was very sensitive to gender stereotypes, took great pride in showing
men that their stereotypes did not apply to her. She described a volleyball game in which
she was the only female participant:

There was a few chauvinistic men there but I proved myself in the end . . . First they said "don't pass it to her." Little did they know I was one of the best players at our school. I started doing these smashes over their heads and won their respect in the end. But you really have to prove yourself to them, but they're alright now.

Sport participation decisions tied to identity issues

A theme in our interviews was that decisions to participate in sports were generally based on the young persons' conclusions that playing sports was consistent with their sense of who they were and what was important in their lives. The ties between gender and these identity conclusions were strong. Statements from many young women indicated that they seldom identified themselves as athletes, even when they were physically active in sports like swimming and skating. They had learned to define sport and sport participation in a very restricted manner, and their definition led them to conclude that if the activity was not competitive, if there were no winners and losers, if there were no formal commitments to achievement and improvement, and if there were no organized teams or matches, then it was not sport. These young women had concluded that being an "athlete" meant being involved in an organized, competitive, physical activity. Therefore, when someone mentioned sports they simply tuned them out and assumed it had little relevance for them.

This orientation toward identity had been intensified through experiences at school for a few young women. For example, a 15-year-old student observed that if girls were supposed to play sports at her school they should not have been assigned a gym so small that they could not play any active games. The boys had better facilities and more resources. She had concluded that the message from school authorities was clear: girls were not meant to take sports seriously. Throughout the interview, it was clear that she did not take sport seriously in any way.

The young men we interviewed were much more apt to see themselves as "athletes," even when they did not play sports regularly. Most of them had at least some experience with soccer, and it seemed that even minimal experience with soccer or cricket provided a basis for identifying themselves as "athletes." Their sense that sports were masculine activities served to reaffirm this conclusion. However, there were a few exceptions to this. Some young men who lacked skills in popular sports, especially soccer, had received such negative feedback that they had taken great care to avoid any participation in organized sports. They had become physically inactive or had restricted involvement to informal physical activities done on their own or in the company of a close friend or family member.

Sport participation decisions tied to constraints of money, parents, and girl/boyfriends

Lack of money as a constraint

A lack of money had a significant impact on the sport participation of both young women and men. This is one of the primary ways that social class influences sport participation. Money was related to transportation, equipment, facilities, and programs in which there were entry fees, user fees, or membership dues. For example, an 18 year old who had participated in dance and gymnastics for nearly nine years indicated that money had long been an issue in her mind even though her parents had supported her involvement. She explained in the following way:

> I felt very bad, my mother wanted me to carry on but I felt guilty. When I started, the other girls, their dads were solicitors [lawyers] and bank managers and doctors and we were really the lowest of the low. My dad's a carpenter, you know . . . It didn't bother me until I started realizing that prices kept going up and I needed new changes of leotards and tracksuits.

A 15-year-old high school student from a working-class family also noted that her sport participation was limited because, "Whenever you want to go somewhere (money) is always a problem . . . First problem is how to get there, second problem is money."

The shortage of money affected both men and women. But it sometimes affected women more since money was needed by some to overcome the constraints imposed by parents who were worried about their safety. For example, having access to a car and not requiring public transport enabled some young women to participate in sports during the late afternoon and evening.

Parental rules as constraints

Our data indicated that parents were more "protective" of their daughters than they were of their sons. Girls' schedules were more closely monitored, and parental expectations were more clearly stated when it came to where their daughters could go to play sports, who they could go with, and when they had to return. These expectations caused the young women to be careful in selecting and becoming committed to playing sports. For example, joining a school team sometimes presented problems because practices or matches did not end until dusk or later, and the trip home would have to be made after dark (and the sun set before 5pm on the short days between mid-October and early March in England).

Many of the girls were required to make special arrangements with parents or friends if they expected to be out after dark. When we asked about this issue, most of the young women seemed to accept these expectations as "normal" and they voiced no objections. But it was clear that their awareness of and response to these expectations had an impact on their decisions about sport participation. Many young women were also expected to give their parents a relatively accurate accounting of their leisure activities. The legitimacy of their accounts was enhanced if they pointed out that they would be with a close friend. Therefore, while young men often hung around with a group of nameless "mates," young women were more likely to say they spent time with a "best friend."

This tendency to refer to a "best friend" who is known by parents seemed to be partly linked to the "conditional permission" girls received from their parents to participate in leisure activities away from home. For example, a few young women said their parents encouraged them to do things after school and on weekends as long as they met other conditions such as not staying out past dark, being home in time to assist with the family meal, or cleaning the house. In discussing this issue a 16 year old said, "I think my parents encouraged me. Well, if it was dark they weren't too keen on me staying [after school]. If there was someone to walk [home] with I'd play; if not, I wouldn't stay."

Fairness did not seem to be an issue when this form of parental protectiveness constrained the sport participation of girls and young women. The constraints were accepted without question. In fact, they were defined as indications of parental concerns for their safety and well being.

The young men and boys in our sample seldom mentioned parental constraints. They freely used public transportation, even after dark, and made decisions about leisure activities without seeking permissions from parents. They seemed to take their independence for granted, and they saw their safety and well being as things to be handled on their own.

Expectations of boy/girlfriends as constraints

In the case of dating relationships, the sport activities of young women were often altered when they had boyfriends. Young men were more likely to be the dominant persons in the relationships described by our interviewees. They more often chose to do things on their own than was the case for the young women who had boyfriends. For example, when an 18-year-old male was asked about how his girlfriend might influence his decisions on sport participation, he told us, "I do what I want." Then he said that once he made up his mind to do something it would be okay if his girlfriend went with him when he played sports, but if she didn't, he'd go without her. Similarly, a 16-year-old member of a roller hockey club indicated that his girlfriend was important in his life, but she knew better than to interfere with his hockey. Another hockey player, a 19 year old, said his girlfriend usually attended his weekly games, but she could not go to the last game because the car was too full of male players and their male friends.

In our interviews with young women we heard different stories. They gave priority to their relationships, and their sport and leisure activities were often chosen because they fitted in with what their boyfriends liked and did. For example, a 17 year old who ice skated three times a week before she met her new boyfriend explained that she had "cut skating down to once in a blue moon . . . I started 'going with' my boyfriend and I just lost interest in skating really . . . He skates very badly . . . We tried skating together, but he's not really keen on it . . . If it weren't for him, I think I'd go every night . . . I don't have the money to do much; I rely on my boyfriend really."

Sport participation decisions tied to memories of PE and school sports

Many young people, especially the young women, referred to school-related experiences when discussing their attitudes toward sports and sport participation. What had happened on school teams or in physical education (PE) classes served as the basis for what they expected in future sport experiences. Some memories were positive, but more often they were negative and subverted interest in sports. The major themes in these negative memories revolved around boredom and lack of choice, feeling stupid and incompetent, and receiving negative evaluations from peers.

For young women, physical education was often associated with feelings of discomfort and embarrassment. Usually it was not the physical activities themselves that turned them off. Instead, it was the bad memories associated with the rules and arrangements pertaining to required clothing and the changing/showering routine that typically accompanied PE classes. For example, a 13-year-old girl told us:

> I don't like it. I don't like going in the gym when you have to have bare feet; there's always a risk of passing [warts] and athlete's foot . . . That makes me shiver. I don't like that. And I don't like showers either. I think we should have separate showers. We've got them but they're not in use. There's a lack of privacy. It's totally open. You're not allowed to take your towel in with you. You've got to hang it up on the rail and walk through . . . Most of us in our year forge notes to get out; you know, headache, heavy cold, whatever. Mostly it's because they don't like cold weather and having to wear shorts . . . And the gym for girls is too small to do anything.

Privacy and appearance issues were important for young women. Unless sports were organized to allow the young women to control their physical appearance in ways that fitted their definition of who they were, they were not likely to participate. For example, a 14 year old said she never liked physical education classes because she was made to "go running round the streets in these horrible short skirts."

A few of the young women also had bad memories about the actual activities in physical education courses. A 14 year old remembered the following experience: "I didn't like gym . . . because I was bigger than everyone else, and if we had to do things like going over benches and if we had to crawl through, I hated that cos' me and my friend were big." She had enjoyed ice skating when it was offered as an option, but it only lasted for a short time. She had played netball with the school team but had dropped out after playing goalkeeper during a 14–0 loss by her team. She explained that after the game "Everyone was going, 'oh, it's your fault,' and I felt a bit bad. And it was cold and I just had to stand there."

The young men we interviewed were less likely to express negative memories about past experiences. It seemed that their physical education classes and sport activities were organized in ways that fitted more closely with their interests and skills than was the case for young women. But we also suspected that young men were less likely to admit that they did not like the sports activities played in physical education and after school. None of the young men complained about the cold weather or about being required to wear shorts or about the showers. The only negative memories they discussed were related to being teased or called names by their peers during activities or games, especially soccer games. Apparently, braving the cold weather and handling interaction in a locker/shower room were seen as compatible with how these young men saw themselves and their connections to peers.

Conclusions

Our study clearly shows that sport participation is an integral part of young people's lives, and it is best understood in the context of their lives as a whole. It is the result of decisions, and those decisions are tied to other concerns and issues. Sport participation in the lives of young people seems to occur when they decide it will help them extend control over their lives, present themselves to the rest of the world as a competent person, and reaffirm the way they think about themselves. Sport participation patterns shift over time depending on opportunities, constraints, social relationships, memories of the past, and changes in the lives and self-conceptions of young men and women. Although economic factors are important in this process, opportunities and constraints related to gender and gender relations are especially influential in decision-making processes.

We found that traditional cultural practices related to gender were taken for granted by most young men and women in our sample. None of the young men and only a few of the young women demonstrated awareness of issues or inequities related to gender, even though their decisions about sport participation clearly reflected the ways in which traditional gender definitions had been incorporated into their identities and their lives. Overt resistance to traditional ideas about gender was rare, but the actions of a number of the young people did challenge those ideas in subtle ways.

The major goal of this study was to provide the British Sports Council with information about how young people integrated sport participation into their lives. Our report listed many practical recommendations for those in the Council who drafted sport policies and worked with young people. We emphasized that policies should be based on an awareness that sport participation was but one part of young people's lives, and that programs should be designed with an understanding of what is important to young people as they cope with challenges and make decisions about their lives.

Our report also emphasized that current forms of gender relations constrain the decisions of girls and young women, and that policies and programs must deal with gender issues and be sensitive to the need for changes in gender relations. For adolescents looking toward becoming adults, policies informed by this awareness would make sport participation a more attractive alternative in many of their lives.

References

Coakley, J. and White, A. (1992) "Making decisions: gender and sport participation among British adolescents," *Sociology of Sport Journal* 9(1): 20–35.

White, A. and Coakley, J. (1986) *Making Decisions: The Response of Young People in the Medway Towns to the "Ever Thought of Sport?" Campaign*, London: Greater London and South East Regional Sports Council.

8

BECOMING AN INTERNATIONAL ATHLETE

Making decisions about identity

Christopher Stevenson

The genesis of this work on the careers of athletes came out of one fascination and two frustrations. I have always been fascinated by how social life works, and in particular how the social world of sport works. For as long as I can remember, I have always looked around me and noticed how people behave and have noticed the patterns – I have not understood them, but I've noticed them and wondered about them. And this was particularly so in my experience of sport. One of the things that I noticed very quickly about sport was how contingent everything was: not only during the playing of the game itself – the best team, the most prepared team didn't always win, the ball often seemed to take funny bounces, the referee often seemed to make strange calls at the wrong time, and so on – but also in terms of peoples' lives in sport. I heard the talk about cause and effect – for example, "work hard and you will succeed," and "talent will always show through" – but I realized that life in sport, or anywhere else for that matter, really was not like that. I looked at my own life in sport, as a water polo player in England and in Canada, and later as a rugby player and rugby referee in Canada, and realized just how lucky I had been in some instances (being a left-handed water polo player got me some opportunities that others, right-handers, did not get), and how in other instances I wished I had done things differently, and maybe the outcome would have been different too (worked harder, done more weights, changed clubs/coaches – and I would have made the team). So the fascination was with how did it work – surely it could not all just be chance?

The two frustrations came in my early attempts to try to find some answers. First, I thought that socialization theory was the place to look, and so I worked for over ten years in this area reading the literature and doing my own research. But in the end I was frustrated by its inability (as I saw it) to tell me what I wanted to know. And so, as I explain in the chapter following, I turned to interactionist theory which provided me with a whole new set of exciting revelations about how the social world worked. The second frustration was with survey research. I had done a lot of this, again trying to find answers to my questions, giving questionnaires of all sizes and descriptions to all sorts of different athlete groups. But time and time again I ended up wanting to know much much more than the survey data would tell me: How did that happen? How did that affect their lives? How did that influence the choices they made? Eventually I turned to qualitative research – interviewing and participant observations. Of course, I realized that, yes, these brought with them their own sets of problems and frustrations – but I felt the chances of finding the answers I was looking for were so much better.

And so, for the research described in this chapter I decided to look at the life histories of elite athletes and to use in-depth interviews as my tool so that I could ask the "how" questions. I also decided to use an interactionist theoretical perspective as a means of trying to understand what was happening in the athletes' lives. As a result I have been able to look at a number of different aspects of the athletic career: the early stages of the athletic career (1990a); the process of specialization on one particular sport (1990b); the athletes' perceptions of fairness (justice) in the selection processes to representative teams (1989a); the other factors (contingences) which influence "making it" in sport (1989b).

I am now extending this work to look at the careers of master athletes, particularly master swimmers, since that is what I am now doing myself. Do the same processes which seem to help us understand the careers of elite athletes also help us understand the careers of older, non-elite, more recreation-oriented and fitness-oriented athletes? I hope we shall be able to find out.

How do athletes become athletes? This is the question which drew me to this research. Where do athletes come from, and how is it that only some people get to be members of national teams, get to go to the Olympics, get to be professional athletes? The popular images we have from biographies and journalistic reports about such elite athletes – the Michael Jordans, Wayne Gretzkys, Janet Evanses, and Martina Hingises – is that somehow their journeys to the top were predestined. They were so good, so talented, that their progression to stardom was inevitable and unproblematic – a triumphant parade, almost. Yet, my own experience of sport, and those of my friends around me, was really not at all like that. My sport career, our sport careers, were not at all smooth sailing. And we saw so many talented people dropping by the wayside who lost interest, did not get picked for a select team, took up with boyfriend/girlfriend, fell out with the coach, decided to play in a band, got blocked by sport bureaucrats, and so on. We all know, sort of intuitively, that success in sport is not just merely a matter of having the necessary talent.

So, what are the processes, the real processes, which make a successful athletic career happen? At first I looked at the socialization literature to provide some answers. Certainly this research has been useful in telling us about the influences of parents, siblings, peers, teachers, coaches, etc. – as well as the effects of such variables as gender, race, social class, culture, and so on. But, ultimately, I found that it really could not tell me why one person would "make it" and why another person, perhaps equally talented, would not. It could not tell me much about the process – and that was what I was interested in. And so I turned to another theoretical approach to the problem – an interactionist approach. This approach to understanding and explaining social life and social behavior argues that individuals are actively engaged in the development of their own social lives – they make choices, they evaluate their options, they are reflexive (that is, they think about themselves, their situations, and the other people involved in those situations), and they are motivated above all by a desire to do what is the best for themselves (whatever they discern that to be). This interactionist approach also emphasizes the central concern of identity. Individuals are seen as being actively involved in the process of identity formation; that is, active in developing, appropriating, and supporting those "role identities" which they perceive to be desirable or valuable. McCall and Simmons (1978: 65) describe role identity as "the character and the role that an individual devises for him[/her]self as an occupant of a particular social position." Hewitt (1989) has characterized this as a combination of a social identity and a personal identity. From this perspective, then, individuals choose to try to develop or continue to maintain particular role identities, of basketball player, say, or age-group swimmer, because of the value to themselves which they see in that role identity – the social, material, emotional benefits which they can see themselves deriving from their involvement in that role identity. All of the decisions and choices they make in the pursuit of those careers, those specific athletic role-identities, can be seen as attempts to maximize the potential rewards from those involvements, as well as minimizing the potential costs.

This study

Taking this approach, I decided to investigate the careers of some members (N = 29) of Canadian and British national teams. I chose the men's water polo teams in both countries (N = 10), the women's field hockey teams in both countries (N = 8), and the men's rugby teams in Canada and England (N = 11). I had quite pragmatic reasons for these choices – I had personally been involved in water polo and rugby in both England and in Canada, and so I knew people who could give me access to the national team members. I also had colleagues who were active in field hockey at the national level, and who knew the people who counted in both countries, and so could give me access to those teams. I decided to choose the "rookies," the first-year players on each of these teams, because of their recent elevations to the national teams.

In order to obtain the data that I needed to explore the questions in which I was interested, I felt that personal one-on-one, tape-recorded interviewing was the way to go. I wanted so much in-depth information about the sporting lives of these elite athletes and the various decisions they had had to make in the course of their careers, and I needed to be able to follow up interesting lines of information and to explore their feelings and emotions about the choices they had made. I would not have obtained this kind of data if I had used questionnaire surveys.

But using this methodology has its own problems. It is a very time-consuming means of collecting data. Each interview took between one and two hours to complete. Then there was the problem getting to wherever the athletes happened to be (their homes, universities, coffee shops, practice sites, and so on) and making preparations for the interview. Arranging to meet people is not always easy. Some people's schedules were incredibly complicated; others were only available at six in the morning or after ten at night; some people had "forgotten" about the appointment and could not do it when I showed up, so we had to reschedule. Then there is the need to make the interviewees feel relaxed and comfortable, so that they will honestly and openly answer the questions and provide you with the "real" truth about their lives, and not just the "truth" they think you might want to hear or the "truth" they think might put them in the best light. Some people are very keen to tell you all about themselves – like turning on a tap and sitting back to listen – in fact, sometimes it is hard to turn them off, or to make sure they are talking about what you want them to talk about. Others are shy, closed and monosyllabic, and it is a lot of really hard work to get them to tell you about their lives and the decisions they have had to make and how they feel about those decisions.

Introductions and involvements

So what did I find out about these athletes and how their careers had unfolded? Well, the first thing I discovered was the enormous diversity there was in their career paths. At face value, it seemed that each one was so unique that there was little commonality with any other. Some began competitive careers in their sports at 7, 9 or 13 years of age, while others waited until late teens or even early twenties. There were fathers involved, mothers involved, friends, teachers, sisters and brothers, coaches, and friends of the family. Early in their careers these athletes were often involved in a large number of sports simultaneously – soccer, volleyball, netball, ice hockey, swimming, equestrianism, gymnastics, dance, and so on and so on. Sam [these names have been changed], when he was young, "used to plague my Mom and Dad's lives" in order to be allowed to play sport. Susan did too:

> I did every sport I could. I just did sports all year long . . . I have two brothers and we used to play hockey and we used to play football . . . When I was little I used to do everything they would do . . . just anything and everything sports-wise that was going.

So, it was quite a daunting prospect to have to make some coherent sense out of all this diversity. What I had to find out was how, out of all of these involvements, a commitment to a specialized involvement in one particular sport could emerge. What I found useful was to make a distinction between their introductions to their sport and their involvements and commitments to their sport. I found that these processes, though obviously interdependent and intertwined, were in fact distinct. Just because someone is introduced to a sport, or indeed introduced to any sort of involvement, it does not mean that they will necessary or inevitably become committed to it. Now, of course, some did – eleven out of the twenty-nine athletes, all males. From almost their first introductions, these athletes seemed to know that they had found "their" sport. "From the very first practice, I fell in love with water polo," said Ron. Bob was the same way, becoming immediately committed to rugby, although admittedly his mother had to force him to try it initially:

> I was always the one that my Mother would say, "Go with your Father to the rugby game." My other brothers wouldn't, so I always went. And my Dad would go out training and she would say, "Go with your Father, go out training with him."

For the rest of their careers, these athletes did not remember having any conflicts or doubts about their choice of sport. But for the other eighteen athletes I interviewed, it was a very different matter. There was uncertainty, there was conflict, and in some cases there was a need for a radical redirection of their energies and commitments. There seemed to be two types of circumstances in which all this occurred – either there was pressure to make a choice from among a number of simultaneous involvements, or an athletic career in one particular sport had to come to an end before another career, which took them to elite status, could begin. For a majority of these athletes (N = 12; 6 male, 6 female) a moment eventually came when they had to make a decision between a number of sports in which they were involved. For example, Hilda had for years been trying to juggle her involvements in badminton, athletics and field hockey; Steve was competing in skiing and water polo; Martha was excellent at both netball and field hockey, doing one at school and the other at a community club. Eventually a time came, often in their teenage years, when a choice had to be made between these involvements because of the increasing demands of time and energy. Hilda remembered:

> I used to be in the County junior badminton squad. And then . . . one year I did pretty well [in high jump] and was ranked third or fourth in the country for my age. I was invited to join the Junior National High Jump squad, which also happened to fall on the Saturday of Junior County trials for field hockey, and it also fell on the Saturday for badminton squad training. So, we then had a big dilemma . . . I had a big decision then.

In all cases, the athletes resolved their problems by making an independent decision, although many of them did consult with parents, friends, teachers, siblings, and so on. Hilda recalled talking to "my sister, my PE teacher, people at the hockey club, my high jump coach, badminton coach, and all the rest." For some, the choice was a reasonably easy one to make: "No, it wasn't hard [it was] water polo all the way," But others found it a much more difficult decision to make: "It was a tough decision, you know," and "I was really serious about rugby. I was [high school] captain for three years. But . . . water polo!"

In the cases of the other six athletes (4 males, 2 females) who had to make decisions about their sporting careers, one athletic career had to come to an end before another athletic career could begin. Each of these athletes had been pursuing a sporting career for some years; for example, Eddie had been a football player all through high school and university and had gone on to a professional career, Tessa had been a competitive swimmer from the age of 8 to 16, and Kate "was first and foremost a netball player." Despite these, often long-term, commitments to the sports, various circumstances conspired to bring these careers to an end, forcing the athletes to make further career-determining decisions. The careers of four of the athletes ended involuntarily: that is, circumstances out of their control ended their involvements in these sports. Eddie was "cut" during training camp after two years as a professional football player. Jon was considered "too slow" by his new college basketball coach. Tessa ended her swimming career because of a personality conflict with her coach:

> I hated that decision . . . and it was a shame because I love swimming and I loved what it did for me . . . I remember telling my Dad and just bawling my

eyes out . . . About eight of us quit at one time, and some of the others a little later. Most of them never went back. I was lucky because I went on to another sport.

The other two athletes chose to end their first careers themselves, voluntarily. Each of them decided to de-emphasize his involvement in one sport while increasing involvement in another. Dave began to realize his limitations in volleyball, even though he was playing at an intercollegiate level, and began to pursue a previously incidental interest in rugby. Dougal quite simply shifted his involvement from running to swimming, even though he personally much preferred running: "I was winning races [in swimming], so it just seemed logical at the time to continue doing that, although I didn't enjoy it to begin with."

At some point, then, each of these eighteen athletes had to make decisions about which sport to choose, or whether to pursue other sports, and at what level. What I found most interesting in these decisions were the two considerations on which they were made. The predominant factor seemed to be the individual athlete's evaluation of relative "potential for success" which each sport offered. This was a very conscious and deliberate determination by the athletes of their chances of "success" (however they defined this) in the various sports. Hilda's comment, "It was a question of what I was going to get furthest in," was echoed by many; for example, Susan, "Field hockey is so important . . . that I will give up, like, gymnastics. It was fun, but . . . where I'm going is field hockey." Similarly Jon, on reflection, realized his aptitude for rugby:

> I was probably a better rugby player than I was a basketball player. Rugby is more my natural game, more aggression and stuff . . . Some of my friends would say to me, you know, "You should really be playing rugby instead of basketball because you play that better."

A second factor in these decisions was an appraisal of the "people" who were involved in the various sports. The sport chosen tended to be the one with the more positively evaluated "people." Some of the athletes talked in generalities about the "crowds" who played the different sports, or in terms of "team spirit" or "social life" associated with the sports. But others were quite specific about their evaluations of people. Dave commented: "I didn't like the people involved in [volleyball] . . . The social part of rugby is fun too, I like that . . . These guys got a good sense of humour and stuff, they're easy to get along with." Val felt similarly:

> [Tennis] could get really bitchy . . . It was all very self, self, you know. I didn't find hockey that way. It's a team game. I mean, I feel happy in a team . . . a bit of a team spirit, it's really good. I prefer it to tennis.

Commitments

We can see, therefore, that the athletes made self-conscious and self-reflexive decisions deliberately to choose the athletic role identity and career in which they saw their best possibilities for both athletic success and an association with people they liked or whose support they valued. But having chosen these particular sport involvements, how did their commitments to them develop? What were the processes through which this initial involvement in their sport became deeper, more intense, and all-encompassing? It seems that these commitments were created through the combined effects of entanglements, commitments, and reputations and identities. And it was in the working out of these processes that, once again, the athletes' active, self-reflexive decision-making played a critical part in determining the course of their sport involvements.

Entanglements

Entanglements are those relationships which act to involve an individual more and more deeply in a role or an activity – like the sticky web of a spider, tying the individual up in more and more strands. Such entanglements, for example, with parent, siblings or friends, seemed to be critical in the development of the athlete's commitment to his or her sport. For example, some of the athletes' parents were involved as their age-group coaches – indeed Ned's father actually created an age-group team just so that his son could play. Clive described how his brother "dragged me down" to water polo practices. Eddie's brother-in-law was "heavily involved in rugby" and invited him to "come on out and play." Susan's friends all played field hockey. Bill's friends played rugby, and Gary's friends played water polo. These webs of relationship drew the athletes deeper into their sporting involvements, and they chose to allow themselves to be drawn in because of the value they placed on those relationships.

Commitments

What seemed to cement these involvements even further were the effects of commitments. These are the set of obligations, whether real or felt, which ties the athlete even more closely into the activity. Some of them are the typical responsibilities to attend practices and games, the obligations to teammates and coach because the team relies on you to be there, and the obligations to display the appropriate attitudes and behaviors once you are there. But many of the athletes also expressed their feelings of obligation towards their parents, because of their involvements in the earlier stages of their careers, the enthusiasm they had shown, and the time and money they had invested. Val describes her parents as "a driving force" behind her athletic career, because of her "Mum and Dad being so keen on me playing hockey." Bob continued as designated son/rugby player, "because of my commitments with my Father . . . [and his] desire to have me play international rugby and how much that meant to him." Once again, the athlete is put into a decision-making position – choosing whether or not to meet the obligations.

Reputations and identities

The process of involvement that began with entanglements and commitments soon becomes consolidated by reputations and identities. Many athletes quickly achieved some form of success. These successes rapidly produced valued identities and reputations that were constantly being confirmed by their peers, their parents and others. These identities therefore acted to reinforce the athletes' decisions to continue their involvements in their sports – the sport role identity was now demonstrably producing valuable rewards. Martha remembered being recognized as one of the better players at her high school, "I think through my time at school I was captain all the time." They became stars of their teams and of their peer groups. As Jon recalled: "I always related rugby season to being popular. When it started in September, me and my best friend were both stars on the team it seemed, and got the girls, and I was very popular. So I always loved rugby season."

Conclusions

So what can we conclude: that the athletic career is not necessarily all that straight-forward; that some athletes (most, perhaps, and certainly it seems, most women) have decisions to make at some point in their athletic careers concerning their future involvements in sport. Some have to choose which single sport they will continue to pursue from the two or three sport involvements which they have maintained so far. Other athletes are confronted with a dilemma because of the termination or winding down of a career in another sport. In either situation, the decisions that the athletes make seem to be based on considerations of the "potential for success" which the chosen sport offers, and the kind of "people" who are involved.

Both of these considerations are understandable from an interactionist perspective. I explained previously that, from this perspective, the individual is seen as actively engaged in developing and confirming those role identities which he or she perceives to be desirable or valuable. The decisions and the choices the athletes make in the pursuit of their careers, i.e., the specific athletic role identities, can be seen as attempts to maximize the potential social, material, and emotional rewards from those involvements (as well as minimizing the potential costs). The seeking after athletic success, which appeared to motivate many of the athletes' decisions, can be understood as a deliberate search for certain role identities that are recognized by the athletes and by others as valuable and desirable. The immediate commitment to "their" sports on the part of some of the athletes can be explained by the success they immediately achieved. Val, for example, described her happiness with field hockey, "It was really good. I used to come home with arms loaded [with prizes]." Those who had to choose between sports or decide on a new involvement also spoke of the importance that "potential for success" played in their decisions. As Dougal remembered:

> My main sport was running . . . [but] I wasn't getting anywhere, I wasn't winning races. Whereas with swimming, I didn't enjoy it but I was getting quite successful. I was winning races, so it just seemed logical at the time to continue doing that, although I didn't enjoy it to begin with.

The importance in these decisions of the evaluations of the "people" involved in the sports can also be understood from this perspective. These can be seen as attempts by the athletes to affiliate themselves with those individuals whose own identities they value, either because of their social status, or because of the "role support" which these individuals may provide for the athlete's developing role identity. As one strives to develop and maintain a particular role identity, and to perform it correctly, the notion of role support expresses the crucial part that approval, reinforcement, and correction by others plays in this identity confirmation process. These athletes' own words reveal the importance of "people" in their decisions to commit themselves to particular role identities and athletic careers. Dave did not like "the people involved in [volleyball]," but thought that the guys in rugby were "easy to get along with." Also Sue recalled, "All my friends played field hockey. I didn't know what field hockey was, but I thought, 'Well, my friends are playing it so why don't I?'" Val commented, "If Mum hadn't played hockey . . . I wouldn't have been as interested." As an extreme example, Bob said:

> You have to go to our house – pictures all over the walls of my Dad, the [club and international] teams he played for. And I was the designated son to carry on that tradition. So I always had to make that sacrifice. I sort of got into a rut that I had to say "Yes," and then it just sort of kept on.

Thus, we can see the athletes making self-conscious and self-reflexive decisions deliberately to choose the athletic role identity and career in which they saw their best possibilities for both athletic success and role support. Having chosen their sporting involvements, the processes of entanglements, commitments, reputations and identities act to draw the athlete deeper and deeper into a commitment to that athletic role identity and career. Of course these processes have already been at work as part of the decision-making processes for those athletes who have had to decide between competing sport involvements. Thus, the athletes evaluated their relationship entanglements and decided which ones were more important and which were of lesser importance – those they could ignore and those they had to take into account. What were the implications for their own chances of being able to perform a desirable role identity, and what were the chances of obtaining valuable role support from their relationships with these various people? Similarly, with commitments – which obligations were important and which were not? Which could be ignored with regard to the successful maintenance of their role identity, and which could not? The interactionist perspective suggests that such decisions are made on the basis of a cost–benefit evaluation of the consequences of meeting or breaking these obligations. Where relationships with parents or any other valued significant other are involved, the stakes are high. How desirable is the involvement in that sport role identity? What social, material, and emotional rewards are likely? But what are the social, material, and emotional costs of maintaining those obligations? And the part that reputations and identities plays is obvious. The more rewards the athletes receive from their athletic role identities – "star" of the basketball team, popular with the "in"-crowd – the greater the cost of not performing that role identity well and the greater the incentives to continue to maintain it.

As it turned out, the athletes whom I interviewed had made career and identity decisions that had led to successful outcomes – they were selected for the national teams. Many other athletes have made decisions which have not turned out well – at least, not in the same way. We know, of course, that all kinds of other contingencies seem to be at least as important in the making of a sports career, such as being in the right place at the right time, being seen by the right people, taking advantage of opportunities when they become available, changes in the coaching staff, and so on. Nevertheless, this research does suggest that the image of the simplistic inevitability of the athletic career is not an entirely accurate representation of reality. The careers of these athletes seemed to be neither inevitable nor unproblematic, not withstanding their unquestioned abilities – rather they were contingent on certain choices which they had made. There were many twists and turns, and a few blind alleys, along the way. I hope this research also illustrates the usefulness of the interactionist approach in helping us to understand the bases of the critical decisions that these athletes made.

References

Hewitt, J. P. (1989) *Dilemmas of the American Self*, Philadelphia: Temple University Press.

McCall, G. J. and Simmons, J. L. (1978) *Identities and Interactions*, New York: Free Press.

Stevenson, C. L. (1989a) "Perceptions of justice in the selection of national teams," *Sociology of Sport Journal* 6(4): 371–9.

—— (1989b) "The athletic career: some contingencies affecting the selection of national teams," paper presented at North American Society for the Sociology of Sport, Washington, DC.

—— (1990a) "The early careers of international athletes," *Sociology of Sport Journal* 7(3): 238–53.

—— (1990b) "The athletic career: some contingencies of sport specialization," *Journal of Sport Behavior* 13(2): 103–13.

9

COMING OF AGE IN NORTH AMERICA

Socialization of Dominican baseball players

Alan M. Klein

Dominicans often boast that at the birth of a boy their hospitals automatically place miniature baseball gloves in the beds. Exaggeration or not, no other country has developed as many Major League players per capita as the Caribbean nation of the Dominican Republic. The 1997 season opened with 57 Dominicans (from a country of 7 million) on Major League rosters, and hundreds waiting in the wings of various minor leagues.

The origins and rise of this island baseball power were the subject of numerous articles in US newspapers in 1987. These stories all concluded that poverty created and fueled this dynamo. While at first the explanation seemed reasonable, further reflection made me wonder why similar levels of widespread poverty had not created comparable levels of excellence in baseball playing countries like Mexico, Venezuela, or Puerto Rico. I decided to explore the question. I would soon learn that another equally powerful factor accounted for the establishment of high caliber baseball as early as the turn of the century: the social economy of sugar production. Managers at the many US-owned sugar refineries bet heavily on baseball contests played against rival refineries. To field the best teams they offered outstanding athletes the opportunity to skip work. Since cane cutting is some of the most backbreaking work found anywhere, no better incentive could be offered. The color barrier in North American baseball prevented Dominicans from exporting their talents until the 1950s. While Dominicans now have regular access to lucrative major league careers, they continue to face subtle cultural and organizational impediments to the pursuit of their dreams.

My research would quickly grow from assessing the game within the Dominican Republic to looking at the interface between the USA and Dominican baseball. Beginning with the 1987 season, I carried out a primarily ethnographic investigation, but also included oral and archival histories of players of previous eras, as well as survey research. My goal was a book-length ethnography, a comprehensive analysis of the sport in which Dominican baseball would be treated as a complete culture unto itself. I would look at its structure, history, unique relationship with North America, and its role in the larger society. This chapter draws on one part of my research in which I examined the socialization of Dominican baseball players who had already signed on professionally and were playing the Dominican Rookie League. I looked at the process by which they learn not only to be baseball players with promise, but also how they learn what North American teams expect of them. Four years and seven field trips later I completed the work which appeared under the title *Sugarball: The American Game, The Dominican Dream* (1991, Yale University Press).

As with so much of ethnography, the path set out upon is rarely the path completed. My initial strategy was to observe the Dominican professional league and the amateur leagues that fed them, but somewhere during my first months there I was introduced to the baseball academies (*los hogares de beisból*). These are training camps for players who have been signed by a team. Having stumbled upon the academy, I still had to get access to it, which meant obtaining the go-ahead from a major league club. The first and foremost stumbling block for ethnographic research is gaining access. I approached half a dozen major league teams with my project, but only when I included a proposal that would allow the teams to help their players overcome some of the culture shock that accompanies their moves to the USA were my efforts met with success. The Los Angeles Dodgers gave me entry to their academy outside the capital city of Santo Domingo.

By the early 1950s, Dominican baseball had become a feeder system for certain major league teams. Thirty years later most teams saw how cost effective signing Dominican talent was. Not part of the US baseball draft, Dominican youths were being freely recruited and signed for $4,000 as compared with six-figure signing bonuses given to most decent picks in the USA. An enterprising team could sign thirty Dominicans for what it would have cost them to sign only a decent draft pick at home. Since there are limitations on how many visas for foreign players the Department of Labor grants to major league baseball, each team must take care to award them to the best possible rookies. Having signed so many Dominicans, Major League teams needed a way to develop them to the point where they might enter the North American minor league system – hence the baseball academy.

The Dodger academy, Campo Las Palmas, afforded me the opportunity to observe, travel with, and interview the players and personnel in any context I wanted. I needed to pursue two tracks: gathering data for my own general sociological interest; and developing a set of proposals on how to foster better adjustments on the part of the Dominican players coming to North America. Without intending to, I had begun a study that was as much applied sociology (or anthropology) as it was purely ethnographic. In time I would design and implement a language program for the academy which might prove useful for other teams. Of equal importance, I tried to present the process of preparing a Dominican player as being social–cultural as much as it was athletic. The players coming to the academy were young men from a biological standpoint. They had already become socialized in their Dominican context, but upon signing with a team they had to become socialized once again, a process that involved some unlearning as well as learning anew.

The study

It was essential to see Campo Las Palmas as much more than a facility for churning out baseball players. For those studying sport in an international context involving industrial and developing nations, culture becomes the crucial variable. It is the study of culture that illuminates many of the issues and difficulties that come up in the course of Dominican rookies trying to make it in North American baseball; and North American clubs trying to train Dominican rookies to succeed by their standards. The academy as a cultural interface is very much evident in the role of Campo Las Palmas as the first North American run institution with which Dominican rookies come into sustained contact. The academy also acts as a remedial center in which young men from very under-privileged backgrounds are taught how to function in settings most of us take for granted (e.g. using toilets properly, dental hygiene). This cultural interface emerges again in the academy's function as a psychological assessment center (built upon North American cultural assumptions) in which the staff are only interested in evaluating the psychological make-up of the player: How easily does he take instruction? How psychologically stable is he?

Campo Las Palmas consists of a director (Dodger Vice President, Ralph Avila), his coaching staff, a crew of people to maintain the 400-acre complex, and group of up to forty rookies. The rookies would spend up to two years learning, or rather relearning, the sport from the Dodger perspective. The Dominican government has decreed that no one under the age of 17 is to be signed, but birth certificates are routinely lost or forged so that even younger men might try out for the Dodgers.

For the young man gaining entry to the academy there is relief (at least temporarily) from poverty. Youths from all over the island are either invited to come to the academy or show up at the gates during certain times of the year in which try-outs are granted. If they impress Avila they receive a signing bonus of $5,000 (in 1987 it was $4,000) and $750 a month salary during the two years they will play as Dominican rookies. In a nation in which the average annual income is $1,300, these young men are in positions substantially to relieve the burdens that plague their families. Thousands of young men play in amateur leagues hoping to enter one of these academies. Campo Las Palmas is the immediate promise of what is hoped will be a much greater future: a career in base-ball. Status immediately accrues to the youngster who signs, and with it a new and more onerous responsibility: having to hold onto that status. One ex-major leaguer summed it up: "It's very prestigious playing in the States. Everybody knows you now. They follow you. But unfortunately, in the Dominican Republic when a player gets released, you wouldn't believe the shame. You're worthless. You're a failure. If you don't make it, it's like you broke the dream."

While the people running the Dodger academy understand the sensitive remedial role that their facility plays, they are nevertheless faced with having cooly to determine which of the young men in their charge will be most likely to make it to the majors. According to Avila:

Only 3 percent of the ballplayers we sign make it to the big leagues. The other 97 percent fail and have to come back here and go to work in the factories or in the sugar cane fields. We can see the physical part of a player almost right away. Hitting, nobody knows, but if you got power, you're gonna show it as soon as you make contact. We can see this stuff in the first week. The rest of the month [first month], they're gonna show us their habits: their drive, their dedication, determination, desire, and durability, the five "Ds."

An ethnography of Dominican players must, of necessity, look at how players are socialized into their roles. What makes this process difficult is that these young Dominicans must be doubly socialized: first into baseball rookie status, then into North American rookie status. Further complicating this process is the fact that many young men in these academies take longer to reach the level of emotional maturity as defined by North Americans. It is not simply that they must master North American rookie standards, but they are also being judged by their ability to do so as quickly as North American rookies.

Socializing the rookies

When carried out in a group, rather than individually, socialization takes on the look of a rite of passage, the type of coming of age initiations found the world over. Classic examples of this process include US military basic training and fraternity pledging, but comparable examples can be found in any age-graded, single-sex initiations. Typically, the group being socialized is temporarily isolated and intimidated; old ideas and attitudes are eliminated before being replaced by new ones. This part of the socialization process involves external agencies (adults of one sort of another) working to remove individual differences among the initiates, then fashioning a group identity before allowing them to take on adult status. At Campo Las Palmas, Avila and his staff carry this out by creating a spartan atmosphere of intimidation in which all the rookies' time is micromanaged and the specter of failure (and success) is constantly dangled before them. In their boot-camp treatment of players the academy is socializing as an external agency.

The rookies, however, also form their own entity, in part as a response to the external agents and in part as a group with shared experiences. This is internal or peer socialization. In particular, they become a bachelor subculture: a group of males bonded by common experience and generating behavioral and ideological attributes that glorify manhood. Traditionally, sport has fostered the creation of such subcultures which exclude women and non-conventional males. In Dominica these young men form links based on their shared experiences, anxieties, and fears.

Thus, external and internal forces are at work to socialize these young men. External socialization comes through the structure imposed upon them by the academy. First and foremost, as members of the Dominican rookie Dodger team, they form a common identity in playing rookies from other major league organizations. This process is accelerated by wearing the official Dodger uniforms, residing at Campo Las Palmas, traveling to contests in the team bus displaying the Dodger logo, and the constant instruction on what it means to be a Dodger. Eager to identify with their "parent" club, Dominican rookies quickly forge their new identities each time they don their uniform and other Dodger paraphernalia. They gaze at the poster-size portraits of Dominicans who have made good in the Dodger organization which grace the walls of many of the buildings at the academy.

Dodger personnel also seek to instil a sense of humility and even fearfulness in these rookies so that they do not develop into "headcases". This is done through a constant litany on life in the USA being full of doubt and difficulty:

> You gotta be thinking baseball all the time, not money or women. [In the US minor leagues] you travel in buses with no air conditioning, sleep in lousy hotels, eat strange foods with people you can't talk with. You have a manager, and you don't know if he don't like you as a Black or as a Latino. You don't know who you're gonna be facing. The four or five years you spend in the minors, you're gonna be suffering. And that's if you even get there. Most of you won't.

Of course there is the simple reality that the organization will only allow those who achieve the goals set out for them to pass on to the next hurdle. Faced with a stern regimented program that demands much of them, and the ability of the organization to promote or eliminate them, there is ample reason to integrate as much as possible. The only place the players would want to stick out would be on the field. Thus, the academy seeks to remove various traits, replacing them with new ones that might make the journey ahead more fruitful.

The players also develop a sense of identity that serves as a source of internal socialization. During the period of observation, they clearly sought to work out as a coherent and smooth running group. This would have various components: mentoring and leveling, in order to begin competing as a unit.

Upon signing with the Dodgers the rookies become paid professionals. They compete in the Dominican Rookie League against other major league affiliates. Playing two seasons of the year, these rookies rack up competitive experience as a group and benefit from all the mutual dependency one would expect of such a demanding schedule. For newly arrived rookies, the first weeks in the academy can be intimidating. In the strange and structured surroundings the rookies find they have none of the familiar supports available. Older players will often take on mentoring roles:

> The guys who have been here awhile, like me for instance, help out the new guys. I'm a shortstop working with that new guy over there from Puerto Plata. Once these guys get signed, they are taken on [included]. As long as they don't have swelled heads we get along.

The rookies gladly accept any hand outstretched that would make their transition easier:

> Well, at first I felt strange with the kids [at the academy]. But I already got to know them better. They were nice to me because last year another Venezuelan guy had been here. I was a little nervous early on, but I already knew Eleodoro from before, and he told me how things worked here. It helped to get into things quickly.

On occasion a new arrival will be overly defensive, and this may be manifested in a belligerence toward others. At this point the group may use a leveling strategy psychologically to knock him down to the point where he will fit more easily into the group:

The new guys are taught by those who have been here a while. Like, I help that new guy, the second baseman over there. If they have an attitude – well that's different. We turn our backs on them, the hot dogs. We have a new guy, Norberto, and he is that way. Last week we played and the umps called him out twice sliding into second base. Afterward the ump told me that he thought it was close but the guy was a jerk, so he called him out. We all laughed and later told Norberto about it. He was angry with us that we didn't stick up for him. I think he'll get the picture soon.

While there was considerable camaraderie, there was also a very real competition among the players for a finite number of slots in the USA. This too becomes part of the Dominican baseball identity formation, a blend of joy for other compatriots who make it, while rankling a bit at having been passed over:

I didn't feel too great about it [watching another in his cohort be promoted to the US]. Yes Alan, there is some jealousy. Especially among us pitchers there sometimes is. Most guys really hope the other guys make it. I think most guys here realize that they could sign up with another club if things here don't work out, and that makes us less jealous.

The fully mature rookie is one who integrates the new styles of baseball, who identifies with the organization, learns a certain amount of discipline, but also looks out for himself to the point of lining up other possible organizations should he be blocked in some way. For many, planning for such eventualities is nothing more than the kind of thinking they had to do in the streets.

Getting socialized in North America

For foreign players identity construction accelerates as they move to North America. I would often hear more established minor or Major Leaguers lament: "I was young. I could have used more education to be better prepared to live in the United States." The initial problems involve language, food and customs, and go on to things more subtle such as how to read behavior and intentions. From the perspective of the organization, Dominicans are, like other players, expected to learn how to make these adjustments in a certain period of time. Here the assumption is that an 18 year old is a man who should be able to cope with certain situations. From the point of view of the Dominican, these are often frightening situations, but issues of masculinity, and for many, years of street life have already dictated that you show no fear or indicate confusion or need. Hence, rather than actively engaging their English-speaking teammates in how to order food in a restaurant, they might, like one of my interviewees, just order "Chicky [chicken] and fries" for six months. Many also find that the North American diet is part of the alienation they constantly feel in strange cities like Great Falls, Montana, or Dubuque, Iowa. Compared with suddenly being thrust into an American or Canadian city with little Latino presence, life and socialization at the academy was smooth. In response, Dominicans find that playing up to their potential is often difficult.

For some, the cultural demands are excessive and they become depressed or belligerent. Others simply leave but rarely return to the Dominican Republic; rather they head for the center of Dominican existence in North America: New York City. Most make the transition to life in North America, painful though it may be. My interviews with various directors in Major League baseball pointed up that they commonly fail to promote Dominicans because of what they see as an attitudinal problem or a personality flaw. Individuals with these problems are termed "headcases" in baseball circles. While the condition does not pertain exclusively to Latinos, it is commonly associated with them. Being emotionally demonstrative is very much a Dominican attribute, part of the cultural make-up. But often in baseball circles this characteristic is interpreted as "hot-blooded Latino" behavior. For Dominicans, their emotional openness is tied up with notions of machismo and personalismo (masculinity and individuality). These are valued attributes in their own culture but often viewed as belligerent and showy in North American circles. The Dominicans must learn these differences (as must the organization for which they play) as part of the socialization process. When players do not understand such differences there is a tendency to become insulted and insular, with the likelihood that their play might suffer.

I delineated three categories of players facing this situation:

- the headcase;
- the headstrong;
- the head of the class.

The headcase

The headcase suffers from not having completely understood the cultural differences. Often his play suffers and his progress through the minor leagues is impeded. Major Leaguers who have this label find it hard to shed and are often traded.

The headstrong

The headstrong player also suffers from not being able to overcome the cultural differences, but is disciplined and talented enough to prevent it from affecting his play. He can move through the farm system and manages to keep his frustration to himself and/or to his Latino companions. No less a personage than Hall of Famer and Dominican Juan Marichal has articulated the ways in which Dominicans are often wrongly viewed by North Americans:

> I know what I did was wrong [getting into a fight and being labeled as hot-headed]. But the Americans don't understand about Dominican ballplayers, about Dominican people. To fail means something else to a Dominican ball-player. If you don't make it in the States you can find a job and make money. If you don't make it and you're Dominican, your whole family loses. If someone does something that threatens his career, his chance to make a living and be rich, he's gotta do something about it. I did. I don't want to hurt anybody. But if you think that somebody wants to hurt you, you reach out to hurt somebody, anybody.

The head of the class

The head of the class is the player who has learned that the cultural differences exist and has developed a bicultural ability (i.e. able to function in both Dominican and North American contexts). This category of player is most likely to be embraced by the club, the media, and the fans in North American cities. He is commonly better educated in his homeland, or simply bright, confident, and mature. What Major League teams fail to see is that, despite their physical maturity, many of these young Dominicans have deprived pasts to overcome, and their education or socialization process would take longer. I was able to document a number of cases of Major League players who early on in their careers acted out and constantly seemed at odds with their environments, but after being traded seemed to do a 180-degree turn, becoming role models. This was, I concluded, simply the socialization process taking its own cultural time.

Conclusion

Identity construction or the socialization of a professional ballplayer was, in the Dominican case, a complex and layered process. For many it began in the academy and ended in mid-career. The problem was that decisions about careers were hanging in the balance. Major League organizations were too quick to label players on the basis of behavior that was unacceptable in North America, without understanding the cultural roots or processes that led to it. The result was that the organization lost out by failing to develop a player after investing, sometimes heavily, in him. The players lost out by being falsely labeled and feeling oppressed for one reason or another. At times this may have undermined their ability to showcase their talents. I felt that if both sides saw the process of identity construction as ongoing they might be more predisposed to see the road from Santo Domingo to Los Angeles as a lengthier socialization process for Dominican players and the injurious practice of labeling might be avoided.

10

BECOMING 100 PERCENT STRAIGHT

Michael A. Messner

In 1995, as part of my job as the President of the North American Society for the Sociology of Sport, I needed to prepare an hour-long presidential address for the annual meeting of some 200 people. This presented a challenge to me: how might I say something to my colleagues that was interesting, at least somewhat original, and above all, not boring. Students may think that their professors are especially dull in the classroom but, believe me, we are usually much worse at professional meetings. For some reason, many of us who are able to speak to our classroom students in a relaxed manner, using relatively jargon-free language, seem to become robots, dryly reading our papers – packed with impressively unclear jargon – to our yawning colleagues.

Since I desperately wanted to avoid putting 200 sport studies scholars to sleep, I decided to deliver a talk which I entitled "Studying up on sex." The title, which certainly did get my colleagues' attention, was intended as a play on words, a double entendre. "Studying up" has one generally recognizable colloquial meaning, but in sociology it has another. It refers to studying "up" in the power structure. Sociologists have perhaps most often studied "down" – studying the poor, the blue- or pink-collar workers, the "nuts, sluts and perverts," the incarcerated. The idea of "studying up" rarely occurs to sociologists unless and until we live in a time when those who are "down" have organized movements that challenge the institutional privileges of elites. For example, in the wake of labor movements, some sociologists like C. Wright Mills studied up on corporate elites. Recently, in the wake of racial and ethnic civil rights movements, some scholars like Ruth Frankenberg have begun to study the social meanings of "whiteness." Much of my research, inspired by feminism, has involved a studying up on the social construction of masculinity in sport. Studying up, in these cases, has raised some fascinating new and important questions about the workings of power in society.

However, I realized that when it comes to understanding the social and inter-personal dynamics of sexual orientation in sport we have barely begun to scratch the surface of a very complex issue. Although sport studies have benefited from the work of scholars such as Helen Lenskyj (1986, 1997), Brian Pronger (1990) and others who have delineated the experiences of lesbians and gay men in sports, there has been very little extension of their insights into a consideration of the

104

social construction of heterosexuality in sport. In sport, just as in the larger society, we seem obsessed with asking "how do people become gay?" Imbedded in this question is the assumption that people who identify as heterosexual, or "straight," require no explanation, since they are simply acting out the "natural" or "normal" sexual orientation. We seem to be saying that the "sexual deviants" require explanation, while the experience of heterosexuals, because we are considered normal, seems to require no critical examination or discussion. But I knew that a closer look at the development of sexual orientation or sexual identity reveals an extremely complex process. I decided to challenge myself and my colleagues by arguing that although we have begun to "study up" on corporate elites in sport, on whiteness, on masculinity, it is now time to extend that by studying up on heterosexuality.

But in the absence of systematic research on this topic, where could I start? How could I explore, raise questions about, and begin to illuminate the social construction of heterosexuality for my colleagues? Fortunately, for the previous two years I had been working with a group of five men (three of whom identified as heterosexual, two as gay) mutually to explore our own biographies in terms of the earlier bodily experiences that helped to shape our gender and sexual identities. We modeled our project after that of a German group of feminist women, led by Frigga Haug, who created a research method which they call "memory work." In short, the women would mutually choose a body part, such as "hair," and each would then write a short story based on a particularly salient childhood memory that related to their hair (for example, being forced by parents to cut one's hair, deciding to straighten one's curly hair in order to look more like other girls, etc.). Then the group would read all of the stories and discuss them one by one in the hope of gaining more general understanding of, and raising new questions about, the social construction of "femininity." What resulted from this project was a fascinating book called *Female Sexualization* (Haug 1987), which my men's group used as the inspiration for our project.

As a research method, memory work is anything but conventional. Many sociologists would argue that this is not really a "research method" at all. The information that emerges from the project cannot be used very confidently as a generalizable "truth," and in this sort of project the researcher is simultaneously part of what is being studied. How, my more scientifically oriented colleagues might ask, is the researcher to maintain his or her objectivity? My answer is that in this kind of project objectivity is not the point. In fact, the strength of this sort of research is the depth of understanding that might be gained through a systematic group analysis of one's experience, one's subjective orientation to social processes. A clear understanding of the subjective aspect of social life – one's bodily feelings, emotions, and reactions to others – is an invaluable window that allows us to see and ask new sociological questions about group interaction and social structure. In short, group memory work can provide an important, productive, and fascinating insight on social reality, though not a complete (or completely reliable) picture.

As I pondered the lack of existing research on the social construction of heterosexuality in sport, I decided to draw on one of my own stories from my memory work in the men's group. Some of my most salient memories of embodiment are sports memories. I grew up as the son of a high school coach, and I eventually played point guard on my dad's team. In what follows, I juxtapose my story with that of a gay former Olympic athlete, Tom Waddell, whom I had interviewed several years earlier for a book on the lives of male athletes (Messner and Sabo 1994).

Many years ago I read some psychological studies that argued that even for self-identified heterosexuals it is a natural part of their development to have gone through "bisexual" or even "homosexual" stages of life. When I read this, it seemed theoretically reasonable, but did not ring true in my experience. I have always been, I told myself, 100 percent heterosexual! The group process of analyzing my own autobiographical stories challenged the concept I had developed of myself, and also shed light on the way in which the institutional context of sport provided a context for the development of my definition of myself as "100 percent straight." Here is one of the stories.

When I was in the 9th grade, I played on a "D" basketball team, set up especially for the smallest of high school boys. Indeed, though I was pudgy with baby fat, I was a short 5′ 2″, still pre-pubescent with no facial hair and a high voice that I artificially tried to lower. The first day of practice, I was immediately attracted to a boy I'll call Timmy, because he looked like the boy who played in the *Lassie* TV show. Timmy was short, with a high voice, like me. And like me, he had no facial hair yet. Unlike me, he was very skinny. I liked Timmy right away, and soon we were together a lot. I noticed things about him that I didn't notice about other boys: he said some words a certain way, and it gave me pleasure to try to talk like him. I remember liking the way the light hit his boyish, nearly hairless body. I thought about him when we weren't together. He was in the school band, and at the football games, I'd squint to see where he was in the mass of uniforms. In short, though I wasn't conscious of it at the time, I was infatuated with Timmy – I had a crush on him. Later that basketball season, I decided – for no reason that I could really articulate then – that I hated Timmy. I aggressively rejected him, began to make fun of him around other boys. He was, we all agreed, a geek. He was a faggot.

Three years later, Timmy and I were both on the varsity basketball team, but had hardly spoken a word to each other since we were freshmen. Both of us now had lower voices, had grown to around 6 feet tall, and we both shaved, at least a bit. But Timmy was a skinny, somewhat stigmatized reserve on the team, while I was the team captain and starting point guard. But I wasn't so happy or secure about this. I'd always dreamed of dominating games, of being the hero. Halfway through my senior season, however, it became clear that I was not a star, and I figured I knew why. I was not aggressive enough.

I had always liked the beauty of the fast break, the perfectly executed pick and roll play between two players, and especially the long twenty-foot shot that touched nothing but the bottom of the net. But I hated and feared the sometimes brutal contact under the basket. In fact, I stayed away from the rough fights for rebounds and was mostly a perimeter player, relying on my long shots or my passes to more aggressive teammates under the basket. But now it became apparent to me that time was running out in my quest for greatness: I needed to change my game, and fast. I decided one day before practice that I was gonna get aggressive. While practicing one of our standard plays, I passed the ball to a teammate, and then ran to the spot at which I was to set a pick on a defender. I knew that one could sometimes get away with setting a face-up screen on a player, and then as he makes contact with you, roll your back to him and plant your elbow hard in his stomach. The beauty of this move is that your own body "roll" makes the elbow look like an accident. So I decided to try this move. I approached the defensive player, Timmy, rolled, and planted my elbow deeply into his solar plexus. Air exploded audibly from Timmy's mouth, and he crumbled to the floor momentarily.

Play went on as though nothing had happened, but I felt bad about it. Rather than making me feel better, it made me feel guilty and weak. I had to admit to myself why I'd chosen Timmy as the target against whom to test out my new aggression. He was the skinniest and weakest player on the team.

At the time, I hardly thought about these incidents, other than to try to brush them off as incidents that made me feel extremely uncomfortable. Years later, I can now interrogate this as a sexual story, and as a gender story unfolding within the context of the heterosexualized and masculinized institution of sport. Examining my story in light of research conducted by Alfred Kinsey a half-century ago, I can recognize in myself what Kinsey saw as a very common fluidity and changeability of sexual desire over the life-course. Put simply, Kinsey found that large numbers of adult, "heterosexual" men had previously, as adolescents and young adults, experienced sexual desire for males. A surprisingly large number of these men had experienced sexual contact to the point of orgasm with other males during adolescence or early adulthood. Similarly, my story invited me to consider what is commonly called the "Freudian theory of bisexuality." Sigmund Freud shocked the post-Victorian world by suggesting that all people go through a stage, early in life, when they are attracted to people of the same sex.[1] Adult experiences, Freud argued, eventually led most people to shift their sexual desire to what he called an appropriate "love object" – a person of the opposite sex. I also considered my experience in light of what lesbian feminist author Adrienne Rich called the institution of compulsory heterosexuality. Perhaps the extremely high levels of homophobia that are often endemic in boys' and men's organized sports led me to deny and repress my own homoerotic desire through a direct and overt rejection of Timmy, through homophobic banter with male peers, and the resultant stigmatization of the feminized Timmy. Eventually I considered my experience in the light of what radical theorist Herbert Marcuse called the sublimation of homoerotic desire into an aggressive, violent act as serving to construct a clear line of demarcation between self and other. Sublimation, according to Marcuse, involves the driving underground, into the unconsious, of sexual desires that might appear dangerous due to their socially stigmatized status. But sublimation involves more than simple repression into the unconscious. It involves a tranformation of sexual desire into something else – often into aggressive and violent acting out toward others. These acts clarify the boundaries between oneself and others and therefore lessen any anxieties that might be attached to the repressed homoerotic desire.

Importantly, in our analysis of my story, the memory group went beyond simply discussing the events in psychological terms. The story did perhaps suggest some deep psychological processes at work, but it also revealed the importance of social context – in this case, the context of the athletic team. In short, my rejection of Timmy and the joining with teammates to stigmatize him in ninth grade stands as an example of what sociologist R. W. Connell calls a moment of engagement with hegemonic masculinity, where I actively took up the male group's task of constructing heterosexual/masculine identities in the context of sport. The elbow in Timmy's gut three years later can be seen as a punctuation mark that occurred precisely because of my fears that I might be failing in this goal.

It is helpful, I think, to compare my story with gay and lesbian "coming out" stories in sport. Though we have a few lesbian and bisexual coming out stories among women athletes, there are very few from gay males. Tom Waddell, who as a closeted gay man finished sixth in the decathlon in the 1968 Olympics, later came out and started the Gay Games, an athletic and cultural festival that draws tens of thousands of people every four years. When I interviewed Tom Waddell over a decade ago about his sexual identity and athletic career, he made it quite clear that for many years sports was his closet:

> When I was a kid, I was tall for my age, and was very thin and very strong. And I was usually faster than most other people. But I discovered rather early that I liked gymnastics and I liked dance. I was very interested in being a ballet dancer . . . [but] something became obvious to me right away – that male ballet dancers were effeminate, that they were what most people would call faggots. And I thought I just couldn't handle that . . . I was totally closeted and very concerned about being male. This was the fifties, a terrible time to live, and everything was stacked against me. Anyway, I realized that I had to do something to protect my image of myself as a male – because at that time homosexuals were thought of primarily as men who wanted to be women. And so I threw myself into athletics – I played football, gymnastics, track and field . . . I was a jock – that's how I was viewed, and I was comfortable with that.

Tom Waddell was fully conscious of entering sports and constructing a masculine/heterosexual athletic identity precisely because he feared being revealed as gay. It was clear to him, in the context of the 1950s, that being known as gay would undercut his claims to the status of manhood. Thus, though he described the athletic closet as "hot and stifling," he remained there until several years after his athletic retirement. He even knowingly played along with locker room discussions about sex and women as part of his "cover."

> I wanted to be viewed as male, otherwise I would be a dancer today. I wanted the male, macho image of an athlete. So I was protected by a very hard shell. I was clearly aware of what I was doing . . . I often felt compelled to go along with a lot of locker room garbage because I wanted that image – and I know a lot of others who did too.

Like my story, Waddell's points to the importance of the athletic institution as a context in which peers mutually construct and reconstruct narrow definitions of masculinity. Heterosexuality is considered to be a rock-solid foundation of this concept of masculinity.

But unlike my story, Waddell's may invoke a dramaturgical analysis.[2] He seemed to be consciously "acting" to control and regulate others' perceptions of him by constructing a public "front stage" persona that differed radically from what he believed to be his "true" inner self. My story, in contrast, suggests a deeper, less consciously strategic repression of my homoerotic attraction. Most likely, I was aware on some level of the dangers of such feelings, and was escaping the risks, disgrace, and rejection that would likely result from being different. For Waddell, the decision to construct his identity largely within sport was to step into a fiercely heterosexual/masculine closet that would hide what he saw as his "true" identity. In contrast, I was not so much stepping into a "closet" that would hide my identity; rather, I was stepping out into an entire world of heterosexual privilege. My story also suggests how a threat to the promised privileges of hegemonic masculinity – my failure as an athlete – might trigger a momentary sexual panic that can lay bare the constructedness, indeed, the instability of the heterosexual/masculine identity.

In either case, Waddell's or mine, we can see how, as young male athletes, heterosexuality and masculinity was not something we "were," but something we were doing. It is significant, I think, that although each of us was "doing heterosexuality," neither of us was actually "having sex" with women (though one of us desperately wanted to). This underscores a point made by some recent theorists that heterosexuality should not be thought of simply as sexual acts between women and men. Rather, heterosexuality is a constructed identity, a performance, and an institution that is not necessarily linked to sexual acts. Though for one of us it was more conscious than for the other, we were both "doing heterosexuality" as an ongoing practice through which we sought to do two things:

- avoid stigma, embarrassment, ostracism, or perhaps worse if we were even suspected of being gay;
- link ourselves into systems of power, status, and privilege that appear to be the birthright of "real men" (i.e., males who are able to compete successfully with other males in sport, work, and sexual relations with women).

In other words, each of us actively scripted our own sexual and gender performances, but these scripts were constructed within the constraints of a socially organized (institutionalized) system of power and pleasure.

Questions for future research

As I prepared to tell this sexual story publicly to my colleagues at the sport studies conference, I felt extremely nervous. Part of the nervousness was due to the fact that I knew some of them would object to my claim that telling personal stories can be a source of sociological insights. But a larger part of the reason for my nervousness was due to the fact that I was revealing something very personal about my sexuality in such a public way. Most of us are not accustomed to doing this, especially in the context of a professional conference. But I had learned long ago, especially from feminist women scholars, and from gay and lesbian scholars, that biography is linked to history. Part of "normal" academic discourse has been to hide "the personal" (including the fact that the researchers are themselves people with values, feelings, and, yes, biases) behind a carefully constructed facade of "objectivity." Rather than trying to hide or be ashamed of one's subjective experience of the world, I was challenging myself to draw on my experience of the world as a resource. Not that I should trust my experience as the final word on "reality". White, heterosexual males like me have made the mistake for centuries of calling their own experience "objectivity," and then punishing anyone who does not share their worldview by casting them as "deviant." Instead, I hope to use my experience as an example of how those of us who are in dominant sexual/racial/gender/class categories can get a new perspective on the "constructedness" of our identities by juxtaposing our subjective experiences against the recently emerging worldviews of gay men and lesbians, women, and people of color.

Finally, I want to stress that in juxtaposition neither my own nor Tom Waddell's story sheds much light on the question of why some individuals "become gay" while others "become" heterosexual or bisexual. Instead, I should like to suggest that this is a dead-end question, and that there are far more important and interesting questions to be asked:

- How has heterosexuality, as an institution and as an enforced group practice, constrained and limited all of us – gay, straight, and bi?
- How has the institution of sport been an especially salient institution for the social construction of heterosexual masculinity?
- Why is it that when men play sports they are almost always automatically granted masculine status, and thus assumed to be heterosexual, while when women play sports, questions are raised about their "femininity" and sexual orientation?

These kinds of questions aim us toward an analysis of the workings of power within institutions – including the ways that these workings of power shape and constrain our identities and relationships – and point us toward imagining alternative social arrangements that are less constraining for everyone.

Notes

1 The fluidity and changeability of sexual desire over the life course is now more obvious in evidence from prison and military populations, and single-sex boarding schools. The theory of bisexuality is evident, for example, in childhood crushes on same-sex primary schoolteachers.
2 Dramaturgical analysis, associated with Erving Goffman, uses the theater and performance to develop an analogy with everyday life.

References

Haug, Frigga (1987) *Female Sexualization: A Collective Work of Memory*, London: Verso.
Lenskyj, Helen (1986) *Out of Bounds: Women, Sport and Sexuality*, Toronto: Women's Press.
—— (1997) "No fear? Lesbians in sport and physical education," *Women in Sport and Physical Activity Journal* 6(2): 7–22.
Messner, Michael A. (1992) *Power at Play: Sports and the Problem of Masculinity*, Boston: Beacon Press.
—— (1994) "Gay athletes and the Gay Games: in interview with Tom Waddell," in M. A. Messner and D. F. Sabo (eds) *Sex, Violence and Power in Sports: Rethinking Masculinity*, Freedom, CA: The Crossing Press, pp. 113–19.
Pronger, Brian (1990) *The Arena of Masculinity: Sports, Homosexuality, and the Meaning of Sex*, New York: St. Martin's Press.

11

THE GAME BEGINS AT HOME

Women's labor in the service of sport

Shona Thompson

Although I did not start collecting the data for this project until 1990 the research "journey" really began for me nine years earlier, in 1981. That year my country, New Zealand, was plunged into a state of civil disorder by the arrival of a men's rugby team representing apartheid in South Africa. This visit contravened an international Commonwealth Heads of Government agreement designed to avert further boycotts of major sporting events (such as the one that occurred at the 1976 Summer Olympics in Montreal, when most of the African countries left to protest New Zealand's presence and our persistent sporting contact with South Africa). The connection between the Montreal Olympics in 1976, rugby in New Zealand in 1981 and my research on tennis in Australia in 1990 may seem obscure, but it goes like this.

Increasingly embarrassed at being seen to condone apartheid and incensed by the Rugby Union's blatant disregard for international relations and public opinion, an unprecedented number of New Zealanders vehemently protested against the South African rugby tour in 1981. Women joined the protests in huge numbers and were often the leaders, motivated among other things by their long-felt anger at how this almost exclusively male sport had dominated public life and exploited their domestic labor. It quickly became obvious that a highly effective form of protest was for women to stop doing the work which had previously supported this amateur sport – the laundry, providing food for players, shopping for, driving or coaching young sons who play, keeping children quiet while husbands watched it on television, etc. Through these seemingly simple actions of resistance we came to realise the extent to which women's domestic work had contributed to a sport played by men.

Being part of the 1981 protest movement was, for me, a "consciousness-raising" experience. I began to understand how women could have relationships with the institution of sport which far exceeded their experiences, or lack thereof, as players and that these relationships could have everyday and political consequences. It was several years, however, before I had an adequate theoretical framework and the opportunity to explore this further. During a sabbatical leave in Canada in 1984 I began reading feminist literature which helped provide the theoretical and methodological "tools" for the research. Then in 1989 I went to Australia to begin work towards a PhD, intended to be generally about women's relationships to sport played by others.

At first I was not sure whether the phenomenon I had observed in New Zealand would exist in another country, but I knew I was onto something when I came across a bumper sticker for sale in a local newsagency which said, "If a mother's place is in the home, why am I always in the car?" I also soon learned that my research would be controversial. Men seemed particularly uncomfortable with it. Male sport administrators suggested that I must emphasise the "ugly parent problem" (read "ugly mother'), or that I should find ways to prevent disgruntled mothers from opting out of providing the necessary support for their child, thereby destroying the administration's investment in a promising young player. A funding grant from the Australian Sports Commission was awarded only on condition that I include men in the research, and investigate the work done by mothers and fathers. Afterwards, I have tried several times to have some of the findings published in the West Australian Tennis Association's magazine, only to be turned down by successive editors.

I think the responses to this research highlight the tensions which often surface when findings are viewed on the one hand as obvious "commonsense" knowledge, while on the other, the very process of having put the social phenomenon "under the microscope" means it has not gone unquestioned and therefore can no longer be taken for granted. I like that tension.

"I've grown up with it. It's just part of my life. I do it without thinking." This comment, made by a woman I have named June, was in reference to the work she did to support the tennis played by her husband and teenage son. I had asked what their participation in the sport required of her and she replied:

> Well, meals. They have a particular diet that they like to follow pre-match, and certain food that they like to eat when they're playing . . . There's always their gear, making sure their gear is ready, their tennis whites, their shorts and T-shirts and track suits, washed and ironed, that sort of thing. And their meal and their drink and their towels.

June was one of forty-six women I interviewed as part of my research to investigate the impact on women's lives of having a member of their immediate family play sport. Being in Perth, Western Australia at the time, I chose to focus on tennis because in this part of the world it has one of the highest participation rates by men, women and children, and is an important part of local organised recreational sport. This allowed me to explore the various, sometimes interrelated relationships women may have with one sport within the context of it being a significant and valued part of the culture.

The women interviewed were identified in three groups, defined by their relationships to the sport. Sixteen were mothers of elite junior tennis players, fifteen were wives/ domestic partners of men who played competitive amateur tennis and a further fifteen were women who played tennis themselves. As the interviews progressed, I discovered there was considerable overlap between these three categories. June illustrated this. She was contacted because her husband was a local A-grade player, but during the interview I discovered that all her three children played tennis (one also at men's A-grade level), and she had played the sport herself for approximately eighteen years. It had become a family preoccupation, leading June to say, "I can't imagine my life without tennis because it *is* our life. I've said that so many times, 'tennis is our life'." This situation was common, particularly if the husband/father was a tennis player. It usually meant, as it did for June, that the amalgamation of work associated with tennis was enormous. I will, however, discuss each of these three groups separately.

Mothers: it's what I do

The women interviewed who were mothers of junior elite tennis players were aged between 39 and 52, and their tennis playing children were between 10 and 17 years. The children had all been selected by the West Australian State Tennis Association into a representative squad which made them eligible for subsidised group coaching sponsored by the hamburger chain, McDonald's. This meant they attended coaching sessions 2–5 times per week and were required to play in a designated number of tournaments. In addition they usually played regular club-based competition during weekends. It became an intense schedule, as Sonia explained:

> It's just tennis all the time. It's not just tournaments, it's pennants, it's state squad training, it's state team training, lessons with his own private coach and on the days he doesn't play you still arrange for him to have a hit with someone, because he needs to play it every day. And of course he plays tennis for his school now. So it's *every* day.

By far the greatest demand on the children's mothers was having to provide transport – driving their children to and from tennis commitments. On a schedule largely determined by the tennis administration, this driving dominated and constructed the women's lives. Kath explained:

> Of course I'm always watching the clock because I have to pick [daughter] up from school at half past three and be at [her tennis training venue] by quarter past four, four nights a week.

For Peggy, the impact of this routine had become obvious only after she stopped doing it. Her son had recently acquired his driver's licence and was now driving himself to tennis. She said:

> There was a terrible lot of running around, really terrible. I just can't believe the difference since he's been driving. I don't think I realised. I was forever running, I couldn't stop. I'd race home from somewhere, run in and do something quickly then, quick, back in the car, we had to be at such and such a place at such and such a time, and off I'd go.

For Yvonne it had been particularly stressful:

I think I was always tired. I hate driving. I'm a nervous driver and the driving was every afternoon, always having to be somewhere by a certain time. I really found it a strain, physically and mentally.

Added to this were her concerns that it had been unfair on her other two children:

I felt it affected the girls because I was always rushing around after him. Sometimes you wouldn't get home 'til 6.30–7.30pm. Then you'd have to get dinner, that sort of thing. I felt they missed out a bit.

The most demanding driving was associated with the after-school sponsored squad training sessions. These took place between approximately 3.30pm and 7pm on weekdays at many different community tennis clubs located around Perth, which is a large, sprawling city without an extensive public transport service. The tennis clubs were selected irrespective of the location of the various schools these junior players attended. A combination of disparate locations, long distances, tight time schedules during peak traffic hours, inadequate public transport and concerns for the safety of their children, especially in the early evening, meant these mothers saw no viable alternatives to driving their children to tennis themselves. It begged the question however, where were the fathers?

Parallel to these interviews, I did a survey of both mothers and fathers of another group of junior tennis players in Western Australia. This was a separate project, designed to accommodate the requirements of the Australian Sports Commission National Research Centre which provided the funding. It required both parents to complete a time-usage diary for a week and cite, from a long list of supporting activities, those which they had done. In summary I found that the support labor done for a child's tennis differed between parents in both quantity and type. Overall, the mothers were more involved in their children's sport than the fathers. Whereas it was possible for some fathers to spend no time committed to their child's sport, this was not possible for any of the mothers. The activities in which fathers were involved were more sport related, such as playing tennis with the child or attending special public events such as important tournaments. Mothers' labor was generally more everyday, private and related to childcare, such as driving their children to and from training, taking them to medical services, providing food, laundered clothing and serviceable equipment. Furthermore, what the fathers did for their children's sport tended to be fitted around their other commitments, whereas the mothers tended to fit their other commitments around their children's sporting needs. For example, one mother recorded in a four-hour block:

4pm   Come home [from work], prepare veggies, do a load of washing.
5pm   Take [daughter] and [son] to tennis, come home, prepare meal.
6pm   Pick up [daughter], come home, have meal.
8pm   Pick up [son].

Another recorded between 7am and 2pm during a junior tennis tournament:

Took [son] to tennis, watched for a while. Went home, did some washing. Back to tennis at noon, watched for a while, games delayed by rain. Went home for lunch, cleaned house, more washing. [Son] rang, tennis cancelled, went to pick him up.

By contrast, accounts from the fathers' time-use diaries included these two examples:

Finish work, drive from city to [tennis club] to pick up [son].
Played golf, drink after golf, watch [son's] tennis practice, drive [son] home.

Referring back to the group of mothers I interviewed, Jill illustrated common differences in relation to paid work when she said:

Sometimes I used to leave work and collect them [from school] and then take them [to training], go back to work and make up the time I'd taken off to collect them and then go back to get them.

None of the interviewed mothers were in full-time paid employment or employment which could not somehow accommodate the demands of the 3.30pm to 8.00pm training sessions. The children's fathers, all but one of whom were living in the same household, were in full-time paid employment and the main income providers. These gendered economic relations played a large part in determining whose responsibility it was to do the driving. The priority of men's work rationalized their inability to provide this kind of support for their children's tennis. As Dianne explained:

[Husband] does as much as he can but his job doesn't allow, well it allows him . . . in that he can come and go as he likes, he doesn't have to explain himself, but his job is such a high pressure job that he can't really afford the time.

One conclusion which could be made is that in this culture the opportunity to participate and excel in competitive tennis is available only to those children with a parent who has unrestricted access to a car and is free from the necessity to be in paid labor at times demanded by the sporting administration. In this case, that parent was the mother, supported by traditional middle-class economic structures within nuclear families. These material relations combine with ideologies of parenting which incorporate sporting experiences as part of childcare. Rosemary, who was a full-time homemaker, commented on the work she did for her children's sport by saying, "I don't even think about it, it doesn't bother me. It's just the job I do."

Wives: he plays more now

When I asked the women who were domestic partners/wives of tennis players what was the biggest demand their adult partner's sport made of them, the most common replies were about laundry and childcare. For example, Lorelle replied, "Well, I suppose laundry. He can go through three or four sets of clothes in a day." I interviewed Anthea at 8.30 one morning and she told me she had already done two loads of laundry. She continued:

> I do, and I'm not joking, three loads of laundry a day. I have got so much iron-
> ing it's astronomical. Three loads of washing! Okay, I have quite a small
> machine but still, three loads, for two people, a day? He changes his shirt
> about three or four times a day because of the sweat. It is a helluva lot of
> washing. I can't believe it. The neighbours always see a full thing of washing
> on the line, it's just constant, absolutely constant.

Anthea recognised very clearly how her domestic labor facilitated her male partner's
tennis. They had been living together for nine months and, explaining his tennis
schedule, she said:

> I suppose, because now we are living together, I can cook and everything, so I
> do all the cooking, and the pressure is off him. Whereas he used to come home
> and have to do this, that and the other thing, now that pressure is off him and
> so he plays more tennis.

Anthea was an interesting case. She and her partner were both 27 years old. They had
no children and were both in full-time paid employment making comparable salaries.
The domestic work she did which facilitated and serviced his leisure was not, therefore,
rationalised by unequal economic relations or associated with providing childcare.
Anthea illustrated how it could be driven entirely by gendered divisions of labor which
deem housework and the care of others, including other adults, as women's work, done
in the name of love, heterosexual marriage and the ideology of wifehood. This care
extended to men's sport and leisure interests which Anthea illustrated when she said:

> The day before, if he has an important match, he enjoys something like pasta
> for dinner or some high carbohydrate meal. If I'm away I've always got it in
> the freezer so he just has to choose it out and heat it up.

In this section of my research I draw parallels with Janet Finch's work (1983). Finch
referred to studies of women married to clergymen, doctors, policemen, academics,
diplomats and railway signal operators to demonstrate how, in the so-called partnership
of marriage, the man's work both structured the woman's life and elicited her contribution to it. My argument is that the same economic structures and ideologies which
elicit a woman's contribution to her husband's work also operate to have her contribute
to his leisure.

Anthea was perfectly happy with the situation, but there were several women I interviewed who were not. The points of dissension related to childcare and reciprocity in
leisure. The women who expressed resentment at their husband's tennis were those who
did not play the sport themselves and who, because of this, were left with the greater
share of childcare. Pauline, for example, said "I suppose I used to get resentful of it.
I guess when the kids were younger and I was stuck at home."

For Maria and Tania the situation had led to immense bitterness and marital
disharmony. Maria, at 60 years of age, was married to a man who throughout their
40 years together had played a considerable amount of medium-grade tennis. She
referred to their six children as "my children" because, she said, she had brought them
up herself:

When the children were little I'd go off my brain. I was *very* angry. He was a butcher and I'd have buckets of bloody aprons soaking, and buckets of nappies [diapers] soaking . . . and piles and piles of laundry and six kids and I'd say *please* don't go [to tennis] this afternoon, but he'd go. He was ruthless.

Tania, aged 27, had two children under 3 years old. She explained the greatest demand of her husband's tennis:

Me having to be the main parent. I'm bringing them up single handed . . . I don't have the partner I expected and the children don't have a father. I suppose I'm like a sole parent really. There couldn't be that much difference.

Such sentiments were not expressed by the tennis players' wives who also played the sport. Tennis clubs were places where children could be taken, which helped facilitate women's play. I have written in more detail about this elsewhere (Thompson 1992) but the point here is that childcare was shared frequently at the tennis club, allowing both parents to play. For example, Brenda explained: "I would sit out with the children and then I would play the next set and [husband] would sit out with the children. We did that for a couple of years."

The conditions of play were not always equal, however, and the women gave several scenarios where the man's tennis would take priority. For example, Karen said:

I was playing a lower level of tennis so if I had to run to the back of the court to say [to a child] "get off that thing and back down on the ground" or something, it was better that it was me.

Despite the greater expendability of their tennis, the women who played and enjoyed the sport alongside their husbands had a far greater sense of leisure opportunity reciprocated. It may not have altered the domestic relations which serviced the tennis, but it changed how the women felt about it. Sarah recalled:

Well, when we were first married and in the city, I would have had his lunch ready and had afternoon tea ready and had his clothes ready, etcetera, etcetera. But not long after, we moved to [a small country town] and then the pattern changed and we both, I mean, I still, I was only "The Housewife" so naturally I did the laundry and the meals but I was doing it for both of us to get ready to go to tennis, not the devoted wife sort of putting the tennis gear out and everything for him to go. We *both* went.

Furthermore, sharing this interest was seen as having contributed to a successful marriage. In the context of describing how there had been two broken marriages among members of her tennis club, and in both cases only one of the couple had been a player, June commented:

Had I been in that situation, had [my husband] not involved me, maybe that would have been the path our lives would have taken, because tennis to him was almost a full-time job, you know. You work at it, you work hard to play well and you play all the time, and if I hadn't been involved I imagine I would have been quite grumpy. It would have occupied far too much of his time.

Anne, aged 72, had met her husband at a tennis club. She said, "We've had a happy life, a very happy life, and tennis has been a big part of it really." The message seems to be: if you can't beat it, join it.

Players: it falls on women's shoulders

I referred earlier to my article about the women tennis players I interviewed (Thompson 1992). It mainly discusses how women's tennis in Western Australia was organised and experienced in gendered terms, mostly separate from "mainstream" tennis, invisible to the women's families and making no demands upon other family members. Here I will discuss the role women players served in their local community tennis.

The women players I interviewed were all members of the local Veterans (Masters) Association which meant they were forty or older and had enjoyed long tennis playing careers. In fact, among the fifteen interviewed they had accumulated 599 years of play. Most of this had been experienced as members of the sixty-one affiliated community tennis clubs scattered through the suburbs of Perth. These clubs are sited on public land controlled by local government and are administered voluntarily by and for club members who lease the land for a nominal fee. A club's viability, therefore, depends heavily upon voluntary labor to maintain facilities and a congenial social atmosphere which keeps members satisfied with and committed to their club. The work required for this was done disproportionately, and often unrecognised, by female members. Betty, who for years had produced her club's regular newsletter said:

> Women do far more work in the club. I worked it out once exactly what positions they had and the percentage of men and women [that were doing the work]. I put it in the [club] newsletter but nothing was said about it.

Marilyn's club was in a predominantly working-class suburb. When I asked her about fundraising activities, her response came in such a way that, by the time she had finished speaking, her answer had been a revelation to herself:

> Well, I would say, at [club], when we want something we have a special fund-raising drive. When we wanted the pergola built or a new lawnmower bought or something like that then it's a fundraising group (pause), which is run by the social committee (pause), which is 90 percent women! Yeah!

Marilyn's response highlighted the strong connection between fundraising and the activities of those responsible for the social aspects of tennis culture. Linda observed how these were both tasks done by women:

> I've discovered that in some of the clubs in the city, it seems to me that there's a lot of ongoing fund raising and it predominantly falls on the women's shoulders in terms of their greater involvement in the social committee, their

running of raffles, running of gala days. Everything that will happen like that will fall on the women's shoulders. It just does. Men just don't do that.

Within the tennis club administration the women were disproportionately represented on social committees but rarely held positions of decision-making power. None of the women interviewed had been their club's treasurer, for example, and only two had been club president. In both cases they were the first and only women to hold the position.

Social events invariably meant sharing food and, again, this was women's work. Alice explained:

> The women do all the catering sort of things . . . The women organise the booze and organise some salads and spread the crockery and things like that. All the womanly sort of things.

Quite apart from special social events, the work involved on regular club days was usually delineated along gender lines. Traditionally, men worked in the bar serving the alcoholic drinks, women worked in the kitchen serving the tea and coffee. Changes to this tradition were considered signifiers of progressiveness within a club, although it rarely meant less work for women. For example, Betty said:

> It's rostered now . . . You're either rostered for bar or making the tea. There's usually a husband and wife team if possible on the bar and the women usually make the tea.

More affluent clubs had moved to paying someone to "do the teas", but in every case that person was a woman.

Much of the work done by women members of tennis clubs in Western Australia was an extension of domestic labor, household management and caring roles. Research focusing on lawn bowls clubs in Queensland, Australia (Boyle and McKay 1995) illustrated how women members were similarly exploited, contributing considerable domestic labor for the benefit of the male club members and providing a greater share of the voluntary work which maintained the social structure of the club.

Summary

This research set out to "make visible" women's unpaid domestic labor which facilitates and services the participation in sport of others. It should be noted that it surveyed women who were still "in the system". In other words, I did not interview women who for some reason had said, "I'm not doing this" and had opted out. The big question is, of course, what would happen to sport as we know it if more women got out. From my experience in 1981, when this happened to rugby it had a huge impact on the sport, from which it took deliberate effort over many years to recover. Of course, it is difficult to imagine women withdrawing their enormous contributions to sport in this way. This support work is widespread and driven by emotional ties through family relationships and the women's identities as good mothers, wives and community citizens. Constructions of gender, ideologies of motherhood and wifehood, economic relations and the ascribed significance of sport all mutually reinforce this phenomenon. Furthermore, as the rewards from sport increase, my prediction is that these constructs will likely become even more strongly reinforcing.

References

Boyle, M. and McKay, J. (1995) "'You leave your troubles at the gate.' A case study of the exploitation of older women's labor and 'leisure' in sport," *Gender & Society* 19(5): 556–75.

Finch, J. (1983) *Married to the Job: Wives' Incorporation in Men's Work*, London: George Allen & Unwin.

Thompson, S. M. (1992) "Mum's tennis day: the gendered definition of older women's tennis," *Loisir et Société/Society & Leisure* 15(1): 271–89.

LEARNING EXERCISES AND RESOURCES

Projects and discussion topics

1 In Chapter 6, Donnelly and Young realized the value of rookie mistakes for understanding the process of becoming an athlete. Think about your own rookie mistakes, all those foolish or embarrassing things you may have done or said when you were a novice in a sport. At what point did you begin to see yourself as a full-fledged participant in that sport? When did you say to yourself, I am now a scuba diver, a white water kayaker, a triathlete, or whatever? Knowing what you know now, at what point do you think the other more established participants began to value and accept you as a fellow participant? Compare your answers with others in the class or in your discussion group. How do your experiences and those of others fit with or deviate from the findings of Donnelly and Young?

2 Successfully negotiating the process of becoming an athlete often involves resolving the contradictions between the public image of an activity and what it was actually like as a participant, or between your expectations and your experiences. (See Chapter 6, or the notes on Klein 1993 in the Additional Books and Articles following Part 3, for examples of such contradictions.) Generate a list of contradictions that you have faced in your own sport experiences. Why do you think the public image and/or your expectations were different from your actual experiences? Compare your list with others in the class or in your discussion group. How do you account for differences or similarities?

3 In Chapter 7, Coakley and White found that, for high school students, a combination of conditions and characteristics had a powerful effect on whether an individual was likely to continue participation in sport and physical activity. These included school experiences in sport and physical education classes, individual perceptions of talent and ability, gender, a sense of how sport and physical activity fitted with how individuals saw themselves as adults, and social class. Consider how these, and other conditions and characteristics in your own high school experience, affected your own decisions about sport participation (or non-participation). If you and others in the class or in your discussion group are all participants, interview some non-participants to determine what factors were involved in their decisions. What things stand out as important in your data?

4 Use an interview with an elite athlete or the biography/autobiography of an athlete to identify the career contingencies involved in their development as an athlete. (Remember that unless they are superstars whose privacy is constantly being

violated, many top-class athletes are quite approachable.) What factors in terms of their social and family relations, their personal characteristics, being in the right place at the right time, the decisions they made, etc., led them to elite status in their sport? Compare and contrast your subject with the examples given by Stevenson in Chapter 8. What accounts for differences or similarities noted in your comparison?

5   If there are foreign scholarship athletes on your campus, or immigrant students involved in sport and physical activity participation, request interviews with a small sample in order to discover the differences in sport culture between their country of origin and your country. What did the individuals have to learn, and unlearn, in order to reconstruct their identity as an athlete in a new country? At what point did they feel their identity was reconfirmed by their new fellow participants?

6   Chapter 10 by Mike Messner deals with the development of male gender and sexual identity. In a class or group discussion, consider the ways in which you, and others you know, have negotiated your own gender and sexual identities through your sport and physical activity participation. If sport and physical activity is involved in developing a particularly narrow view of what it is to be a male in your society, how is sport and physical activity involved in becoming a female in your society?

7   In Chapter 11, Shona Thompson suggests that wives and mothers make a major contribution to the economy of amateur sport. Select one such woman for a case study. Generate a list of tasks that she performs in relation to her children's/husband's sport participation and determine the number of hours for each task. Then assign a cash value to each task based on how much it would cost to employ a person or a service to carry out the task (e.g., laundry, taxi, fund raising, restaurant bills, etc.). The total for one person in one sport provides an interesting insight into the true costs of sport. What would occur in populations where women's free labor in sport was unavailable?

Films and videos

Film and video annotations are provided by Steve Mosher, Department of Exercise and Sport Science, Ithaca College, Ithaca, NY 14850, USA.

Feature-length films

- *Breaking Away* (1979), 100 mins, CBS/Fox Video.
  A romantic but never condescending depiction about coming of age in Middle America, *Breaking Away* also ably depicts the role sport plays in the lives of late adolescent working-class boys, in the awkward transition from high school to the work force or college. Using the Little 500 bicycle race held annually at the University of Indiana as the focus point for a potentially explosive town–gown confrontation, *Breaking Away* nonetheless manages to present believable characters in believable situations. The central story in the film focuses on Dave's (Dennis Christopher) struggle to "break away" from his family's "cutter" tradition of work in the local quarry and become the first member to attend college. Dave's struggle is made more difficult because, while he has already separated himself from his friends by becoming an able bicycle racer, he depends on their support and friendship. The

climactic race allows Dave and his friends to use sport as a means of self-validation while at the same time engaging in class warfare.

- *He Got Game* (1998), 131 mins, Touchstone Pictures.
  From the poetic opening scenes of a cross-section of American children (boys and girls, country and city, black and white) playing basketball in schools and on playgrounds, *He Got Game* offers Spike Lee's deeply personal and intense vision of contemporary basketball. All of the potential clichés surrounding the all-too-familiar battle between white college recruiters and professional sports agents for the opportunity to exploit the black high school superstar are submerged beneath a powerful story of father and son reconciliation. Jesus Shuttlesworth (NBA star Ray Allen) has to choose between two lucrative basketball futures, while at the same time struggling with the question of forgiving an absent father (Denzel Washington). The film also highlights an adolescent struggling to create an adult identity, and recreate an athletic identity. The hypocritical and mercenary nature of the battle for Jesus's basketball services is vivid and realistic, while the poignancy of the story of family life in the inner city is refreshingly authentic and free of stereotypes. *He Got Game* is a wonderful dramatic companion piece to either *Hoop Dreams* (1995) or *Hardwood Dreams* (see below). The striking stylistic similarities of the opening montage with Lee's *Malcolm X* (1992) will offer students a powerful image of two very different Americas.

Shorter films and educational programs

- *Hardwood Dreams* (1994), 56 mins, Turner Home Entertainment.
  This short film chronicles a year in the life of the basketball stars of Morningside High School in Los Angeles. Similar in style and scope to the better known *Hoop Dreams*, this modest film carries with it an authenticity in that it is a film about black people made by black people and intended for a largely black audience. The narrative and images are deeply personal in nature. They show the constant struggles in the daily life of inner-city youth. At the same time they explore the importance of a state sports championship at a school where the main battle is to retain its students as long as possible so that they may be able to overcome disadvantages grounded in the context in which they live.

Additional books and articles

- Albert, Edward (1991) "Riding a line: competition and cooperation in the sport of bicycle racing," *Sociology of Sport Journal* 8(4): 341–61.

Eddie Albert, a sociologist and competitive cyclist (road racing), reminds us that rookies not only have to learn the formal rules of a sport, but also a whole set of informal rules – a way of participating in the sport that is constructed by the cyclists themselves. Novices and outsiders may think that cyclists in road races are all individuals competing against each other. But the social order of the peloton, and the paceline of the breakaway group, stipulate that competing cyclists must cooperate with each other (e.g., taking turns to lead and draft each other). So strong is this unwritten rule that cyclists may direct severe sanctions against individuals who refuse to cooperate. Thus, experienced cyclists trust that rookies will cooperate, and have the skill to ride in a straight line at fairly high speeds while in close proximity to other cyclists. And rookies must learn to become trustworthy (see Donnelly 1994 below), or fail to have their identities as racing cyclists confirmed by established cyclists.

- Donnelly, Peter (1994) "Take my word for it: trust in the context of birding and mountaineering," *Qualitative Sociology* 17(3): 215–41.

In Chapter 6, Peter Donnelly and Kevin Young raised the idea that trust was involved in constructing an athletic identity. Peter Donnelly develops this idea in an article dealing with two activities in which it is sometimes necessary to trust the claims that an individual is making about his or her achievements. He outlines the conditions in which it might be necessary to resort to trust in the two activities, and then examines the way in which social relations in the climbing and birding subcultures come into play with regard to testing the veracity of an individual's claims. Novices are the individuals who can be tricked most easily, and untalented but experienced participants may enhance their egos by exaggerating their achievements to a novice who has not yet learned the skills of testing trust. Learning to become an athlete (i.e., taking on an athletic identity) also involves learning who, and how, to trust, and how to be trustworthy. Trust relationships are also evident in sports such as cycle racing (see Albert 1991 above), and professional wrestling, where it is necessary to trust that individuals will play their part and demonstrate appropriate skills.

- Fussell, Samuel W. (1991) *Muscle: Confessions of an Unlikely Bodybuilder*, New York: Avon Books.

This is more of a journalistic account than a sociological study, but it provides some delightful insights into the world of competitive bodybuilding. After graduating from Oxford University, the author (an American) decided, after several frightening experiences in New York City, to take up bodybuilding. Four years and a great many experiences (including steroid use) later, and 80 pounds heavier, he was competing in Southern California. He had constructed his identity as a bodybuilder at the same time that he was building his body, but he remained detached enough to provide this fascinating account of experience and identity.

- Jacobs, Glenn (1970) "Urban samurai: the karate dojo," in G. Jacobs (ed.) *The Participant Observer*, New York: George Brazilier. pp. 140–60.

This is an older study, done at a time before martial arts films had become so popular and before martial arts clubs (such as the karate dojo studied by Jacobs) were a regular feature of urban and suburban landscapes. However, even though many things have changed since Jacobs carried out his research, the study is valuable for the way in which it describes systematically the culture of the dojo, and what novices must learn in order to participate and progress through the ranks of the colored belt status system. In addition to learning how to acquire status, rookies also learn to play appropriate roles in the highly status-structured environment of the dojo. Few sports provide such a clear-cut status system, or are carried out in such an authoritarian environment where the master outlines so specifically the norms and values required of rookies.

- Messner, Michael A. (1992) "The Meaning of Success," "The Embodiment of Masculinity," and "Friendship, Intimacy, and Sexuality," Chapters 3, 4 and 5 in *Power at Play: Sports and the Problem of Masculinity*, Boston: Beacon Press. pp. 42–107.

Michael Messner's interest in masculinity and sexuality is evident in Chapter 10 of Part 2. In these three chapters, from Messner's book-length study based on interviews with 30 retired male professional athletes, he deals with the issues of developing both an athletic identity and a masculine identity, and the way in which those identities overlap. The identities and experiences of these former athletes were consistent with the rather narrow dominant view of what it is to be a man in American society. Their masculinity was based on (a) trying to become wealthy and famous; (b) developing relationships with other men based on misogyny and homophobia; and (c) a willingness to take risks with their bodies, regardless of the consequences for their health. As a consequence, these men experienced a number of contradictions. For example, while developing physical competence in their sports, many incurred serious injuries and suffered chronic health problems. Also, even though they represented a type of masculine ideal, they had a constant sense of insecurity about their manhood. Furthermore, although they experienced fame and public recognition, their identities as athletes and men discouraged them from forming close relationships with other men and with women.

- Wacquant, Loic (1992) "The social logic of boxing in black Chicago," *Sociology of Sport Journal* 9(3): 221–54.

Loic Wacquant was a French student who came to the University of Chicago to complete a doctorate in sociology. His focus was urban life and race relations in a major American city, but he became fascinated by the significance of a boxing gym in Chicago's South Side community. He started to work out at the gym, and to carry out field work. The study analyzes the complex social world of the boxing gym, and its relationships with the surrounding community. Wacquant notices that the regulars at the gym are not from the very lowest levels of ghetto life, but come from backgrounds where they still have some ambition for a better life and the discipline to follow the extremely strict training regimen of boxers. He notes how the gym is a part of ghetto life, but shows that the process of becoming a boxer both separates and shelters individuals from the harsh realities of a neighbourhood without hope or opportunity. Wacquant's work uses an approach developed by French sociologist, Pierre Bourdieu, in order to provide some striking insights into the experience of becoming a boxer in the USA. (See also Sugden, John 1987, "The exploitation of disadvantage: the occupational subculture of the boxer," in J. Horne, D. Jary and A. Tomlinson (eds) *Sport, Leisure, and Social Relations*, London: Routledge and Kegan Paul. pp. 187–209.)

Part 3

DEEP IN THE EXPERIENCE
Doing sports

As Donnelly and Young noted in Chapter 6 of Part 2, the process of constructing and reconstructing an athletic identity is ongoing, as is the process of having that identity confirmed and reconfirmed by one's peers in a specific sport subculture. However, while these processes are ongoing, only occasionally do they become the focus of attention. In the meantime, athletes get on with their lives and careers in sport, make meaning out of their participation in an infinite variety of ways, and enjoy a tremendous range of experiences as a consequence of their participation. The chapters in Part 3 provide just a small sample of those experiences in sports ranging from high school football to women's ice hockey, from skateboarding to college basketball and women's professional golf.

Sociologists and anthropologists have taken a variety of approaches to studying the lives of athletes. In general, they have used the concept of subculture to describe the cultural systems of sports. While all athletes live in the larger culture and, to a greater or lesser extent, share the values, norms and beliefs of that culture, they also share, and produce, a set of values, norms, beliefs, meanings, and social relations specific to their particular sport subculture.

In Chapters 6 and 9 of Part 2, for example, Donnelly and Young, and Klein, described individuals struggling to learn the values, norms and beliefs of the rugby, rock climbing, and North American baseball subcultures. One approach in such studies has been to provide a detailed description of the values, norms and beliefs of the sport subculture. Another has been to describe an individual's progress in a sport as a career, and to examine the contingencies (i.e., steps or conditions that must be met before progressing to the next stage) that influence an athlete's career development (see Chapter 8 by Stevenson).

A more recent approach used in research on subcultures examines how meaning is produced and social relations are developed. This is done in addition to providing detailed descriptions of subcultural values, norms, and beliefs, and is incorporated into an examination of sport subcultures in the context of the larger society. Past research was often based on the assumption that sport was a reflection, a mirror, of society. But this passive approach did not tell us anything about the dynamics of the relationship between sport and society. So we now have gone beyond that passive approach to consider how sport involvement is actively concerned in helping to reproduce status quo values, norms and beliefs in a society, and how sport may be involved in challenging and resisting that status quo in order to bring about social change.

In Chapter 12 Douglas E. Foley (for example, like Messner in Chapter 10) shows how sport is implicated in the reproduction of social inequality. While Messner was concerned with the way in which sport helps to reproduce gender and sexual relations – specifically, a very narrow definition of masculinity – Foley shows how high school sport in the USA is involved in reproducing a whole set of gender, racial, and social class relations. Foley originally intended only to study the Chicano civil rights movement in a small town in the southern part of Texas. But, as a former athlete, he became interested in the high school sports scene in "North Town." He was struck particularly by the rituals surrounding high school football – the pep rally, the homecoming game, the politics of the Booster Club, the powder-puff game, etc. – and the insights they provided into social relations in the community as a whole.

These social relations are played out by a cast of characters including the players (strongly identified as Anglo or Mexicano), the cheerleaders and pep squad members, the "band fags," the ordinary fans and the rebellious Mexicano *vatos*, the Booster Club members from the town's predominantly Anglo business community, and the Mexicano coach. While gender relations, racial relations, and social class relations are all, to a greater or lesser extent, in a process of change in the USA, Foley shows how traditions such as high school football help to maintain (reproduce from generation to generation) gender, racial, and social class inequality. His findings challenge the widely held notion in the USA that social relations always change in progressive ways and that inequalities are being eliminated. The processes described by Foley suggest that social relations can change in regressive ways as well.

Becky Beal, in Chapter 13, directly addresses the issue of resistance in skateboarding, a non-mainstream sport. Skateboarding is one of a whole series of countercultural activities having their origins in the 1960s. Others include surfing, frisbee, and hot dog skiing. More recent additions are mountain biking, snowboarding and windsurfing. All these activities have had as their basis a rejection of the more overt norms, values, and beliefs of mainstream sports – e.g., a dominant coach, hyper-competitiveness, ascetic training regimens, and a distinct lack of fun. Becky spent a great deal of time hanging out with, and interviewing skateboarders to gain insights into their subculture. She found that many boarders were very conscious of how they resisted aspects of mainstream sport. They emphasized cooperative behaviors and they avoided a strict hierarchy of status and authority. They shared with the dominant sport culture an emphasis on skill development, but they worked hard to prevent equating the acquisition of differential skills with the value of the sport experience or the value of the athletes engaged in the sport.

While there is a tendency to perceive such resistant sport subcultures in a homogeneous and static way, they are usually full of contradictions. They are continually in a state of flux in relation to the dominant sport culture. For example, Beal notes the contradiction between the progressive values of skateboarders, and the fact that the predominantly male participants were quite sexist. Also, while most resistant subcultures begin with and often maintain a set of values that are in opposition to mainstream sport, the lure of competition, sponsorships, and professional status often pulls the top athletes in these activities, and sometimes the whole sport, into the dominant sport culture. For example, skateboarding has been partially incorporated into the dominant sport culture, and even the most anti-commercial, anti-competitive participants will sometimes be drawn into an organized and sponsored competition just for fun. Hot dog skiing began with exactly the same values that Beal describes for skateboarding, but the entire sport has now been bureaucratized and professionalized as a set of Olympic and World Cup activities called freestyle skiing. It was evident at the Nagano Winter Olympics in 1998 that snowboarding was in a similar state of flux, somewhere between resistant subculture and incorporated mainstream sport.

In Chapter 14 Nancy Theberge takes us inside the world of women's elite amateur ice hockey at a top Canadian club. She shows another example of resistance at work as women struggle with issues surrounding the meaning and expression of their physicality. What does it mean to play like a girl? Are there essential differences between the way males and females play the same sport? These questions have become very important as women begin to participate in physical sports such as rugby, wrestling, and ice hockey that have long been associated with men and masculinity. The questions themselves do not have any essential answers – rather, the answers emerge out of political struggles over rules and definitions between competing interest groups, and out of the processes by which meanings are produced in subcultures and in the larger culture.

Theberge shows quite clearly that the participants love the physicality of the game, and that women's hockey involves vigorous physical contact despite rules against body checking. But she also shows how the women themselves, particularly those who previously played games in which checking was allowed, struggle over the issue. They understand fair body checking as a valuable skill in the game, but they are also aware of the risk of injury. This awareness is particularly acute among amateur players who have full-time jobs. Theberge also shows us that this struggle exists also at the ideological level because the outlawing of body checking was initially a deliberate attempt to re-establish the difference between men and women. The game is marketed, and presented by the media, as different from the men's game. Promotions emphasize skill and speed rather than violence. This struggle will continue for some time as many women begin to embrace the physicality of contact sports at the same time as many men, and women, continue to see sport as one of the last arenas in which to assert and reaffirm male and female differences.

In Chapter 15, Douglas E. Foley takes us more directly into the research process to look at what sport means for the aboriginal population in the USA. Like Messner in Chapter 10, Foley employs the new life history method, again combined with some auto-biography, to explore both his relationship with the subject of his research, Jay White Hawk, and the consequences of publishing the research for Jay White Hawk and his family. Jay is a Mesquaki Indian from Iowa, and he played on the same high school football team as Doug. The themes of reproduction and resistance are simultaneously evident in this chapter as it becomes clear that being a good Indian and good athlete did nothing to change, and even helped to reproduce, the race relations in a small Iowa town.

The emergence of the American Indian Movement, a native resistance movement emphasizing a revival of aboriginal cultures to combat incorporation as subordinates into Euro-American culture (an unequal status quo), eventually resulted in the Mesquaki athletes withdrawing from participation in high school sport. But, just as interesting in this chapter is Foley's account of the way in which the publication of his study affected Jay White Hawk, and even caused some rethinking of race relations in the town. Sometimes sociological and anthropological research is designed as an intervention for a specific social problem but, as Foley shows, even where intervention was not intended, our research can have surprising consequences.

Chapters 16 and 17 take us away from the themes of reproduction and resistance to address two important aspects of the lives of elite and professional athletes: the effects of fame; and relationships with fans. Patricia and Peter Adler are sociologists who often carry out joint research projects. The study they summarize in Chapter 16 was undertaken while they were both employed at a university with a strong Division I men's basketball team. Division I includes universities with the most elite sport programs in the National Collegiate Athletic Association in the USA. It is the division out of which most National Basketball Association (NBA) players are recruited. Because of some previous research on sport, Peter became a counselor to the players, and enjoyed fifteen minutes of fame when he was designated as the only team sociologist in the USA. This brief experience of fame led to an interest in, and empathy with, the star players on the team. These players were nominally student athletes, but they enjoyed and were victimized by all of the glory that high profile athletes receive.

The Adlers show how fans and the media create different identities (selves) for the athletes, and how the athletes feel pressure to live up to their media-generated identities. They explore the factors that inhibit and enhance the sense of pride and self-importance felt by the athletes, and show the price that most athletes pay in trying to live up to the glory that is heaped on them. It is important to consider these aspects of the lives of university athletes when we watch, for example, the annual Final Four NCAA Basketball Tournament, and to consider how it might be possible to temper some of the highs and lows of glory.

Todd Crosset spent a season traveling with and studying the Ladies Professional Golf Association (LPGA) tour, and in Chapter 17 he focuses on the relationships between the golfers and their fans. Crosset notes the value of a press pass for an individual with limited funds conducting this type of field research. In this case it gave him free access to the players and courses, and free meals. The LPGA provides a relatively unique context in which to study the player–fan relationship. In addition to their proximity on the course, fans have more access to the players during a women's professional golf tournament than in most other sports. For example, some of the fans sponsored golfers when they were rookies on the tour, and players regularly have meals with fans, or stay at the homes of fans in the various cities where they play.

Crosset found that the best way to understand the relationship between the golfers and their fans was as a reciprocal gift-giving relationship. The players give the fans the gifts of their skills, their autographs, and their time; and the fans give the players applause, status, and more material gifts. However, this reciprocity is fragile and Crosset provides examples of three ways in which it might break down. In each example the breakdown was the fault of the fans, not the players. Perhaps Crosset does not identify examples in which the players caused breakdowns because he came to identify with the players more than the fans. Or perhaps he did not observe or hear about player examples. Or perhaps the LPGA players also have a sense of self-importance that results from their fame.

In the final Chapters of Parts 1 and 2 we saw how the mothers of young athletes, and the wives of male amateur athletes, become implicated in supporting and facilitating the athletes' participation. But what if the athlete is a full-time professional? Sport is not an avocation for these individuals – it is their career, their identity, and their life. Do the husbands and wives of professional athletes get caught up in this world, or are they able to carry on with their own lives? They certainly do not have to get caught up in the mundane chores of laundry, meal preparation, and driving because professional athletes usually have a supportive infrastructure to provide these services.

There are so few female professional athletes that we were unable to explore the lives and experiences of their husbands. The final chapter of Part 3 is by Wendy Thompson, the pseudonym of a wife of a National Hockey League player. (Wendy is using a pseudonym because of concern that her revelations about the lives of hockey wives may be used against her husband in the insecure career of a professional athlete.) She shows us once more how male sport is constructed on the labor of women. She demonstrates quite clearly that being married to, or living in a common-law relationship with, a professional athlete is not nearly as glamorous as we might expect. Thompson looks at two aspects of their lives: the way wives are incorporated into their husbands' careers; and the effects of celebrity.

Wives are incorporated into careers when players are traded because all the details of moving fall to them. They are incorporated by management influences because wives are not allowed to travel with teams, or even attend away games. However, they are expected to engage in voluntary work for the team. They suspect that failure to abide by either of these management constraints would result in sanctions against their husbands. The most striking aspect of incorporation is the tyranny of the league schedule. When wives were pregnant, they often chose to have induced deliveries when the team was playing at home. This enabled their husbands to be with them as they gave birth.

When combined with this process of incorporation, their husband's celebrity, and the public misconceptions about what the life of a player's wife is like, lead to identity problems for many of the women in Thompson's study. The wives had often given up their own careers. They spent a great deal of time alone, and they had difficulties establishing relationships with other people outside the sport because of the prevalence of pseudo-friends who were just attracted by the glamor of their husbands' jobs. Thompson reminds us vividly that the players on our favorite teams often have wives and children whose lives and experiences are not nearly as exciting as we might expect.

The seven chapters in Part 3 take us inside the lives and experiences of athletes. They not only provide a small sample of the wide range of rich experiences of people involved in sport, but they also provide insights into the relationships between sport and society. They show us how sport may be implicated in reproducing both positive and negative aspects of the social relations in a society, how sport is involved in reproducing social inequality, and how sport might be involved in attempts to resist the status quo, or at least establish alternatives to it. A few of the chapters in Part 3 also give us insights into the positive and negative aspects of celebrity in the lives of athletes, and into athletes' relationships with their fans and families.

12

HIGH SCHOOL FOOTBALL
Deep in the heart of South Tejas

Douglas E. Foley

When I went to a small South Texas town (pop. 8,000) to study the Chicano civil rights movement, I had not intended to conduct a study of high school sports. But I was an ex-small college football and basketball player and had coached basketball in an Iowa high school and in the Philippines as a Peace Corps volunteer. Given my love of sports, I became part of the local sports scene without much fanfare. I quickly realized what all "sports sociologists" know, that sports is a window into the larger society. How "North Towners" conduct racial, gender, and class relations is apparent in how they organize and play football.

This great insight hit me during my first pep rally. I was immediately struck by the fact that all the white players walked in first. They were followed by all the Mexicano players, who made up about 65 percent of the team. No one else seemed to notice what I found very odd. In addition, the cheerleaders and pep squad members were all young women. They were busy supporting their "men" who were about to do battle for the honor of the town. Meanwhile, all the social "nobodies" were sitting in the stands playing their part as the adoring, dutiful underclass. The exceptions were the rebellious Mexicano youths called "vatos" (cool dudes). Forced by school rules to attend, they sulked in the wings of the gym and made fun of the "square" kids who cheered wildly. There it was, American society writ large in one little insignificant small-town pep rally.

At that moment, I decided to follow the team through the season. I eventually attended all the games, rode on the player and pep squad buses to away games, attended as many practices as possible, hung out with the coaches, and interviewed a number of players, coaches, and Booster Club supporters. Doing the fieldwork evoked many memories of my own high school sports scene, and I included some in a book and an article about North Town High (Foley 1990a, b). When I look back on this fieldwork, I am enormously pleased with what I produced. I was a young scholar fresh out of Stanford. What I lacked in experience, I made up for in youthful enthusiasm and energy. I trusted my instincts and let my love of sports guide me.

At first, many of the kids distrusted me and called me "narc," but as time passed I became "Doc," the guy who was writing a book about kids and sports. I was this strange adult who they could invite to their beer keg parties and tell their secrets. I was the adult who listened and who did not "rat them out" to teachers and parents. Like any good anthropologist, I was able to get "inside," to accept and be accepted by a group of strangers, if only for a brief time. Now I am too old to do this type of research, but I am glad that I revisited my youthful pleasures and passions. It taught me some important lessons I missed as a player.

When I was a kid and a player, I never thought of sports as a popular cultural practice that reinforces societal patterns of inequality. Where I grew up, no one looked at sports with such a critical eye. As a working-class white kid who played on teams with native American athletes, I experienced some of these inequities. But I was such a gym rat, and so dedicated to becoming a player, I lacked the emotional and intellectual distance to see the darker side of sports. While in South Texas, I saw things that forced me to look anew at sports. I hope that this piece does the same for you.

The study: North Town

The setting of my study was "North Town," a small (8,000 population) South Texas farming and ranching community with limited industry, considerable local poverty, and a population that was 80 percent Mexican-American. North Town High had an enrollment of 600 students. Its sports teams played at the Triple-A level in a five-level state ranking system. North Town High usually made a habit of winning their conference and occasionally the bi-district. As in many other Texas towns, people took their football very seriously.

Shortly after arriving in North Town I attended my first pep rally. Students, whether they liked football or not, looked forward to the Friday afternoon pep rally. Perhaps nothing is more uniquely "American" than these events that are supposed to whip the student body into a frenzy to support the team. The exchange student from Norway found its blaring brass band and bouncy cheerleaders strange and exciting, "very different from our high school sports." Meanwhile, the coaches and players were upfront on the stage stammering through cliché-filled speeches about beating the "Tigers." The crowd seemed to accept their inarticulateness as a virtue. They were strong and silent types. Men of action, not words.

Meanwhile, the cheerleaders were on the gym floor doing dance and jumping routines in unison for the crowd. They were acknowledged as some of the prettiest young women in the school, and they aroused the envy of students who had reputations as "nobodies" and "nerds." Male students incessantly gossiped and fantasized about these young women and their reputations. Particularly the less attractive, "uncool" males plotted the seduction of these young women. They reveled in the idea of having them as girl friends, but they often accused the cheerleaders of being "stuck up" or "sluts." Most of their talk about cheerleaders was sheer fantasy and laced with considerable envy. Only those males with very high social status could actually risk relating to and being rejected by these dangerous, status-confirming young women.

Many young women who were not athletic or attractive enough to be elected also fantasized about becoming a cheerleader. Such young women joined the pep squad as an alternative. The North Town pep squad comprised a group of fifty young women in costume who came to the games and helped the cheerleaders arouse crowd enthusiasm. The pep squad also helped publicize and decorate the school and town with catchy team-spirit slogans such as "Smash the Seahawks" and "Spear the Javelinos." In addition, they helped organize after-game school dances. Their uniforms expressed loyalty to the team, and pep squad members were given a number of small status privileges in the school, such as being released from classes early for pep rallies and away games.

The other crucial part of any pep rally is the marching band. Indeed, some community members scrutinized the quality of the marching band as carefully as they did the football team. Although the band director, Dante Aguila, disliked turning music into a team-like competition, he did it to conform to community wishes. Like sport teams, marching bands competed in local, district, and statewide contests, attempting to garner high rankings. Individual band members could also achieve top rankings in various instruments, but the emphasis was on attaining a high group ranking. A certain segment of the student body began training for the high school marching band during their grade-school years. Band members were generally in the advanced academic tracks and perceived by the more marginal, deviant students as "goodie goodies," "richies," and "brains." Not all band members were top students or rich, but they were generally loyal, school-oriented students. Many female band members were "cool" and socially prominent, but others were studious homebodies and uncool.

On the other hand, "real men" supposedly did not sign up for the North Town band. According to the football players, only the physically weaker, more effeminate males were in the band. Consequently, males in the band were often derisively labeled "band fags." The only exceptions were a few "cool guys" who did drugs and had their own rock and roll band. Regrettably, males who emulated jocks and hoped to hang with them picked on band fags. However, the players themselves, rarely picked on band members. They were too powerful and prestigious to use this as a status-boosting strategy. Consequently, they showed physical restraint towards obviously weaker males. Such a show of restraint enhanced the players' social status among peers.

In anthropological jargon, the pep rally, with its inarticulate heroic male warriors, adoring cheerleaders and pep squad, maligned yet irrepressible "band fags" and audience of loyal "nobodies," is a major American cultural ritual. Among other things, this ritual reproduces what feminists call the patriarchial order of male privilege. One can see this pattern especially well in a curious event called the "powder-puff football game." Exactly how widespread powder-puff football games are, I cannot say, but students from all over Texas and various states report similar practices in their high schools. In North Town, a powder-puff football game is staged by the junior and senior classes on the Friday before the seniors' final game. A number of the senior girls dress up as football players and form a touch football team to play the junior girls. The male football players serve as coaches and referees. Some also dress up as girls and act as cheerleaders. Perhaps a quarter of the student body, mainly the active, popular, successful students, drifted in and out to have a laugh over this game.

This event struck me as a priceless example of what anthropologists call "rituals of reversals." During such events people break or humorously play with their everyday cultural rules and roles. Such reversals are so clearly marked as being out of the ordinary that everyone knows the participants are "just playing." No male who is acting like a female will be accused of being a girl or homosexual, nor will the women be accused of wanting to be men. In this instance, however, it is crucial to note that the males used this moment of symbolic inversion to parody females in a burlesque and ridiculous manner. Males used this event to act in silly and outrageous ways. They pranced around in high heels, smeared their faces with lipstick, and flaunted their padded breasts and posteriors in a sexually provocative manner. This was their way of expressing their social and physical dominance. Conversely, the females took few liberties with the male role being played. They donned the football jersey and helmets and huffed and puffed soberly under the watchful eyes of the boys. They blocked and shoved with considerable gusto. They tried to play a serious game of football. They wanted to prove that they were equal. Their lack of playfulness was a poignant testimony to their subordinate status in this small town.

Another part of any football season is the annual homecoming celebration. It also reproduces male privilege but has a much broader community function as well. Ideally, North Town graduates return to the homecoming bonfire and dance to reaffirm their support and commitment to the school, team, and town. Typically, the local paper plays up the homecoming game, and it draws a bigger crowd. On this particular homecoming day, three groups of boys with pickup trucks created a huge pile of scrap wood and burnable objects in the school parking lot. Unlike the school pep rally, a number of adults and ex-students joined the band, cheerleaders, pep squad, and players and coaches. The mood was even more festive and informal than the after-school pep rallies. The adults attending laughed about the "borrowed" packing crates and were pleased that others "donated" things from their stores and houses to feed the fire.

During the homecoming game, a king and queen and their attendants were presented and crowned during half-time. The royal court, typically the most popular and attractive students, was elected by the student body. The queen and her court, dressed in formal gowns, were ceremoniously transported to the crowning in convertibles. The king and his attendants, who were often football players, escorted the young women from the convertibles to their crowning in their dirty, sweaty uniforms. After the game, the king and queen and their respective courts were presented at the homecoming dance. The dance was primarily for high school students, but ex-students, especially those in college, were noticeably present at the informal beer parties after the dance. The homecoming pep rally, crowning, dance, and informal beer parties struck me as a particularly heightened expression of tradition and community solidarity.

Another major aspect of any football season is how the community, beyond being spectators and fans, actively involves itself in the football ritual. North Town was the type of community in which male teachers who had athletic or coaching backgrounds were more respected than other teachers. North Town school board members, many rugged farmers and ranchers, generally preferred that their school leaders be ex-coaches. In addition, the North Town Booster Club – composed mainly of local merchants, farmers, and ranchers – had the all-important function of raising supplementary funds for improving the sports program and for the post-season awards banquet. The Booster Club was the most direct and formal link that coaches had with North Town civic leaders. According to many ex-coaches, players, and fans, North Town had a long history of Booster Club and school board interference. North Town students and adults often expressed fears and suspicions that the school board and Booster Club imposed their racial and class preferences on the coaches and team. In this case, the role of the Booster

Club illustrates nicely that the football ritual reproduces class and racial inequalities as well as gender inequalities.

Early in the season, the North Town Booster Club became outspoken against coach Trujillo, their "weak Mexican coach." He was generally perceived as too "nice" and not enough of a "disciplinarian." Prominent Anglos frequently compared him unfavorably to an earlier, highly successful Anglo coach who had a much more military style. Early in the season, conflict surfaced over the selection of the varsity quarterback. Coach Trujillo chose the son of an Anglo businessman, an underclassman, over a senior, the son of a less prominent Anglo. The less educated Anglo faction lambasted the coach for giving preference to the children of socially and politically prominent families. Several other controversial player decisions also occurred, but selecting the varsity quarterback, the symbolic leader of the team, was especially sensitive.

Later in the season, the Booster Club also became critical of how coach Trujillo handled the selection of the freshman quarterback. The local restaurants staged many coffee-drinking debates over which of the two freshman quarterbacks should start, the "strong-armed Mexican boy" or the "all-around, smart Anglo boy." The Anglo boy was the son of a prominent car dealer and Booster Club activist. The Mexican boy was the son of a migrant worker and small grocery store manager. Eventually, the Anglo boy became the starter, which aroused several prominent Mexicano political leaders to blast coach Trujillo as a *vendido* (sell-out) for succumbing to the Booster Club and "their freshman coach," whom they considered a racist "redneck." These incidents generally illustrate how prominent citizens from all races can and do put considerable pressure on coaches. The Booster Club was a particularly powerful voice, and its racial and class prejudices clearly enter into some decisions about players.

Having briefly portrayed the racial and class politics that surrounded player decisions, I must add that on a day-to-day basis, there was considerable racial harmony among players. North Town Mexicans and Anglos played side by side with few incidents during the regular season. Although the team never quite lived up to pre-season predictions, they did win six of their ten games. More importantly, these young players displayed a great deal of team unity in the face of much racial squabbling among the adults.

But what about the players? What did they think about their sport and being athletes? Only a very small percentage of players were skilled enough to play college or professional football. As already suggested, the social rewards from playing football are mainly local and cultural. Small town football is a way "to meet cute chicks" or to get preferential treatment from teachers to retake a test or get out of class early. Some players parroted a chamber of commerce view that football builds the character and discipline needed to succeed in life. Others evoked patriotic and civic ideals about beating rival towns and "showing that South Texas plays as good a football as anybody."

On a more personal level, however, playing was a way of proving that you were a virile man. Players talked incessantly about being "hitters" and "studs." They were always trying to prove that they could inflict pain and play with pain. But not all young men found an honored place in society through sports. A few simply ignored football and excelled in other forms of self-expression and achievement from art to science. Most non-playing males fitted into the football ritual as spectators, academic advisors to the players, hangers on, band members, and sports fans.

One group of non-players stood out, however, because of their marginal racial and class position. The most conspicuous anti-footballers were working-class Mexicanos

137

called "vatos" (cool dudes) who were into a hip, drug-oriented lifestyle. They considered sports straight and "kid-stuff for suckers and suck-asses." Nevertheless, the vatos used sports events to stage and display their machismo. They went to games to establish "reps" as tough guys who beat up kids from other towns and "hit on their chicks." After each game, the vatos regaled me with tales of their foray into enemy territory – the fights they won, the women they conquered. They saw themselves as warriors who were not under the thumb of "dumb coaches" and restrictive training rules. They were tough, unconventional North Town patriots who helped establish the town's reputation as a cool, hip place.

In actual fact, many "straight" North Town football players actually shared some aspects of the vatos' rebellious life style. They often broke their strict training rules by drinking and smoking pot at private teen parties. Publicly, however, most jocks acted like all-American boys. Unlike the rebellious vatos who flaunted their drinking and drugs publicly, jocks hid their pleasures and represented themselves as "clean cut" and "straight." If jocks got caught breaking training, prominent men in the community tended to explain away these infractions as natural male temptations. Most fathers believed that "boys will be boys." Players were rarely criticized publicly the way rebellious vatos, non-playing males, and young women were. As long as they were not outrageously indiscreet through public drunkenness or getting a "trashy girl" pregnant, their training infractions were forgiven. They often seemed to revel in their privileged role and were not above telling "I-got-drunk/stoned-before-the-game stories" to the school "nobodies."

To sum up, North Town football is a powerful metaphor of American capitalist culture (Foley 1990a). Football is an enjoyable, seemingly innocent popular cultural practice, but it is deeply implicated in the reproduction of the local ruling class of white males, hence class, patriarchal, and racial forms of dominance. All too often, coaches and players become ensnared in the local politics of the Booster Club. Local sports, especially football, socialize every new generation of youth into the local status hierarchy, both inside and outside the school. Each new generation of males learns to be individualistic, aggressive, and competitive within a group structure, thus better prepared for military and corporate life.

References

Foley, Douglas (1990a) *Learning Capitalist Culture: Deep in the Heart of Tejas*, Philadelphia: University of Pennsylvania Press.
—— (1990b) "The great American football ritual: reproducing class, race, and gender inequality," *Sociology of Sport Journal* 7(2): 111–35.

13

SKATEBOARDING

An alternative to mainstream sports

Becky Beal

I love sport and have been involved in organized sport for most of my life as an athlete and as a coach. Yet I have never been able completely to engender a deep loyalty to any team or sport organization. My inability fully to assimilate the norms and values of the sports in which I have participated has provoked my interest in investigating people who actively seek sport activities outside of the mainstream. Accordingly, I chose skateboarding as a topic for my doctoral dissertation because it is considered by many to be different from the traditional sporting culture.

The incident that generated my interest in skateboarding as an alternative sport occurred when I watched a group of young people in downtown Denver, Colorado. Dressed in long black pants and long sleeved T-shirts, smoking cigarettes, and listening to loud rock and roll music, these skateboarders were using a fountain, a sculpture, and stairs as their playground. As I pursued this, it became evident that skateboarding is largely seen by the adult world as unruly and the participants as lacking respect for others and their property, as illustrated by the "no skateboarding" signs posted in numerous shopping malls, parking ramps, and university walkways. I noticed that one response to this was the very popular "skateboarding is not a crime" bumper sticker. It appeared to be an activity fueled by those who were seeking an alternative to mainstream sport.

The world of skateboarding was new to me, and I brought with me many stereotypes, especially about skateboarders being teenagers who defied adult authority by openly displaying indifference for school, their own health, and public property. Although I found some participants who confirmed my stereotypes, many more challenged them. Even with similar demographic backgrounds (e.g., teenagers, white, male), their interests varied greatly. For example, some of the skaterboarders were committed Christians; others were racist skinheads, feminists, and environmentalists; there were honor students, high school drop-outs, and a practicing artist.

To investigate the ways in which skateboarding might be alternative, I spent two and a half years (1989–92) observing and interviewing skateboarders in the state of Colorado. Because I am not a skateboarder, I was surprised that the vast majority of participants were keen to talk with me, but I quickly realized that they were eager to talk with someone who took their activity seriously. I found a variety of perspectives and styles, yet there were some common concerns and characteristics that will be the focus of the following chapter. The original research is published as "Disqualifying the official: an exploration of social resistance through the subculture of skateboarding," *Sociology of Sport Journal*, 12(3): 252–67 and as "Alternative masculinity and its effects on gender relations in the subculture of skateboarding," *Journal of Sport Behavior*, XIX(3): 204–20.

The participants

To determine whether skateboarding was an alternative sport I needed to document the norms and values and then compare them with the prevalent norms and values of mainstream sport. My first task was to contact participants who were willing to be interviewed about the values they held and the reasons why they skateboarded. For each interview I covered four main areas: the participants' background; their interest in skateboarding; their perception about similarities and differences that skateboarding had with mainstream sport; and their perception about what characterized a "cool" or "uncool" skateboarder. I also allowed the skateboarder to direct the conversation around any other pertinent information or special interests.

I met most of my participants by stopping them while they were skateboarding on the streets, and asking if I could talk with them. (They called themselves "skaters," and the act of skateboarding they called "skating".) I met other skaters through interactions I had with their parents. In addition, I met one female skater through mutual membership in a local feminist group. These initial contacts led to many others and over a two-year period I spoke with forty-one skaters, two skateboard shop owners, and several parents and siblings. Thirty-seven of the participants were male and four were female. In addition, all were Anglo except for two who were Hispanic males. The average age of those participating was 16, but ranged from 10 to 25 years. The participants had skated for an average of four years. Of the forty-one participants, I interviewed twenty-four more than once and had ongoing communication with six of these. This gave me a vital source of feedback which helped to refine my questions and conclusions.

I also wanted to observe skaters to document their behaviors and to verify whether these supported what they claimed to value. I spent more than 100 hours observing skateboarders, many of whom I had not interviewed. For example, I would go to the local skateboard parks and to public areas which were often used by skateboarders where I would watch and take notes about their interaction.

The skateboarding scene

Unlike mainstream sport which is formally organized and competitive, the popular practice of skateboarding is run by the participants and does not emphasize competition against others. With the exception of commercialized events such as the X-games, skateboarding is not sponsored by an official organization. I found no equivalent to a "little league" for skateboarding. Consequently, it was the skaters, the participants, who created and controlled their sport.

A typical skating session included a small group who would seek the best spots in town for doing tricks. Skaters frequently sought areas where there were ramp-like structures such as a loading dock or areas that had parking blocks, stairs and handrails. When a spot was found the skaters would practice certain tricks such as "ollies" and rail slides. "Ollies" are the basic skill one needs to perform a variety of tricks. An ollie is the ability to "get air," and is done by applying downward pressure on the board generating the opposite reaction which propels the board upward. When skaters master an ollie, they can then jump their board on a variety of structures and slide along them. Ollying to a handrail or onto a parking block and sliding the skateboard along that surface is a very common trick. Skaters would occasionally create games such as follow the leader.

Another significant difference I found between skateboarding and more traditional sport was that skateboarders did not focus on competition and the subsequent ranking of individuals. That is not to say that skill levels were not recognized, but skill was not the determining factor for high status. When I asked the participants to describe what makes a skater "cool," their overwhelming response was someone who was both skilled and cooperative. The skaters' focus on cooperation should not be equated with a lack of motivation or skill. The vast majority of skaters took risks and tried hard. In fact, they reveled in challenging their own limits. The emphasis on both cooperation and skill development is reflected in a 13 year old's comments:

> Well, we don't, we're not like competitive like saying, "I can ollie higher than you so get away from me," and stuff like that, we're like, we just want to do a few things people are doing, and skaters help out skaters . . . and if I were to ask a good skater like some people I can skate with, like Brad Jones, he's the best skater I know in Welton, if I asked him he would like give me tips and stuff, you know on how to do it and that's just how we do it, we want to show other people how to skate.

Common values of the participants

Four themes emerged from the values and behaviors I found in the practice of skate-boarding. Three of the themes demonstrate the differences I found between traditional sport and skateboarding:

- the participants' control of skateboarding;
- the participants' desire to individualize skateboarding and emphasize self-definition;
- the devaluing of competition by participants.

It is significant to note that these values were not extended to females in the same manner as they were to males. The fourth theme is a significant qualification to the above and one that is common in mainstream sport:

- male privilege and dominance in skateboard culture.

Participant control

Many skaters commented on their attraction to a sport in which they were the ones who made the decisions about the activity. Frequent references were made by the skaters about the absence of authority as an important aspect of the sport. For example, Paul claimed that to skateboard "[you] don't need uniforms, no coach to tell you what to do and how to do it." Kathleen noted that skateboarding has "no referees, no penalties, no set plays. You can do it anywhere and there is not a lot of training." Craig contrasted skateboarding with other sports and noted that it "is not as military minded" and "you're not part of a machine, [you] go at your own pace." The skaters asserted that this lack of formality allowed them more freedom to explore and express themselves. For example, Jeff described the skating context as:

> . . . a lot less confined [than organized sport], people are open to a lot of new things when you skate . . . Baseball, basketball, soccer and swimming, I did them all pretty well, but didn't really pursue them that much, skating is so fun because it's so progressive, there's so many things, like in baseball there's not much else you can do once you can hit the ball . . . That's what I like about skating, it's abstract, it's not your average hit the ball and run sport.

Self-definition

Linked with the control that the skaters had over their activity is their ability to define for themselves the significance of their participation. In other words, the participants determine the boundaries and criteria for their sport which allows them to create an activity that fits their needs. The desire for self-definition was commonly expressed by their disdain for formal standards on which athletes are judged. More frequently, the self-definition is demonstrated by the participants' desire to promote individuality, creativity, and self-expression through their sport.

Craig's comment, "there's no such thing as a perfect '10' for a trick," indicates the skaters' awareness about the lack of formal standards in skateboarding. Accordingly, there were no universal criteria by which skaters were judged. Grace's comment illustrates how she questions using other people's standards to evaluate how she gains satisfaction from her sport: "For who's to say what trick is better? I like to do stuff that feels cool, that gives me butterflies in my stomach." Alan, a fifth grade student and skater, wrote a school essay that describes how he is able to express himself because there was no formal judgement: "The reason I love to skate is because its [sic] a challenging [sic] sport. It's the way I express myself. It's something I can do by myself and nobody's there to judge me."

The most frequent representation of the skaters' sense of satisfaction was the creativity and individual expression that occurred. Doug, a 25-year-old skater and public school teacher, commented:

> A lot of them [skaters] are really involved with artistic endeavors, are very artistic. You can see the parallel; it's a kind of freedom of expression that skating is. How do you express yourself playing football, playing basketball? When you're skating it's, basically skating reflects your mood at the time and

how you're skating, what you're doing. You know, it's definitely, you know a
way to express yourself.

Many athletes as well as sport sociologists would claim that one can express oneself
through organized sport, but the point is that these skateboarders felt they had more
opportunity to be creative in skateboarding than traditional organized sport. I would
agree because the skaters defined their sport according to their individual needs.

Competition devalued

One of the most prevalent findings was the devaluing of competition. I contend that this
occurred because skateboarding is primarily an avenue for personal fulfillment. To help
ensure this, the skaters could not adopt a competitive system which grants only the top-
ranked participants a sense of accomplishment. Instead, the skaters embraced a cooperative system that allowed each to define and reach his/her own needs.

The skaters often described their sport as something different from competition. Jeff
stated: "I don't know if I would classify it [skateboarding] as a sport. I suppose I just
find sport as competition, unless you are on the pro or amateur circuit you're not really
competing against anybody." Pamela, an 18-year-old skater made this comparison:

> Soccer is a lot of pressure . . . you have to be as good if not better than everybody
> else, you have to be, otherwise you don't play at all. Skating you can't do that,
> you just push yourself harder and harder [without trying to beat other
> skaters] . . . Swimming is just sort of there, you get timed . . . you go against
> the clock. Now when you skate you don't go against anything, you just skate,
> that's what it is.

While I discussed the issue of competition with Doug, he claimed:

> I don't hear skaters whining about, you know, other people being better than
> them or striving to be, or bumming out because they're not mastering some-
> thing, whereas in other athletics you do. There's a pressure to succeed where
> there isn't in skateboarding because there's not huge goals to attain. How do
> people measure success in skateboarding if you're not skating in contests
> which most people don't. Skaters, even in contests, it's more an attitude of
> having your best run, making all your tricks, as opposed to beating somebody.
> It's not "I got to beat this guy, this is the guy I'm going to beat."

Not only was competition devalued, but also competitive attitudes. Several of my
conversations with skaters were around what made a skater "cool" or "uncool," in other
words, what made a skater authentic. Overwhelmingly, a competitive attitude was seen
as a negative attribute. As noted by Charles, "Skaters who are assholes are people who
brag or skate to compete." This was echoed almost universally, as Jeff noted:

> Nobody really seemed to like competitive natures. For instance, me, Philip and
> one of our friends all found that to be a real turn off. This guy would pull a
> really good trick and rub it in their faces. And then there's Hugh who can do

stuff and doesn't go "Oh, wow, bet you can't." But he's fun to be with . . . and he encourages you, so that's pretty cool.

Authenticity was gained in two main ways: the skaters made an effort at learning to skate; skaters did not compete. Those who had the highest status among skateboarders were highly skilled, but they shared their knowledge and time with others. Cooperation was valued because it enabled others to meet their individual goals and fostered friendships more readily than a competitive atmosphere. As Eric stated:

> In skating you're only responsible for you. If you mess up, you won't mess up the whole team, [you're] not going to lose friends over messing up in skating . . . If you're the worst one on the baseball team others give you shit [and that] makes you feel bad. In skating if you are bad, no one makes you feel bad about that.

The popular, everyday form of skateboarding had little to do with competing against others. It was a means for the participants to challenge themselves without the threat of losing friends or status. As Craig commented, "You never lose when you skate."

Masculine privilege and dominance

It was quite apparent to me that very few females skateboarded. I literally chased down three of the four females who were in my sample to include them in the study, and I rarely saw any other female skateboarders. I was very interested in how the participants explained the dominance of males in skateboarding. After establishing a rapport, I asked them to comment on the obvious lack of females. The responses primarily referred to different natural aptitudes and different interests among males and females. Most of the skaters saw no physical or tangible barriers to female involvement and therefore assumed that females freely chose not to be involved. Even though no physical barriers were present it became apparent that there were attitudinal barriers.

The most noticeable attitude was that females were not taken as seriously as males. Females who skated were perceived as a kind of groupie, and were referred to as a "skate Betty." Doug, explained "skate Betties" in this way:

> They do it because they want to meet cute guys, or their boyfriends do it. It's the alternative crowd; it's like the girls that are kind of into alternative music and that stuff, and kind of skating goes along with it, not as much punk, but not mainstream, and, um, they like the clothes; it's a cool look, I think it's a cool look.

Obviously, this comment demeans females and relegates their role as a skateboarder to the margins of the group because it portrays them not as real skaters, but as people who want to associate with males who are assumed to be real skaters. Additionally, some skaters assumed females to be less physically capable. One example is Brian's comment: "Oh sometimes there are girls that like skaters, like they hang out, but they don't really, they aren't like, they just try to balance on the board." Eric claimed that "it takes too much coordination for a girl, and it's too aggressive."

The four females who participated in the study were quite aware of this attitude. Grace, a 21-year-old skater, believed males felt threatened by her, and thus treated her differently. Specifically, she felt patronized and overprotected by her male friends. For example, they are more concerned when she falls, and more enthusiastic when she learns tricks for the first time. Pamela claimed that she had to be better than the males to be accepted by them. To negotiate being part of the group, all of the females stated that they had to become "one of the guys." This indicates that they did not feel accepted as female skateboarders. It is my contention that even though the vast majority of males did not intentionally discriminate against the females, their attitudes of not fully embracing females as equal skate partners discouraged girls and young women from becoming part of the scene. Few of us feel comfortable doing an activity when we are not welcomed or respected by the other members.

Summary

Skateboarding was an important avenue for the skaters I interviewed to develop physical skills, to challenge their physical and mental limits, and to socialize with like-minded peers. The fact that they wanted minimal adult interference (guidance) enabled them to define their sport and develop their own goals and styles, which frequently brought feelings of satisfaction. In addition, skateboarding was constructed as a masculine realm, making it very significant to teenaged males, but simultaneously the masculine bias tended to discourage female participation.

I would characterize most of the skaters as young people who creatively challenged and questioned rules and regulations in an effort to form their own style. I enjoyed getting to know them. We often socialized over coffee or a meal and occasionally I was invited to "skater" parties. This gave me the opportunity to observe them in different environments. The most challenging circumstances for me occurred when I met skaters whose values opposed my own; most notable were those who made sexist and racist comments. One of these incidents occurred while I was hanging out with Mark and Kathleen as they were practicing new skate tricks on the steps of a county courthouse. A second young male skater joined us. Noting that I was not skating, he asked me why I was there. I told him I was from the university doing research on skaters. He immediately commented: "Have you seen all those niggers up there? I think they have a program for potential drop-outs." This blatant racist comment offended me and my first reaction was to tell him to leave. Part of qualitative research is to investigate the social situation as fully as possible, so this means that I cannot just interview and report the findings of people with whom I get along. As difficult as these interactions were, they helped improve my communication because I had to practice listening to and understanding the views of those who do not agree with me.

14

BEING PHYSICAL

Sources of pleasure and satisfaction in women's ice hockey

Nancy Theberge

My research in women's ice hockey grew out of a more general interest in the relationship between gender and physicality. Literature on sport and gender has emphasized the importance of bodily practice for ideologies of gender, that is ideas about masculinity and femininity that form the basis for gender relations. I had explored this issue at a theoretical level in some earlier work (Theberge 1991) and decided to pursue the topic further in a "hands on" research project.

The historical association of sport and masculinity has been most powerfully celebrated in sports that involve dramatic displays of force and power. Women's increasing involvement in contact sports like rugby and ice hockey poses a particularly significant challenge to this association. I wanted to understand the meaning of this involvement for participants and the broader social and cultural factors that influence the expression of physicality. I chose ice hockey as a setting for the research because of its special grip on Canadian culture.

The project started with a call to the offices of the Canadian Amateur Hockey Association (now the Canadian Hockey Association) in May 1992. The manager of women's programs suggested I attend the upcoming meetings of the Ontario Women's Hockey Association, in Toronto, not far from where I live. This meeting gave me an introduction to the organization of women's hockey. But the most important outcome was that I met a woman who was planning a girls' hockey camp to be held in July on the campus of the university where I teach. I told her of my interest and arranged to visit the camp. There I met a number of people involved in women's hockey, including John. He is the coach of the "Blades," one of the best teams in the country, who compete in a League in Canada.

John was also supportive and I made plans to attend a game and meet the team in November, after the season had started. In this meeting, with John absent, I explained my interests and asked permission to "spend time" with the team, for purposes of doing research. I told the players I wanted to "get an idea of what it is like to play hockey at an elite level."

I then began regular attendance at team events, including games, practices and social events. I also travelled with the team to tournaments. I had complete access to team activities including, most importantly, the change room where the players assembled before and after games and practices. While I began the research as an outsider, over time I became accepted as an unofficial member of the Blades.

I continued my field work through the 1992–3 season and the 1993–4 season, from October to April. After each game, practice or other event, I wrote field notes. Over the period of the field work, I also interviewed players on the team and others in women's hockey who offered insight and information on the issues which I was exploring.

Players ranged in age from 16 to 30 years. They included students and women who worked in a variety of occupations. There is no professional women's hockey. The league in which the Blades compete includes a number of members of the Canadian national team and the level of play is very high.

Physicality in players' athletic lives

My initial appreciation of physicality in players' lives came from time with the team in the change room. After games that were particularly intense, the room was especially animated. Players lingered, often delaying changing from their hockey gear, talking about the game and re-enacting plays. On these occasions, there was a palpable sense of excitement in the room. I came to understand that the shared experience of the practice of the sport was one of the central elements of the construction of the "team as community" (Theberge 1995b).

This sense was reinforced when I asked about "playing the game." In different ways, individuals spoke of the attraction of contact and intense play. Here is one of the most vivid accounts:

> I like the corners. I like the fight for the puck; it's who's going to fight for the puck. It's that one-on-one situation . . . That's where the competitiveness comes in, that's where my aggressiveness comes from: this is mine and I'm not giving it to you kind of thing . . . I like a physical game. You get more fired up. I think when you get hit – not a cheap shot – but something like when you're fighting for a puck in the corner, when you're both fighting so you're both working hard and maybe the elbows are flying, that just makes you put more effort into it. You're using your body that much more which means you're exerting that much more energy. It creates more of the game.

Others described the sense of satisfaction from physical play. A player said:

> It's great to go into a corner and come out standing when someone else is on the ground. You've done your job. You've got them.

Later in the interview she spoke of another skill she felt she had, which is to "keep your cool better than your opponent . . . I can get people to do something stupid, to take a penalty when I know I'm not going to retaliate." She continued that both these abilities are important but:

> I think the most satisfying is the physical. When you run into somebody and you stand up and they're down, that makes you feel a lot better than if you out-smarted somebody. It makes you feel better, the physical part.

At the same time that I was learning about physicality in the players' athletic lives, I was coming to appreciate that there are differing views about this feature. As part of my work with the Blades, I attended a number of events in which officials of women's hockey spoke about the sport. Here, and in interviews, they frequently referred to it as "hockey the way it is supposed to be played." They described it as a game of speed, finesse and playmaking and emphasized the "sportsmanship" of players. A similar emphasis was found by Etue and Williams (1996) in their book on women's hockey.

There was a clearly implied comparison to the aggressive physicality of men's hockey, particularly the fighting and other forms of violence that seem an occupational require-ment in the National Hockey League (NHL) and its feeder leagues. The effort to de-emphasize the physicality of women's hockey seemed somewhat at odds with the impressions I was gathering in my field work and interviews. There are some clear differ-ences between men's and women's hockey. There is no fighting in women's hockey (or nearly none). In my two years with the Blades, only one fight occurred and this was exceptional as it happened at the end of a season when players were less concerned about suspensions that would normally be given for fighting. There are no bone-crunching collisions, vicious cross-checks and other forms of attack that are common in men's professional hockey. But interviews with players, as well as the exhilaration in the Blades dressing room after particularly intense games, suggested that the "alternative construction" belied a more complicated story about physicality in women's hockey. Uncovering that story yielded insights about the relationship between gender, sport and physical practice.

Construction of women's hockey: the place of body checking

A centrepiece of the construction of women's hockey as an alternative to the men's game is the rules surrounding body contact. The rules of play in men's and women's ice hockey are substantially the same, with the major difference being that the rules of women's hockey prohibit intentional body checking, that is intentional efforts to hit, or "take out" an opposing player. To be sure, there is still considerable body contact in women's hockey, both intentional and unintentional. To watch a game is to see players constantly try to outmanoeuvre and outmuscle one another. But the game is noticeably different from the higher levels of the men's sport in that one rarely sees the forceful collisions that are a defining feature of men's hockey at these levels (Theberge 1995a, 1996).

The prohibition of body checking results in a game in which speed, strategy and play-ing skills are featured more prominently than in a full contact game, where a greater emphasis is placed on power and force. This difference is one of relative emphasis: with or without body checking, hockey is a game of skill and strength. While body checking changes the balance, each element remains significant.

It is important to keep in mind that the rules of women's hockey prohibit intentional body checking, not body contact. This distinction is often lost in discussions, including some of the excerpts provided here, where the women's game is referred to as "non-contact."

Until the late 1980s, the rules regarding body contact in women's hockey varied across Canada. A number of the Blades have played both full contact and the current game. Many of these players express a sense of pleasure and accomplishment in receiving and taking a body check well. Here are the comments of two women who have played full contact:

> Contact makes the game a lot more enjoyable. The game of hockey is skate, shoot, score, hit. An intense hockey player has to focus on the hitting. I liked it. I was small. I got hit around a lot. I used to get nailed by some of the big people. But that's part of the game and I got up and skated away. And I put in a few good hits as well. When they took it away, it just made the game a little faster.

> Part of the camaraderie, part of the fun, is hitting . . . When we played against [X, one of the strongest players in the League who is now a Blade] part of the thrill was if we could hit her. Hit her clean. That was part of the fun.

A woman who has not played the intentional checking game offered similar comments:

> I wish I played in this league a couple of years ago when there was body checking. That'd be great. I think hockey should be physical contact because that's the way it was made. Physical. You should be tough to play this game. I played for the boys' hockey team at school and I used to get killed sometimes cause I was so small and they were really big. You get right back up looking for more. I love it.

Others emphasize that body checking is a skill, part of the repertoire of abilities that players can master. A player with experience in playing the full contact game offered the following account:

> It's a certain aggressiveness. You're putting your strength against, your technique against . . . It's a technique that you've learned and you can complete, and maybe you can complete it better than they can. You can prove your flexibility and your stamina, your stability on the ice.

Players' references to checking as "killing," "hurting," and "getting back" are allusions to the view that body checking is one element of the uncontrolled aggression featured in the NHL. As their comments indicate, it is a view they reject.

Another player provided an account of how players use checking to "get the job done":

> I liked the contact. Playing defense it just made it a little bit easier. It's easier to ride the person out of the play. Now you've got to rely on just getting in front of them but not hitting them and if you've got someone that's really fast and

you can't take a piece of them, they're apt to go around you. When there's contact you can take a piece of them to slow them down.

Players who endorse the inclusion of body checking in women's hockey readily acknowledge the attraction of the non-body checking game. Several players who have played both versions spoke of the trade-off and their satisfaction with each. A veteran said:

> I like both games. When they took it [contact] out, I like that because the game is quicker without the contact and that means you have to have more skill. Although, you know it's funny there's a part – when it does go to checking I like that.

She used an analogy in which she described checking as one part of the game:

> It's kind of like writing an essay. If you use everything you're supposed to use properly in your writing, you're much more satisfied than if you use something like dangling participles . . . It's a skill to be able to body check.

Some players support the limitations on contact. One woman said:

> I prefer it without. Maybe just because I've always played without. The women's game being a bit different from the men's game, it may actually be better without it. I like to think of it as more of a finesse game.

Body checking and the risk of injury

When I asked players why body checking had been eliminated from women's hockey, nearly all cited concern about injuries. Following are the accounts of several women who played when the Blades' league was full contact:

> We went to a meeting and we argued that someone on my team had their collarbone broken by another player and this other player was pretty well wiping out quite a few people. And there were other people causing problems and we felt that as females who were not professionals we weren't getting paid to do this, that something had to be done because the game was not enjoyable at all when people are taking all kinds of illegal motions. I mean even if they do get a penalty, what does that do for a broken collarbone or foot?

> People were complaining about cheap shots, about people getting hurt, we all worked for a living, we all had to get up and go to work the next day.

> Because of injuries . . . 'Cause it wasn't clean at all. Girls aren't taught how to hit. 'Cause you don't hit all the way up [through the youth system]. Then all of a sudden you get to senior and there's contact. No one knows how to hit. Sticks are up. Hands are up.

Well to be honest with you checking was fine but I believe that the women weren't taught properly how to check. And there was a lot of injuries, like I was pretty scared of a few people out there just because I know, they were going to hit you with their fists up or whatever. If checking had been taught properly at a young age, just like the boys, they learn checking [from] a young age . . . then maybe it wouldn't be so bad. To take a hit on the boards is fine. It's just, I don't think women know how to check properly.

These comments suggest that the relationship between body checking and the risk of injury is conditioned by other factors. Whether through failure to teach players to give and take checks properly or failure to observe and enforce the rules of play, the body checking game moved past "good clean hockey" to play that was dangerous and, for some, not enjoyable. Players felt that the best way to rid the League of this type of play was to remove body checking.

Another view of the relationship between checking and injuries is that without checking there is an increase in injuries from other, illegal body work. One player said "I think I've had more stupid injuries with the no intentional body checking rule in." She explained the effect of the rule on the practice of the game:

[With no body checking] I'm not expecting some of the hits that I'm getting because some people don't play within the rules. And they can hit you and put you into the boards or whatever when you're not expecting it, which usually I don't, because I think no, we play within the rules, they don't want to get a penalty, they don't want to hurt me.

Another player commented on the relationship between the prohibition of body checking and illegal stick work:

I think most of the players at first liked the idea of no checking, no intentional body checking. Some of them I think have come around and said "hey, yeah, less stick work." So okay, say you get frustrated out there and you hit somebody clean and you know it's coming, like if you know it's coming you're not going to get hurt. That's the way I always feel. If there's body checking I know I'm going to get hit. Fine. I know how to go into the boards a little differently . . . So with that in mind, yeah, I prefer the body checking, myself. It's the game.

When asked why players seem to see an inevitable trade-off between checking and illegal stick work, she explained:

Well because you've got to slow them down somehow. You've got to get in front of them somehow and usually if you can't hit them or at least take a piece of them, that's the only thing left. And that's your stick to slow them down. Unless you can outskate them. Well that's not me.

This player's comments speak to the view that checking is part of the repertoire of a hockey player's skills. When it is not available, players resort to other tactics to accomplish their task. These tactics include illegal and sometimes dangerous practices.

Body checking and other expressions of physicality

The prohibition of body checking does not mean it never occurs. Players sometimes check unintentionally. Some use the skill deliberately. When they do so they are gambling they will not be seen and will get away with it or they are prepared to risk receiving a penalty. The penalty for body checking is two minutes in the penalty box – the same as for slashing, tripping and most other "standard" infractions. A player described a hypothetical situation when she would check. She said a good body check can be "great":

> Just because of the satisfaction of taking the man [sic] out. If you have a nice, good, strong body check and you get called for it, depending on the situation you might say "all right, that was a good body check." You don't really care 'cause you're winning or whatever. But in an important situation you wouldn't take the chance because we're not allowed to body check.

Players follow a code in regard to other expressions of physicality. One principle of the code is that the goalie is "out of bounds," meaning that if the opposition "takes a run" – deliberately skates into – the goalie or otherwise violates her and her space, retaliation is in order. The code also condemns hits to the knees and from behind, and sticks to the crotch. Responses to these transgressions depend on the context and players' judgements and restraint.

Players also distinguish between "smart" and "dumb" penalties. Smart penalties serve a purpose. Dumb penalties hurt the team without accomplishing anything. The value of penalties was the subject of an exchange in the dressing room after a game in which B received a two-minute penalty for upending a player, while C received two minutes for a similar hit, followed by another two minutes for mouthing off to the officials. The general consensus in the room was that B's hit was smart because it took an opponent out of a play while C's was pointless. B teased C that she got fewer minutes for a "smarter" penalty.

Intimidation and retaliation are elements of some player's games. One of the veteran players' said that her game is "passing, thinking, checking, sometimes intimidation." I asked how she intimidates:

Player: Shoves here and there. I usually don't say much on the ice unless they say something to me.
Q: Why and when would you use intimidation?
Player: If somebody was getting out of hand, or if you knew you could do it to somebody and they're going to cough up the puck the next time you see them, or throw them off their game. Someone like [Y, on another team] if she's all of a sudden thinking about you she stinks, so the next thing you know she's whining and crying and that's the end of their game. That's the only time you use it. You never intentionally injure anybody. You just get in their face.

Another player offered an example of physical play for the purpose of retaliation. Like others, she suggested that if there were body checking, there might be "less stick work." When I asked her to explain, she said:

Well because we're not allowed to fight, so if someone does something to you, you can't get back at them otherwise you're suspended. So what we'll do, whenever the ref's not watching, here and there a little stick between the legs, that doesn't tickle, and in the ribs or whatever. That's what's bad about [no body checking] because we do little things like that because it's the only way to get back at a person. You have no alternative.

Players also "talk trash." Here is one player's account:

Talking trash is going up to another person and yacking at them and cutting them up and saying "Ha, I just slammed that over your face," or "Ha, I just blew by you and beat you to the corner. I can't believe you're actually playing this game."

This woman is one of the most skilled in the sport, who is vocal in her disdain for dirty play and stupid penalties. I asked why she talked trash. Her answer indicates ambivalence about the practice and what it says about her as a player:

I think if you have to talk trash you're actually lowering yourself, even if I do it all the time when I get frustrated. I think it's just frustration coming out when you're talking trash. Or, if you've gotten something over on someone that you dislike, or you dislike what they've just done: "Hey, I just beat you and I just did this and let's see why you're here and playing" . . . I don't like it, it's something that possibly may help your confidence by getting something off your chest . . . I see it as more a release.

One of the Blades told me that women's hockey is "very dirty," in players' use of their sticks for "hooking and slashing." To be sure, there are variations among players in their endorsement and use of "dirty play." Nonetheless, pushing and shoving, sticks to the ribs, back and other areas of the body, confrontations that are broken up by officials before they can escalate, and verbal aggression in the form of taunts and trash talking are part of women's hockey at the highest levels.

Physicality and the construction of difference

My research indicates that the effort to portray women's hockey as an alternative to the men's game belies a complicated relationship between the sports. To be sure there is one significant difference in that there is virtually no fighting in women's hockey. Other distinctions are less straightforward. The prohibition of body checking means that there are none of the full-force collisions which feature prominently in men's hockey. At the same time, it means that a skill that some see as "part of the game" and which brings players pleasure and satisfaction is not routinely available to them.

The promotion of women's hockey as different is challenged by other aspects of its practice. The clutching, grabbing, slashing and high sticking that is criticized in the men's game are elements of the women's game, as are intimidation, retaliation and trash talking. While the specifics of the code of conduct in each sport vary and women's hockey rejects the aggressive physicality of the men's game, the cultures of men's and women's hockey are alike in players efforts to "do the job." In this effort, men and women alike attend to but do not necessarily abide by the written rules (Faulkner 1976). Another similarity is that myriad emotions occur in competition, including frustration, aggression and anger. Combined with variations in players' skills and styles, these yield differences in adherence to the standard of "good, clean hockey."

The prohibition of body checking is about much more than injuries and clean play. While both these considerations are important, neither bears a simple relationship to the rules around body contact. Body checking is a particularly dramatic expression of physicality in sport. It is for this reason that the rules and practices surrounding its use are so central to the construction of hockey and the broader cultural struggle over the gendering of sport.

Historically, this struggle was resolved by constructing women's sport as an alternative to men's (Theberge 1989). This meant the differentiation of sports into gender-appropriate categories, and in sports in which men and women compete, the development of adapted models for women, such as six-player basketball. By diminishing physicality, the adapted model minimized the challenge posed by women's participation to the historical association of sport, physicality and gender. The inevitable result, however, was that women's sport was viewed to be an inferior version of "real" sport.

A number of the Blades saw a dilemma in playing an alternative version of hockey. A player described her reaction to a seminar that the team attended in which a representative of women's hockey emphasized the uniqueness of the game:

> When you're playing a sport you don't go out there saying "OK, I'm a woman. OK, I have to play like one." You go out there and you play aggressive, you play your game and that's that, whereas people are trying I think to give the image that it's just an all skill game and it's a woman's game kind of thing.
>
> Basically they were saying that, you know, women don't compare to men. Which is true, when you get to the older ages. I mean there's no NHL calibre women in the game right now and that's fine. Strength factor and everything, I mean people are going to know that no matter what. But you don't have to go around saying that this is a woman's sport, there's no contact, it's totally skill, and make it sound like it's a nothing sport either. I think that's part of the reason why women's hockey went nowhere for so many years.

Another woman, who had played women's hockey when body checking was allowed, also expressed cynicism about efforts to de-emphasize the physical aspects and to promote women's hockey on the basis of its difference from the men's game. She explicitly acknowledged a connection between the rules of play in women's hockey and concerns about its image:

> It doesn't make any sense to me. If they want to do it [promote women's hockey], that's not the way to do it, for my view. Hitting doesn't make you any more of a boy than non-hitting. I just don't know what they are trying to do.

In responses to presentations I have given and some of my published work, I have sometimes encountered disapproval from people who feel that in critically examining the construction of women's hockey I am criticizing the prohibition of body checking. This is not the case. Like many players, I see attractions to both versions of the sport.

At the same time, my research has provided clear and strong evidence of the enjoyment and sense of accomplishment that women hockey players (and all athletes) derive from the physicality of sport. I am suspicious of efforts to promote women's sports by distancing them from images of strength and power. While there has been much to criticize in the model of men's sport, in our efforts to devise alternatives we need to retain features that provide pleasure, satisfaction and a sense of empowerment.

References

Etue, E. and Williams, M. (1996) *On the Edge: Women Making Hockey History*, Toronto: Second Story Press.

Faulkner, R. (1976) "Making violence by doing work: selves, situations and the world of professional hockey," in D. Landers (ed.) *Social Problems in Athletics*, Urbana: University of Illinois Press. pp. 93–112.

Theberge, N. (1989) "Women's athletics and the myth of female frailty," in J. Freeman (ed.) *Women: A Feminist Perspective*, 4th edn, Mountain View, CA: Mayfield Publishing. pp. 507–22.

—— (1991) "Reflections on the body in the sociology of sport," *Quest* 43(2): 123–34.

—— (1995a) "Sport, caractère, physique et différenciation sexuelle," *Sociologie et Sociétés* 27: 105–16.

—— (1995b) "Gender, sport and the construction of community," *Sociology of Sport Journal* 12(4): 389–402.

—— (1996) "'It's part of the game': physicality and the production of gender in women's hockey," *Gender & Society* 11(1): 69–87.

15

JAY WHITE HAWK

Mesquaki athlete, AIM hellraiser, and anthropological informant

Douglas E. Foley

During my South Texas study (Foley 1989, 1990; see also Chapter 12), I became aware of the plight of minority athletes. The racial discrimination stories of Chicano players made me wonder how my old Indian teammates felt about playing on white-dominated teams. Like most whites in my hometown, I grew up thinking my Mesquaki teammates were happy playing on perennial South Cedar Conference Championship teams. It never occurred to me at the time that "our Indians" were victims of white paternalism and discrimination. But after sixteen years of listening to South Texas Chicanos, I wanted to hear what the Mesquakis had to say.

My study of race relations *The Heartland Chronicles* (Foley 1995) focuses on a small (population 1,500) Algonquian-speaking tribe called the Mesquakis who live on 6,000 acres near the small town of Tama, Iowa (population 3,000). Among many other things, the *Chronicles* portrays contradictory white images of Indian students and athletes that range from "super Indians" to "hell-raising Indians." After World War II, white sports became, for many Mesquakis, a kind of rite of passage into adult masculinity. But by the 1970s, the rise of the American Indian Movement (AIM) and an alternative Native American sports scene led to a decline of Mesquaki male participation in the white sports scene (Foley 1993).

In retrospect, my rite of passage article was a good technical account of these historical trends, but I was left wanting to tell a much more intimate story about one Mesquaki sports family. In this chapter, I would like to convey the general situation of Mesquaki athletes through the life story of one man and his family. Ethnographic narratives based on "life histories" are not unlike a good piece of fiction or journalism. They are often very engaging stories with which the reader can identify personally. The difference is, of course, that the ethnographer is recording someone's story as accurately as possible, without the imaginative embellishments of fiction and the commercial considerations of a journalist.

This particular story is about Jay White Hawk and his family, but it has a strong autobiographical flavor as well. It also begins to tell the story of how I did the fieldwork. The story of my encounter and evolving relationship with Jay helps to convey the general character of white–Indian relations in my hometown. In retrospect, my

156

"boyhood friendship" with Jay turned out to be no deeper than most white–Indian friendships in my hometown. But our relationship changed as I dug deeper into his life story and shared it with others in the *Chronicles*. Jay and his family responded in some unexpected and interesting ways.

The story of what happened after I published Jay's life story illustrates nicely the kind of relationship that anthropologists form with some of their key "informants" or "collaborators." These are technical terms used for the people who help anthropologists to write their books. People like Jay White Hawk spent many hours talking with me, teaching me to see things more like an Indian. Without such people, anthropologists, who are "outsiders," could never present in-depth, "insider" accounts of the group being studied.

Moreover, by revealing my personal relationship with Jay, I am portraying more openly how anthropologists produce the stories they tell. In the latest anthropological jargon, my story about Jay White Hawk is written in a "reflexive," autobiographical narrative style. Narrating in a more personal voice helps to convey that I am not some infallible, objective observer simply recording "the facts." By not speaking in an all-knowing "scientific voice," I am trying to convey how intimate and subjective "scientific ethnographies" often are. I want the reader to see that getting closer to the person being studied helps you better capture their life experience. A good ethnographer must not be too distant and aloof. On the other hand, one could argue that I became too emotionally involved with Jay White Hawk. As readers, you will have to decide if I have maintained the subtle balance between intimacy and detachment which is necessary to produce a good ethnographic account.

As I look back on the five years I spent researching and writing *The Heartland Chronicles*, I am convinced that good ethnography is based on intimate human encounters like the one I had with Jay White Hawk. Ruth Behar (1996) says that she only wants to do "anthropology that breaks the heart." The lesson in her work and mine is that social scientists have to learn to write from the heart, yet not sentimentalize and romanticize their subjects. If you can literally "go home" and see the good and bad of home and yourself – see your way of life unsentimentally – then you will grow as a person and as a writer.

My friend Jay White Hawk was one of two fleet-footed star Indian halfbacks on our conference championship football teams of the mid-1950s. He was an especially fearless defensive back who loved to stick his small but muscular 160 pounds into the chests of opposing ball carriers. Jay was also a very promising Golden Gloves boxer with fast hands and a devastating punch. On the academic side, he was an average to indifferent student. Hunting and fishing, and an occasional pool-hall brawl captured his imagination much more than books. Like many Mesquakis, he remembers feeling like an outsider in our high school. Nevertheless, he and a dozen other Mesquaki boys stayed in school because they loved playing sports.

In the post-World War II era, Mesquaki athletes were vital to a winning season. During my study, I collected a number of nostalgic stories told by whites about Tama High School's lost "golden era" of Indian athletes. These white stories of loyal, dedicated Indian athletes evoked some very enduring personal memories. As I listened to whites go on about the good old days, the image of Mesquaki athletes running home after football practice popped into my head. Their long hair waved in the wind as they ran, laughing and joking in Mesquaki. They cut a very romantic image for those of us who grew up on hardscrabble farms and measured our self-worth in sweat and muscle. As a young athlete, I often wondered if I was "man enough" to run three miles home after a hard practice. There I was, the objective professional anthropologist, celebrating Indians as "natural athletes" with exceptional physical prowess.

Despite my lapses into a romantic view of Indian athletes, I persisted with my basic research plan to collect the life stories of several Mesquaki athletes in each decade from the 1950s on. I hoped a 40-year spread of stories would help to explain the precipitous drop in Mesquaki sports participation. Jay was to be just one of my "sample," but as I dug deeper his story took on epic proportions. After collecting the stories of many Mesquaki athletes, Jay became my metaphor for, or symbol of, what happens to most Indian athletes.

Rather than telling Jay's story from the beginning, I would like to start with my first impressions of him 40 years later. Even though Jay, at the age of 57, was decidedly slower-a-foot, and at least 50 pounds heavier, he still seemed to be fighting the proverbial good fight. He never went on to college, and his alternate dream of being a professional boxer had faded. But he had survived various scrapes with alcoholism and the law, and has become a family man with five children. After some lean years, Jay is a reasonably successful small businessman. He and his wife run a traveling food stand that sells "Indian tacos." Although Jay's wife did not invent Indian tacos, her exceptional fry bread is a delicious alternative to the Mexican corn tortilla, especially when heaped with beef, grated cheese, lettuce, and hot sauce.

On the sports side, Jay remains an avid fan and continues to be involved with settlement children. For some years he has organized, with varying degrees of success, a boxing club for Mesquaki youth. Moreover, his own children have participated, to some extent, in the white high school sports scene. His three daughters played on the high school volleyball team, and his eldest son, Danton, even ran the quarter mile briefly in a Division I college sports program. However, Danton never completed his first year of college, nor fulfilled his promise as a runner. He apparently partied too hard and studied too little. Jay's youngest son, James, a record-breaking quarter miler in junior high school and a promising boxer, dropped out of high school and into an alcohol treatment center when he was 15 years old. Both sons recounted a string of racist events that turned them off white schools and sports and, like their father before them, they eventually ended up drinking and dropping out.

In collecting the stories of Mesquaki athletes over the past 40 years, the patterns are clear. By recent Mesquaki standards, Jay's family is a fairly successful, sports-oriented family but, like many Mesquaki families, his kids were underachievers in the white sports scene. Jay's children eventually retreated to a world of inter-tribal weekend recreational sports tournaments rather than play for white teams. Only the most exceptional Mesquaki athletes stayed in the local white high school sports scene. Of those surviving high school athletes, only four went on to play college-level football or basketball at all-Indian schools like Haskall Junior College.

As I talked with Jay about his present life, I recalled that he too had mysteriously dropped out of school after his senior year football season. At the time all this happened, I was on my way to Northern Iowa University with a scholarship to play tight end on the football team and shooting guard on the basketball team. I wondered why Jay was not going on to play football and even felt a little sorry for him, but that is as far as my feelings went. I never believed the stories circulating that the clean-cut Jay was, as local rumor had it, "just like the rest of 'em, just a drunken, shiftless Indian." But I never bothered to ask him why he dropped out and moved to Chicago. I lost touch with him for over thirty years, and during that time he apparently became the number one "hell-raising Indian" in my hometown.

My first inkling of how Jay developed his reputation as a hell-raiser came from an old newspaper article. Before doing any formal interviewing, I spent several weeks reading the newspaper archives. I wanted to fill in my knowledge of what had happend since I left town in 1957. When I got to the 1972 files, I came across a bizarre story about some Mesquakis setting up a roadblock and heisting a load of pigs. To my surprise, the story was about the wild escapades of Jay White Hawk and his friend Eddie Run Far. The paper implied that their roadblock was some kind of payback for earlier racial incidents and tensions. The summer before, a white motorcycle gang got into repeated bar-room brawls with various Mesquakis. After months of sporadic violence, one Mesquaki was charged with murdering a local white. Conversely, several Mesquakis were beaten unconscious with baseball bats in a major street brawl. In the wake of these events, the town declared martial law and closed down all the bars for a week or so. Racial tensions were high enough that both whites and Mesquaki bar-room brawlers remember driving around in cars armed with automatic weapons.

Upon hearing about the murder and baseball batting, the American Indian Movement (AIM) organizers from South Dakota created a state and local chapter. Although AIM was never strong among Mesquaki tribal elders, a number of younger Mesquakis led mass protests at the courthouse and city hall. So when Jay White Hawk, a known AIM activist, and Eddie Run Far heisted a truckload of hogs, the local papers were quick to play up the Indian uprising image. When the sheriff and his Mesquaki deputy jailed Jay and Eddie, Jay became the town's number one "troublemaker." Fifteen years after we won the conference championship, it would seem that the real enemy was no longer opposing running backs. Instead of "sticking" opposing running backs, Jay was "punching out" local white rednecks and leading protests against police brutality in his hometown.

Had I been looking for a jock turned ethnic militant, my anthropological search would have ended there. At this point, I had a nice symbol of ethnic political rebellion. Jay had told me that his experiences in Chicago were filled with heartbreak and poverty. He worked hard on the loading docks and in the boxing ring, but city life ground him down. It was difficult to feed his family and pursue his dream to box. Being unable to rise out of the ranks of club fighters, he returned to the safe environs of communal tribal life. Life on the Mesquaki settlement is "safer" than in harsh urban ghettos because many kinsmen provide material support, and the traditional clan ceremonies provide spiritual and moral support. The settlement is also a "safe haven" away from the daily slights and slurs of racist white society. But Jay experienced the "same old crap" in local white bars, so he decided to bring in AIM to help organize his people to fight back. It would seem that Jay was the classic case of migrating to the city and returning with radical political and racial ideas.

As I dug deeper into the archival records of earlier anthropologists, however, I discovered the personal side of this political story. The archives contained an interview with Jay during his senior year that took place in the now defunct Clifton Hotel. The young anthropologist conducting the interview noted that Jay was a promising young athlete who had gone awry. Local school officials were at a loss to explain his dropping out. Some resorted to the standard white explanation of Indian failure that highlights the allegedly degenerate life of the settlement. During this conversation with the anthropologist, Jay suddenly blurted out that he knew who killed his mother. Filled with anger and on the verge of tears, he vowed that someday he would avenge her death. As I read this surprising interview transcript, I wondered what had happened to Jay's mother to put him in such a state of mind.

Rather than ask him directly, I scurried back to the 1957 local newspaper archives to find the sordid story of his mother's death. In those days, the local newspaper had a way of sensationalizing the misdeeds and misadventures of Mesquakis. The editor, John Hynek, afforded his white readers a steady diet of broken, mutilated bodies on train tracks, in cars or abandoned in fields. In this case, the headlines screamed out: "Three Coats Wrapped Around Body of Indian Woman a Mystery: Govt Attorney Orders Autopsy, Questioning." The story plays up the intrigue of who left this drunken Indian woman to freeze. Why was she wrapped in three coats? Had some guilty companion come back and tried to save her?

Her death was eventually ruled accidental, but when I was finally ready to discuss what happened with Jay, he poured out his suspicions about the white taxicab driver, a white friend, and a Mesquaki rumored to be with her on the night she died. Jay still believes that the white authorities are covering up for the whites and Mesquaki who got her drunk and left her to die in the snow like a wounded animal. Living in a society where such things happen regularly to your loved ones makes you distrust all whites and your future. It makes you want to drink and fight, and Jay was no exception. He left school for Chicago in a drunken rage. School and sports paled before the death of his mother.

Before publishing an extended version of this story in *The Heartland Chronicles*, I showed it to Jay and asked for his permission. He read it slowly and quietly and said little except to nod and say, "Yes, it's OK." After the story came out, many whites apparently talked to Jay about his mother's death. Several expressed the opinion that Editor Hynek had no right to print what he did about his mother. Although Jay's story is particularly vivid and intense, it has much in common with the stories of other Mesquaki youth. At some point, a heady mix of poverty, racism, and personal setbacks closes in on most Mesquaki athletes, and too many self-destruct in the face of bitter personal tragedies. Telling Jay's story the way I did moved local readers in ways that I hoped it would. Various locals who have read my book now admit that Jay's story is fairly typical of what happens to promising young Indian students and athletes.

The story also evoked some unexpected responses from the White Hawk family. Jay's eldest son told me: "Gosh, I didn't even know about that. He's never said nothing. I guess he just toughed it out all these years." Danton seemed to have a new appreciation of his father. His eldest daughter thanked me more directly and said, "I think maybe it will help him bury the bitterness." Rachel seemed grateful that I had taken it upon myself to "help dad." I never thought of what I did as consciously trying to help her father, but when I returned to Iowa for the annual pow-wow the following year, Jay shook my hand. He smiled what seemed like a broader smile than usual and joked about people telling him that I had made him into a hero. They kidded him that Graham

Greene, the native Canadian actor who co-starred in *Dances with Wolves*, would probably play him in the movie version. He also confided that he had been on the wagon for over a year. I went back to Texas feeling that this sports story had a therapeutic dimension which I had not anticipated. I was surprised but pleased.

After a couple of months, Jay called and asked how people on the settlement could get a copy of my book. He wanted others to read it and claimed there was considerable interest. I told him to get the local bookstore to order copies, but he called me back a month later and wanted to know how to get the books directly from the publisher. He perceived the bookstore as uncooperative, so he decided to order and personally sell the book to those who wanted a copy. I gave him the publisher's number, and over the next year he called me several times to report what people were saying about the book. He also made a point of mentioning how many people were buying it. At last count, almost 200 whites and Indians have purchased copies from Jay. This figure astonishes me. I never expected more than a handful of locals to buy and read my book.

Jay was particularly proud of the sales to whites and has consistently claimed that it was beginning to "loosen some tongues." Being a traditionalist, he saw the book, and especially his story, as a powerful moral parable that would move stone-hearted whites to tell the awful truth of racist cops who had murdered and covered up their atrocities. So it would seem that my innocent story about one Mesquaki athlete had become a moral parable about American society and sports. In the great oral tradition of Mesquaki story-telling, Jay wanted my parable retold to teach whites what Mesquakis must do to survive in a their world. He wanted whites to look at themselves through Indian eyes and see what they should do to become better human beings.

In addition, my story of Jay's exploits had apparently made his "hell raising" more understandable, perhaps even heroic to some of his friends and family. On some intimate psychological level a deep, painful secret had been lanced open. Perhaps old events can now be faced and talked about in new ways. Whatever happened for Jay personally, he took my portrait of him as a generous act. He appreciated the fact that I had come home to write about my hometown from both a white and a Mesquaki perspective. He knew that I saw him as one struggling, flawed human being trapped in a racist situation. That seems to have set me up as Jay's surrogate storyteller. In effect, I became a kind of honorary Mesquaki storyteller. In return, Jay became what may be the first anthropological "informant" in history who was also a "literary agent." Ultimately, he paid his respects by selling my book. During my last visit to the settlement, I kidded Jay that I got the best deal, unless, of course, Graham Greene plays him in the movie. Being a shrewd business man and still a tough defensive back, Jay retorted: "Only if you share the royalties, too."

References

Behar, Ruth (1996) *The Vulnerable Observer: Anthropology that Breaks the Heart*. Boston: Beacon Press.

Foley, Douglas (1989) *From Peones to Politicos: Class and Ethnicity in a South Texas Town, 1900–1988*. Austin: University of Texas Press.

—— (1990) *Learning Capitalist Culture: Deep in the Heart of Tejas*. Philadelphia: University of Pennsylvania Press.

—— (1993) "Mesquaki sports as an adolescent rite of passage," *Journal of Ritual Studies* 7(1): 28–44.

—— (1995) *The Heartland Chronicles*. Philadelphia: University of Pennsylvania Press.

16

COLLEGE ATHLETES IN HIGH-PROFILE MEDIA SPORTS

The consequences of glory

Patricia A. Adler and Peter Adler

Our careers in sociology have been fascinating and full of discovery. We have been fortunate to have been able to link our personal biographies to our research endeavors, giving meaning and relevance to our work. Whenever possible, we have studied those things that have been near to us. All along, we have maintained the notion that the best way to study people is to get close to them, to live among them, and to try to share in their lives. Our approach, called ethnography or participant observation, demands that we become part of the settings we study.

The work we did with college basketball players grew out of just such an approach. We both came from strong sports backgrounds. Patti lettered in three varsity sports in high school at a time when girls could not always legitimately play sports. She even wondered what it would be like to have grown up in a society where women could play sports professionally and why established gender roles did not permit it. Peter has been a rabid sports fan for as long as he can remember, frequently wondering what it was like behind the scenes, what went on in the locker room, what the players talked about, and how they prepared for their games.

While in graduate school, we began integrating our interest and knowledge of sport with our professional lives. Our first published article was about "momentum" in sport, examining the social conditions when a team was either streaking or slumping (Adler and Adler 1978). We showed this article to "Apollo," a student in one of Peter's classes who would later become one of the "key informants" in the study of the elite college basketball team that we discuss below. He passed this "pamphlet" on to the coaching staff, who liked it and invited Peter to their offices to get acquainted. Peter's ability to apply the sociological imagination to their world made him a regular speaker at the coach's basketball camps and a sociological advisor to the team. He counseled players on academic matters, and helped orient them to their new surroundings and the options their futures held (or did not hold). Peter was eventually made an assistant coach on the team, and attended team meetings and practices, traveled with the team on the road, and worked in the backstage arena he once glimpsed from afar. Patti took the role of coach's wife with the coaches, boosters, and other wives, and, with Peter, became a close friend to many of the players.

Thus, we were able to able to experience firsthand the complex lives of college athletes. Gradually, we became more closely aligned with the team, experiencing the ups and downs of the season, as wins and losses mounted. So closely associated with the team was Peter that he began to be recognized by fans, since he frequently appeared on television to talk about the team. During one nationally telecast game, he was featured during a halftime segment as "the only sport sociologist working for a college athletic team." This created a media blitz where he was subsequently interviewed by dozens of newspaper, radio, and television reporters. Although he could not approximate the celebrity of the players themselves, these encounters with fans and the media helped us emotionally to understand the feelings of intoxication, self-importance, and ego gratification that the players felt as well. Now we were not only active members in the inner circle of the team, but we were also experiencing the emotions, adventures, and intensity that is so much a part of the big-time collegiate sport scene in the USA (Adler 1984).

The chapter you are about to read (adapted from Adler and Adler 1991) provides a glimpse of how all the attention society places on these young athletes (18–22 years old) profoundly changes their self-images and the ways in which they interact among themselves and with others. We hope that it gives you a sense of how attention, celebrity, and glory alters the personalities of those who are touched by these ephemeral forces.

In the mid-sized city where we lived, the team we studied was "the only game in town." Since there were no professional franchises or other highly successful local sports teams, the athletes with whom we associated were raised to the stature of heroes. They became celebrities so famous that they could not have privacy in public, they were sought after by reporters, and they became role models to community youth. They were thrust into the spotlight of glory, which they found overwhelming.

Athletes experienced this glory in many ways and developed a variety of means to deal with it. Yet from the team's biggest stars to the lowliest freshmen or walk-ons, it changed them in both subtle and noticeable ways. The experience of glory was so existentially gratifying that these athletes became emotionally riveted on it, turning away from other aspects of their lives and selves that did not offer such fulfillment.

Athletes developed "gloried selves" as a result of the intense interpersonal and media attention that accompanied their celebrity. It did not necessarily matter whether that celebrity was positive or negative; in society we accord status and recognition for both fame and notoriety. A "public persona" was created, usually by the media, that differed from their private ones. Eventually, they had to resolve the disparity between how they saw themselves, and the objectified selves that they saw in the media and from their adoring fans.

The allure of glory

The glory experience was exciting, reinforcing, and ultimately transformative. Two self-dimensions were either created or expanded in the athletes we studied: the reflected self, and the media self. These dimensions caused them to become larger than life, aggrandizing themselves in the light of the beacon that was being beamed on them.

The reflected self

As a result of the face-to-face interactions which team members had with people whom they encountered through their role as college athletes, their impressions of themselves became modified and changed. One of the first things they all noticed was that they were highly sought after by strangers. People treated them as objects of awe and fascination. Commonly, fans would approach players and try to talk to them. Carrying on a conversation with these people was often difficult, as Apollo expressed:

> People come walking up to you, and whether they're timid or pushy, they still want to talk. It's like, here's their hero standing face to face with them and they want to say something just so they can have a conversation with them. It's hero worshipping. But what do you actually say to your hero when you see him?

Players were thrust into a "pseudo-intimacy" with members of the public when people recognized them and treated them like friends. Marcus remarked:

> It's a real odd feeling to have these people be walking up to you like they some kind o' friend of yours. They call you by your first name, they want you to make conversation with them. Suddenly everybody in town's on a first name basis with you.

Boosters (supporters of the team who gave large sums of money) jealously fought over the privilege of spending time with players and having them in their houses. Their polite, respectful, and interested treatment often confused players, as Tyrone stated in his freshman year:

> When I'm at some millionaire booster's house I always wondering what they are thinking. Why do they want me here so much? Why are they always smiling when they see me? What's going on? Am I that appealing to them?

It soon became apparent that boosters derived social status from associating with the players, that boosters "basked in the reflected glory" they captured from them. Players realized that they had an attribute that everybody wanted (fame), and it could be transmitted. They experienced a sense of the "Midas touch."

The media self

A second dimension of the self which was created out of the glory experience was one largely influenced by media portrayals. Radio, television, and newspaper reporters covering the team often sought out athletes for "human interest" stories. Team members felt that they had to live up to these portrayals. For instance, some of the players were depicted as "good students," shy, quiet, religious, and diligent. Marcus lamented how this picture affected his interactions with people:

> Other kids our age, they go to the fair and they walk around with a beer in their hand, or a cigarette, but if me and Darian were to do that, then people would talk about that. We can't go over to the [night] clubs, or hang around, without it relaying back to Coach. We can't even do things around our teammates, because they expect us to be a certain way. The media has created this image of us as the "good boys," and now we have to live up to it.

Other players were seized upon for their charismatic qualities. They had naturally outgoing personalities, the ability to turn on a crowd, to put their fist in the air, wave towels, jump up and down exhorting fans to cheer. They capitalized on this media coverage, exaggerating their antics to gain attention and fame. Apollo was such a person, but as he progressed through college his showmanship took over and it turned into a caricature of his original self. The more the media presented this image of him, the more he portrayed this character and the more it consequently developed an outside life of its own. He discussed how his objectified media self constrained him:

> That Apollo image, it's out there. The media like to play something like that, it sells papers. But they wrote about it so often that everybody is expecting me to be that way. I never get to be a real person, to have another side. And, you know, sometimes I don't feel that up. I want to just be concentrating and minding my own business and not be into pumping everybody up on the team. It follows you everywhere you go.

Tyrone, who had a similarly high profile, described how he felt trapped by his braggart media self:

> I used to like getting in the paper. When reporters came around I would make those Mohammed Ali type outbursts – I'm gonna do this, I'm gonna do that. And they come around again, stick a microphone in your face, 'cause they figure somewhere Tyrone will have another outburst. But playing that role died out in me. But people seen me as what the paper said, and I had to play that role.

Everyone shared the media-conferred sense of self as celebrity. The more they interacted with people through their media selves, the more familiar and comfortable they felt with this image. The net effect of having these selves cast upon them was that athletes eventually came to believe in them and to integrate them into their core selves.

Self-aggrandizement

With all of the attention they received, athletes developed gloried selves: an aggrandized image of who they were, their importance to others, and their impact on society. While they wanted to accept this glory, to yield to its intoxicating powers, they felt hesitant and guilty. They wrestled with the competing pulls of their inner desires for exorbitant pleasure and pride versus the normative guidelines of society that inhibit them. Their struggle with factors inhibiting and enhancing their self-aggrandizement yields insight into how and why they ultimately developed gloried selves.

Inhibiting factors

Players knew they had to be careful about both feeling important and showing these feelings. They worked hard to suppress their feelings of self-aggrandizement. *First*, they drew on their feelings of fear and insecurity. No matter what they were hearing about themselves, there were always doubts about how they would perform. These fears haunted them, helping them inhibit, to some degree, their feelings of importance. *Second*, they tried to discount the flattery of others as exaggerated or false. When people referred to them as "NBA material," they graciously accepted these compliments, without necessarily believing them. *Third*, their feelings of superiority were constrained by Coach's actions and the norms of the subculture. Coach actively tried to keep players' self-aggrandizement in check by puncturing them whenever he thought they were getting too "puffed." As one player explained:

> Sometimes Coach, he just drill on your dream – like, "No, Tyrone, no way. You can just git that dream out of your head. Just play ball. There's one out of one thousand make it." Every time the NBA is brought up too much they give you those crazy stats. They don't really want you going "I'm an NBA player – I'm gonna make it one day."

Additionally, the players punctured their teammates by publicly ridiculing each other in their informal dorm sessions. As a result, except for the braggarts, none of the players publicly expressed how fantastic he felt and how much he loved being treated as a star. The players mostly tried to suppress these feelings of excitement, intoxication, and aggrandizement. As Darian remarked:

> You feel it coming up on you and you know you got to fight it. You can't be letting your head get all out of control.

Fourth, Coach helped to normalize their experiences and reactions by casting them within the occupational perspective. His view was that adulation came with the job, and that this job was no more special than any other. All of the attention they got from their fans was recast as something they had to service as part of their job.

Enhancing factors

Yet as tired as they were, as repetitive as this behavior became, they knew that this was unlike any other job. Its excitement, centrality, and secrecy, which did not exist in the everyday world, made this arena different. Athletes were influenced in their feelings of self-importance by the concrete results of their behavior. When the team was winning, their feelings of distinction, grandeur, talent, and invincibility soared. When they lost they felt comparatively incompetent, powerless, and small. Given that this team had an overwhelmingly successful record, they easily concluded that they were fine athletes and local heroes.

One of the results of being the objects of success, personal interest, and intense media attention was that players developed "big heads." They were adored by so many people and their exploits were cast as so consequential that they began to feel more notable. While they tried to remain modest, they all found that their celebrity caused them to lose control over their sense of self-importance. As Marcus described:

> What's happening to you is so unbelievable. Even when you were sitting at home in high school imagining what college ball would be like, you could not imagine this. All the media, all the fans, all the pressure. And all so suddenly, with no time to prepare or ease into it. It got to go to your head. You try to fight it, and you think you do, but you got to be affected by it, you got to get a big head.

Although they fought to normalize and diminish their feelings of self-aggrandizement, they were swept away by the allure of glory, to varying degrees, in spite of themselves. Their sense of glory fed their egos, exciting them beyond their ability to manage or control it. They developed deep and powerful feelings affirming how important they had become and how good it felt.

The experience of glory was thus one that brought feelings of excitement, pride, power, and self-importance. These sensations were immediate and real; they flooded all team members' lives, overwhelming them with feelings of invincibility.

The price of glory

This new, aggrandized self that was being created for and by athletes did not develop without consequences for the players. While they were being pumped up in their athletic sphere, they were being diminished in other facets of their identity. The price they paid for being elevated came in the form of self-narrowing, or self-erosion. They sacrificed the multi-dimensionality of their present selves and the potential breadth of their future selves. Various dimensions of their identities were either diminished, detached, lost, or somehow changed.

Self-immediacy

One of the consequences of athletes' gloried selves was a loss of future orientation. This reaction was caused, in large part, by the absorbing quality of the moment. The responsibilities of school, when they were lying, exhausted, in their hotel rooms hundreds of miles from campus, or on their beds after a grueling practice, seemed remote and distant. Darian described his state of preoccupation:

> I've got two finals tomorrow and one the next day. I should be up in the room studying right now. But how can I get my mind on that when I know I've got to guard Michael Jordan tomorrow night?

Their basketball affairs were so much more immediately compelling, not only in the abstract, but due to the pressure of others making specific demands on them, that it was easy for them to relegate all other areas to the realm of unimportance.

Their absorption in the present was also a result of Coach's manipulations. He knew that only a fraction of players were good enough to make it in the NBA, yet he encouraged them to be focused on their goal to make it as a professional athlete, to be the lucky ones. This was the only way he could get them psyched up for training and games. Thus they all clung to the hope that they would be the ones to make or break those statistics. For instance, Jesse, one of the less talented athletes on the team, expressed the attitude players commonly held toward their present and futures:

> You have to have two goals, a realistic and an unrealistic. Not really un-realistic, but a dream. We all have that dream. I know the odds are against it, but I feel realistically that I can make the NBA. I have to be in the gym every day, lift weights, more or less sacrifice my life to basketball.

Players, then, who had entered college hoping to use their education to prepare themselves for professional careers outside athletics got distracted from those plans and relinquished them. Ironically, they came to college thinking it would expand their future opportunities, yet they sacrificed the potential breadth of their future selves by narrowing their range of vision to encompass only that which fed their immediate hunger for glory.

Diminished awareness

Locked onto a focus on the present and smitten with a vision of themselves obtained through their celebrity status, all team members, to varying degrees, became desensitized to the concerns of their old selves. They experienced a heightened sensitivity and reflexiveness to their gloried self and a loss of awareness of the self-dimensions unrelated to glory. As their gloried selves were fed and expanded, their other selves tended to atrophy and diminish in importance.

This diminished awareness had several consequences. *First*, in becoming so absorbed in their gloried selves athletes relegated concerns outside the realm of their athletic self to secondary, tertiary, or more distant status. This included commitments to friends, relatives, and school. *Second*, their gloried selves made them seem different. Their new personae were swelled, even in interactions with friends. Players referred to this as being "puffed," and each accused the other of it:

> Sometimes I can't even talk to Lew no more. He so puffed in the head you can't get him to talk sense, he's lost touch with reality. It's like it's full of jello in there and he's talking a bunch of hot air.

Third, their gloried selves made them act differently. They distanced themselves from their old values and took potentially career-ending risks. For example, when James, who filled a substitute role, was "red-shirted" (given an extra year of eligibility) due to injury, he was willing to give up this desirable and protected status when Coach asked him to return for a single game. Despite his secondary position, he became easily convinced that the team could not function without him.

Self-detachment

The distinction between athletes' gloried and other selves became more than a separation; the distance and lack of reflexivity grew into a detachment. They experienced a dualism between these selves, as if they occasionally represented distinct individuals and not multiple facets of the same person. Apollo, for instance, struggled with these problems generated by his gloried self. Charismatic and enthusiastic whenever he was in public, he generated enormous amounts of attention and adulation by his outgoing personality. Yet although he had deliberately created the Apollo identity, it eventually began to control him. It led him to associate, at times, with people who valued him only for that self, and it surfaced in interactions with friends when he had not called it forth. As he described:

> I had a summer job working for some booster at a gas station. I figured he wanted to show off that he had Apollo pumping his gas. I'd go into my act for the customers and the other employees, how fine I was, lotta times showing up late or not at all. I figured he wouldn't fire me. But he did . . . Looking back, I can't see how I just up and blew that job. That ain't me. That was Apollo done that, not me.

Thus, associated with the developing gloried self was a loss of critical aspects of individuals' identities and self-conceptions. In order to feed the grandeur of their gloried selves, athletes ignored, modified, or abandoned parts of themselves that either hindered or failed to complement this powerfully gripping self-identity.

Conclusion

The years that the athletes spent in college were memorable. They took away from these times experiences that could fill pages of scrap books, tales to tell their grandchildren and, for some, entry into the professional athletic ranks. For most, though, the end came suddenly, as they were rudely spat back into a society that favored them no more, that refused to give them the perquisites that they had come to cherish, and that forgot them as quickly as they had risen into prominence. To be touched with fame, and to be so stricken by its influences, had profound effects on their selves. Years later, when we saw many of the old teammates at Apollo's wedding, they moaned to us that they had not listened to our warnings to stay focused on their studies and alternative careers. They would not trade those years for anything, but they would do them differently, they said. Some used their athletic ability to play basketball, while others never wanted to pick up a ball again. Unlike other college students, who graduated with their futures in front of them, many college athletes reported that their best days were behind them. Everything they had put into basketball evaporated into a mist of memories, leaving them with no tangible entry into an occupation or profession. When they tried to turn the focus and intensity that they had raised for the athletic realm to other arenas, they were unable to do so. Nothing ever again struck them as engrossing and compelling. Nothing ever again generated for them the sensation of glory to fill the void that had been created. Athletes were left with an inner conflict between their relief at escaping the hounding pressure of publicity, and their secret desire to continue receiving recognition, flattery, and treatment as important people. Ultimately, these conflicts were resolved by a society that, at once, raised them to exalted status and then plummeted them to the depths of mundane, routinized everyday life. With the exception of a few, they found this a hard lesson successfully to absorb.

References

Adler, P. A. and Adler, P. (1978) "The role of momentum in sport," *Urban Life* 7(2): 153–76.
—— (1991) *Backboards and Blackboards: College Athletes and Role Engulfment*, New York: Columbia University Press.
Adler, P. (1984) "The sociologist as celebrity: the role of the media in field research," *Qualitative Sociology* 7(4): 310–26.

17

FANS, STATUS, AND THE GIFT OF GOLF

Todd Crosset

The following piece is a modified version of a chapter from a book I wrote on professional women's golf (Crosset 1995). I started this research as a graduate student in the late 1980s hoping to discover something about changing gender relations. I took off after the tour in my pickup truck, equipped with a sleeping bag and camping gear, in pursuit of data for my doctoral thesis. Even though I expected to "rough it," studying the Ladies Professional Golf Association (LPGA) actually proved to be a boon to my quality of life. I found that friends generally took me in for the week of each tournament and I rarely ended up sleeping in the truck. At the tournament site I enjoyed the luxury of a press pass. With access to the press room I usually received three free meals a day, frequently prepared by the host country club's kitchen staff. The press pass, it turned out, was better than most academic grants which a social scientist receives.

Data were fairly easy to acquire and record. At each site I was given a spot at one of the tables reserved for the press. Press tents or rooms came complete with phones and electricity for my computer. In addition, a media staff person was usually on hand to answer technical questions and introduce me to "gatekeepers" at each tournament site. Most players, caddies, and other folks associated with the tour were willing participants. No one seemed to mind my doing a study, and I did not feel particularly conspicuous.

The ease and comfort of the setting was further complemented by the summer sun and lush bucolic surroundings. Golf courses, after all, tend to be pretty nice places. When I needed a break from research or transcription, the field site presented itself as free entertainment. I grew to enjoy the tournament's drama, silently cheering for players who had given me good interviews.

I chose qualitative methodology for a number of reasons. First and probably foremost, I was trained as a qualitative researcher in graduate school. It is the methodology I feel most comfortable with and qualified to use. I would be skeptical of any exploratory research that attempted to capture the breadth and complexity of the women's professional golf tour strictly through quantifiable data. Social scientists must stay very close to the selected area of study to limit their researcher bias, particularly when exploring aspects of society that fall outside the mainstream. The data collecting tools of qualitative research – participant observation, "hanging out," and open-ended interviews – ensure this sort of proximity.

I have selected this topic from my research because I think it demonstrates the power of sociology and qualitative methods. When I began the research I had no intention of studying fan–athlete relationships. But as I got into the "field" it became clear that fans are a significant part of the athlete's life. There is almost no physical boundary between golfers on the tour and fans, and the two groups often develop complex personal relationships. But the interaction seemed strange to me at first. Fans came to the course with gifts for the players, flowers, and often picked up the tab for players' dinners in local restaurants. In some cases, golf fans gave players the money needed to play on tour (about $30,000 for a season) with no strings attached. Only through observation, and then by returning to "classic" sociological texts, did it become clear to me that fan–athlete relationships are shaped by a system of reciprocity or gift giving.

Introduction

One aspect of the tour that is quite striking is the friendly relations that the professionals maintain with fans. On the Ladies Professional Golf Association (LPGA) tour fan–athlete interactions extend far beyond autograph seeking and signing. Fan avoidance by athletes, which characterizes most other professional sports, is rare. The tour has the feel of a country fair or a neighborhood picnic. Players seem to move in and through this civic event easily.

It is not uncommon for total strangers to approach athletes whom they admire and engage them in conversation. While there is a limit to the interactions – fans do not engage players while they are practicing putting – any player walking to or from the clubhouse is generally open to conversation. The professional might not stop to chat, as they generally have a tight schedule, but if a fan is willing to walk with the golfer, fairly complex interactions can take place.

While the average fan does not interact with the golfers, the golfer's day is filled by interactions with fans and supporters. For most veteran golfers, each city on the tour is a homecoming in a way. Relationships with fans built on these once-a-year inter-actions are re-established and affirmed. In particular, the older athletes talk positively about playing in tournaments where they expect to see loyal friends and supporters whom they first met at a pro-am function or through private housing. There are times when the area around the clubhouse feels more like a family reunion than a major sporting event. It is primarily these interactions that define the players' relationship with fans.

The structure of the tour necessitates that the athletes deal directly with the fans. Management of most tournaments is dependent on citizen volunteer labor. Some golfers choose to stay in the homes of these supporters to cut down on expenses. At the tournament site, the athletes and the fans share the same spaces. There are no barriers to protect the athletes from the fans as they walk between green and tee, and between clubhouse and course. The athletes mix with the fans to such an extent that it is often difficult to distinguish the golfers from the fans.

Some might argue that friendly player–fan relations on the LPGA tour are simply a product of the physical environment of the tournament: a golf course lends itself to such interactions. If this were the full explanation, one would expect to find similar relations between fans and athletes on the men's tour. While there is no real difference in the layout of the course for men and women, the women are said to be more approachable, pleasant, and outgoing in comparison to the men. Comments like Cathy's permeate most comparisons between the men's and women's tour:

> I've heard that we are a lot friendlier than the men on the PGA [Professional Golfers' Association] tour. Amateurs enjoy the women more because men feel they should not be bothered with the pro-am. They are not all like that, but a lot of them are.

A common explanation for the differences in the two golf tours is that "the men don't have to be nice." Corporate sponsorship and television dollars pay for the men's tour: the LPGA depends on putting on good pro-ams and drawing a decent gate, and requires the players to be friendly and accessible. Although this reasoning is highly plausible, it is an incomplete explanation of the women's relationship with their fans.

To reduce these interactions to a simple motivation to sell the tour fails to explain much of what I observed. For example, one night I tagged along with a player, Kim, to a fan's home for dinner. A working-class couple and their family received us, fed us, and gave Kim a new outfit. When the golfer examined the gift she noted, in a rather matter of fact manner, that the color and size of the outfit were all wrong. The wife then offered to return it and bring her a new one the next day. Later I quizzed Kim on her actions, which I took to be rather rude. She laughed at me, and said, "You don't get it, they want me to wear the outfit." It was at that point in my field work that I began to understand that player–fan interactions were more than just being nice to the paying public and Kim was not acting like a spoiled brat but facilitating the process of reciprocity.

Kim laughed at my question because it seemed ignorant. I had failed to grasp a fundamental rule of fan–athlete gift giving on tour – gifts are only gifts if they are received. In this case, receiving the gift meant wearing it at the tournament. Only if the couple returned the outfit could Kim fully receive the gift.

Fan–athlete relations in women's professional golf lie, at least in part, outside the system of rational exchange and within a system of reciprocity or gift giving. The social rules which govern social giving, receiving and giving back, shape fan–athlete relations.

Reciprocity

Studies of social systems based on reciprocity are most often grounded in Marcel Mauss's classic essay "The Gift" (1954). By comparing data collected by various anthropologists, Mauss constructs the bases of "archaic" economies. He contends that, in these "primitive societies," bonds develop around the moral obligations of gift giving. Gifts and obligations are the determinants of status or social place in these societies and define a hierarchy. "The spirit of gift exchange," according to Mauss, "is characteristic of societies which . . . have not yet reached the stage of pure individual contract, the money market, sale proper, fixed price and weighed and coined money" (1954). For Mauss, gift exchange societies are an intermediate system between tribal society and industrial capitalist society.

Gift giving, however, does not completely evaporate with the rise of free market economics. Sociologist have studied the norms associated with exchanges such as: Christmas gift giving (Caplow 1984); blood donations (Titmuss 1971); and material and emotional giving between spouses (Hochschild 1989). These studies support the notion of universal norms of reciprocity (Gouldner 1960).

We can make two primary distinctions between the norms of commodity exchange and gift exchange. First, in a commodity exchange system, success is measured by material gains. In systems based in reciprocity, like art, sport, or parenting, success can be measured by the increased well-being of those subject to it. Success of this sort is more likely to be publicly honored than monetarily rewarded (e.g., Halls of Fame, Mother's Day). Second, a gift establishes a feeling bond between two people, while the sale of a commodity does not necessarily leave a connection (Hyde 1983). We feel tied to those who give us gifts in a way that would seem unthinkable had we purchased the same object from them.

The gifted athlete

My analysis of the fan–athlete relationship is predicated on the idea that athletes are "gifted." That is, their ability comes not of the player's doing; the talent to play golf well was simply there at birth. Doris captured this sense of talent in our interview:

> I feel very fortunate to have been given a talent and I can wake up everyday and hit a little white ball and make a living doing it.

This is not to say that she did not have to work. Indeed, most golfers work extremely hard to hone their talent. Talent is understood as the intangible core of all accomplishments. The athletes work hard to cultivate talent but cannot claim credit for creating it. Lynn noted this distinction between talent and effort:

> We have talent. A lot of people are golfers and they know they will never be able to do it. They will never, as much as they want to, they never will. As a group, we make it look easy.

The giftedness of an athlete is only visible to most people when it has been cultivated by years of practice.

Fan appreciation

For a gift to spark a reciprocal relationship it must be received. Regardless of a player's talent, it does not become a gift to fans until it is received as such by the spectators. The gift of talent can only be received if it is presented in a fashion that is consumable. While in the field, I was repeatedly struck by the average fan's knowledge of the sport and their desire to watch it performed well. While there were a number of gawkers following the most attractive players and a few fans simply following the leaders for dramatic pleasure, the vast majority had a fairly sophisticated understanding of the game. Without it, I must admit, watching the sport would be rather boring.

The manner in which most fans watch the sport necessitates at least a professed knowledge of the sport. Fans seemed to watch in one of two ways: they either plant themselves in one spot and watch the entire field of golfers perform one particular shot or series of shots, or they follow a particular golfer for some portion of the eighteen holes of a round. In between shots, fans discuss the relative merits of a player's club selection, the lie of the ball, distance of a tee shot, a player's read of a putt, and a myriad of other details of the game.

Players reap psychic benefits from the spectators' reception of their prowess. The golfers' view of themselves and their belief in the prowess ethic is affirmed when they are admired by spectators. Applause, for example, is understood as an affirmation of the players' prowess.

This fan appreciation is often deeply felt by the players. Hattie displayed an emotional change when she talked about fan appreciation. This rather outgoing, effervescent player was visibly moved as she recalled the fan reaction to her finest round of golf and her only win:

> Chills going all the way down my body, when they clapped for me [she said in a very quiet shy voice]. When I sank that putt on eighteen they clapped for me [her voice fading to a whisper].

Val's reaction to the fans is similar:

> It is not that all the people are watching you, it is just that it is a good feeling to be playing good and having that amount of people really appreciating what you are doing out there. That is pretty neat.

Clearly, applause has a dual purpose. It is a sign of appreciation for the gift of an excellent or moving performance and, at the same time, it is a gift given in return. There is a certain thrill in knowing that your gift, your talent, was received and appreciated, as the quotes above illustrate. Spectators understand the charge which a performer receives from applause and thus heap collective praises on the performers. Cara expresses this dual function of applause in recounting a day in which she had not played particularly well:

> It is really neat coming up eighteen and having all these people around and cheering. Like yesterday I didn't play very good yesterday, and yet we got a big ovation when we walked up to the eighteenth green, which was fun. That is pretty neat that they come out and appreciate you even though you did not shoot 68 or 69 that day.

People congregating around the final hole at the end of the day applaud all the participants, honoring them and paying tribute, even when the golfer has not performed outstandingly. Applause is the way the audience repays the artist, entertainer, and sportsperson in our society.

The gift of status

Athletes give fans gifts beyond their performances. In a system of reciprocity, the gift will eventually circle back toward its source (Mauss 1954). When players are continually successful, they attract attention. As a result, they gain elevated status. Players can return the gift of status by allowing individuals to associate with them (Mills 1956).

Athletes give the gift of status in a number of ways. Giving autographs is the most obvious example. Like a photograph or a memento, the autograph is an indication of having spent time with the athlete. Golfers often throw golf balls to fans in the gallery and/or hand gloves to children as a way of showing appreciation. Often golfers share their status by giving fans their time and a bit of conversation. Molly expressed her desire to reciprocate this way:

> When someone comes up and says "I loved watching you play today," I'll go over in person and want to meet them and tell them, "Thank you for your support and we appreciate you coming out and watching us." It's just a little personal touch, but it means a lot for those people. And it comes from my heart, it's not just a lot of hot air.

The notion that her expressed thanks "comes from the heart" speaks to the level at which her motivation to respond is felt. Complete strangers who follow a player for the day are frequently thanked by the player at the end of the round. These fans are also often introduced to the player's family, friends, other loyal supporters, and caddies.

On one observation of the tour, I experienced this sort of player appreciation directly. I was following a threesome of low-ranking golfers. It was a particularly hot day. I was one of a handful of supporters and the only one not related to any of the three players. One player showed her appreciation of my support by throwing me an ice-cold bottle of water at the thirteenth tee. I was touched that this player would recognize my unbiased support for all three golfers, and take something from "inside the ropes" and share it with me.

Rubbing elbows with the stars or vacationing where the elite vacation improves the status of the non-celebrity. In interactions with friends, people name drop, relate stories about eating dinner next to a famous person, and recall dancing at hot spots in New York. We have our picture taken with movie stars and athletes and hang them over our desks. All of these practices are intended to give us credibility through association with a famous person's talent or special charisma.

Celebrities, by virtue of their being celebrities, can give status. By simply allowing individuals to associate with them, they give that person higher credibility among their peers (Mills 1956). As this amateur points out, contact with LPGA stars can enhance an amateur's respectability within golfing circles and, in turn, the fan feels a sense of loyalty to the athlete:

> Let's face it though, it is an ego trip for certain people. Let's say I played with Kathy Whitworth or Amy Alcott, the name means something to a fellow golfer. I see that Sherri Turner, who I played with last year, won the LPGA, that's great. I just love to see it. You develop sort of like a "that's my gal" attitude, "that's the one I played with, and she is doing well this year."

In some cases the golfer is the primary beneficiary of gift giving. Golf enthusiasts sometimes give golfers the gift of financial stability by footing the bill for players' expenses. This sort of gift is usually motivated by the fan's desire to give back to the game and/or to support a local golfer. In either case the benefactor is moved by a sense of obligation to reciprocate for what he or she has received.

Breakdowns in the reciprocity system

Despite the real benefits that both athletes and fans gain from their relationship, both parties have to be careful not to violate the expectations of the other. Tension arises whenever one of them does not meet the other's expectations. Confusion abounds and expectations are shattered when players and fans fail to live up to their obligations or feel that they have been let down by others. The data suggest that breakdowns in the system can occur for a variety of reasons; below I discuss three of them.

Conflict in perception of excellence

As stated earlier, at the core of the relationship between fans and athletes is the respect for and appreciation of the professionals' prowess. Failures in the relations between the two groups often center on the fans' appreciation of the game. Although golf fans are generally knowledgeable about the sport, the majority of golf fans lack an in-depth understanding of the professional game. For the most part, players view the fans' lack of knowledge about the game with mild amusement. As Ann explains:

> I found that the fans, one of the things they like the most, clap the hardest for is when you back a ball up on the green. When you put spin on it they love it, they go nuts. The ball can back up off the green and they will go nuts. They don't care. They just like to see it spin because they can't do that.
>
> They really appreciate good bunker play. Because most amateurs cannot play out of bunkers. So if you get the ball anywhere near the pin out of a bunker the people are going to clap. Even though you might not think it is a good bunker shot, they are going to clap.

At other times, players express hostility toward the fans for their lack of knowledge about the sport, and thus their inability truly to appreciate the golfers' talents. The guarded posture toward ignorant fans can at times become hostile. The high-spirited June captures this hostility toward the fan who lacks golfing knowledge when she discussed her reaction to fans questioning a poor performance:

> It just drives me crazy when a fans says (deepens voice) "What happened out there?"
>
> "Oh, shut up buddy, never in your whole life have you done anything like this." They think it is so easy, they have no idea. But what do you say to that guy? "Sorry buddy." I just make a joke of it or I don't say anything. I don't say anything anymore. I mean I don't give a shit what they say.

I mean in one respect they are your fans, and they are pulling for ya, but I am not playing to please this asshole in this town and that asshole in that town. You would go crazy.

Athletes feel a deeper sense of gratitude for support when the fan has some understanding of the difficulty of the game. Questions which demonstrate a fan's lack of understanding can cause players to feel hostility toward the fan because they realize, on some level, that their "giftedness" has not been fully appreciated.

False intimacy

Ann expresses similar hostility toward fans in a discussion of autographs. The asking and receiving of autographs is a form of reciprocity. By asking for an autograph, the seeker pays tribute to the athlete. The athlete repays the fan with an autograph, material evidence that the fan was in the presence of the athlete – a gift of status:

> I was never that much of one for collecting autographs, I never got into that kind of stuff. So it is hard for me to understand why people want my autograph.
> [But] part of autograph hunting is just that you are that close to that person. That has got to be part of it. It is a desire to get a part of that person.
> Now if someone writes me and says I am an autograph collector and here is a special card, I know they are sincere. A lot of times when kids come up, with these little pieces of paper all mashed up. "Would you give me your autograph" or, "Would you sign my shirt." Something like this, that is going to get thrown away in two weeks or something.

Ann wants her autograph to be valued because it is a symbol of intimacy. Players attempt to avoid inappropriate demands on their sense of self, or false intimacy. Fans who seek interaction with players for the sake of it take without giving, forcing a personal exchange without a corresponding commitment to the golfer. Golfers seem far more responsive to fans who have followed them for nine holes, than they are to the autograph seekers who hang out by the eighteenth green and ask every player for an autograph.

Confusion of market and gift economies

The commodification of sport has as impact on behavior and relationships. Many athletes and fans view their relationship as a business contract. Fans complain that they pay good money for tickets and therefore expect to be entertained. Even the last vestiges of reciprocity between fans and athletes – the autograph and the public appearance at children's camps – have been commodified. But the commodification of sport is never complete. At the very core of sports rests a system based on reciprocity. Thus gift and market economies exist simultaneously.

However, misunderstandings can result from a confusion over the incongruous demands of commodity exchange and gift exchange. In the following case, Dorothy is sponsored by friends. Friendship is a relationship governed by the rules of reciprocity. In this case, the business of golf confuses their friendship:

I had some people at my club at home sponsor me for two years, I had a contract for two years and my third year was negotiable. At the beginning of the second year they said, "Well, we'll sponsor you for another year."

It was awful. I was struggling, I wasn't making any money and every time I'd go home I'd hear "When are you going to start making some money for us?"

I had played in about eight tournaments and had made about $300 and they said that the money's all run out so that's it . . . It worked out well actually, because after I lost my sponsors I started playing a little better, so I made some money last year.

The emotional ties to the sponsors combined with the pressure to make money for them was stressful. Despite not having the security of a sponsor, Dorothy feels relieved of the burden of playing for others whom she might disappoint. Fending for herself, she is able to play better.

Conclusion

This research on the LPGA suggests that the relationship between athletes and fans is complex. While the structure of the tour may highlight reciprocity between fans and athletes, I suspect that fan–athlete relations in other sports are framed by this complex web of gifts and obligations within a capitalist entertainment system. Clearly fan–athlete relations have been changed by broader economic forces – athletes sell autographs and fans pay thousands of dollars to play in fantasy camps. But alongside (or is it underneath?) the cool reality of our capitalist sports economy, there is a constant give and take between fan and athlete, of which neither party is entirely conscious. The obligations, hostility, and expectations that define much of player–fan relations are shaped by our tacit understandings of the rules of reciprocity.

References

Caplow, T. (1984) "Rule enforcement without visible means: Christmas gift giving in Middletown," *American Journal of Sociology* 89(6):1306–23.

Crosset, T. (1995) *Outsiders in the Clubhouse: The Social World of Women's Professional Golf*, Albany, NY: SUNY Press.

Hochschild, A. (1989) "The economy of gratitude," in D. D. Franks and E. D. McCarthy (eds) *The Sociology of Emotions: Original Essays and Research Papers*, Greenwich, CT: JAI Press.

Gouldner, A. W. (1960) "The norms of reciprocity: a preliminary statement," *American Sociological Review*, 25(2): 161–78.

Hyde, L. (1983) *The Gift: Imagination and the Erotic Life Property*, New York: Random House.

Mauss, M. (1954) *The Gift: Forms and Reason for Exchange in Archaic Societies*, New York: W. W. Norton.

Mills, C. W. (1956) *The Power Elite*, Oxford: Oxford University Press.

Titmuss, R. M. (1971) *The Gift Relationship: From Human Blood to Social Policy*, New York: Pantheon.

18

WIVES INCORPORATED

Marital relationships in professional ice hockey

Wendy Thompson

It was my father who first pointed out that my life as the wife of a professional ice hockey player would be lonely. Most people believe that our lives are easy and exciting, and that the player's high income makes up for any inconveniences. Our lives have been interesting, challenging, sometimes exciting, and at times (one or two nights each year) glamorous. But it has not been easy.

The most difficult aspects of professional team sports for athletes and their families result from the fact that players rarely have a choice about where they will play. The draft system, and player trades determine which teams an athlete must play for, and even free agents are restricted to the teams prepared to pick up their contracts. If a player wishes to continue to work as a professional athlete, he must move to the city where he is selected or traded. These circumstances, and the particular character-istics of work as a professional athlete, become all-consuming aspects of his life. As a consequence, they become an even more significant aspect of the lives of his wife and children.

Two of my professors saw the potential for research in this particular element of professional sport, and I decided to use my position as the wife of a professional ice hockey player to carry out research on players' wives for my Master's thesis. Although I have kept a journal for the whole of my husband's career on three different National Hockey League teams, I spent one year conducting detailed field research and interviews with the wives of players on one particular team. Although each team has its own particular "group culture" – which also affects players' families – there are striking similarities in the subculture of professional sports. However, I have tried to be careful not to make generalizations beyond the particular team that I studied.

Because I was a member of the group, it was easy for me to contact the players and their families. I was able to bypass the barriers that protect the privacy of these highly public figures. However, because of some of the material that follows (and the potential that it may affect my husband's career) and in order to continue to protect the privacy of my informants, I am writing under a pseudonym.

There were some real problems associated with being a participant observer. I sometimes felt that I was exploiting my friendships. I also felt that, at times, I was interfering with my husband's work. When the team was not winning, the blame was sometimes attributed to the players' personal lives. I was concerned that the managerial and coaching staff would find out about my research, assume that I was causing problems with players' families, and victimize my husband (by trading him, or reducing his playing time) in retaliation. I also experienced some of the limiting factors of the lifestyle discussed in this chapter while I was actually doing the study. However, the feedback from the players' wives with whom I talked was generally positive. They enjoyed sharing their experiences, and appreciated learning that they were not alone in going through the difficulties associated with being "incorporated wives."

So much attention is paid to male professional athletes in team sports that there is a tendency to forget that many are married and have children. Players' wives show up at the occasional charity event or banquet, or in the occasional lifestyle feature in the media. If they are married to baseball players they will be identified in the stands during the World Series. But, for the most part, they are anonymous and invisible. Yet they play an extremely significant role in the players' lives, often taking on more responsibilities than is usual in similar young and high income families.

I interviewed ten women for this study. Eight were married to, and two were living in a common-law relationship with, players on one National Hockey League (NHL) team. As of this time there have been no female players in the NHL (Manon Rhéaume was drafted, but only played in exhibition games). Therefore, for convenience, and to protect the anonymity of the two "partners," I will refer to all of the women as "wives."

Despite the "puck bunny" or "groupie" image of women associated with male professional athletes – an image that does not suggest any level of higher education – nine of the wives had been to university. Five of these had completed undergraduate degrees, and one had a Master's degree. Although none was working full time at the time of the study, their occupations had included: financial advisor, licensed stockbroker, occupational therapist, teacher, corporate secretary, and actor. At the time of the study, most were homemakers with children.

Because of the relatively short season, and the fact that they play only one game per week, players in the National Football League and the Canadian Football League have somewhat different experiences from players in the other three major professional sport leagues in North America – Major League Baseball, the National Basketball Association (NBA), and the NHL. Basketball and ice hockey seasons last up to ten months if teams are involved in play-offs. Teams play over eighty regular season games in addition to exhibition games and play-off games. Teams are scheduled to play on average four games per week during the season, and away games are often grouped to reduce team travel costs. This leads to frequent absences from home, absences that may last up to one week. One of the major differences betwen the NBA and the NHL is in the average player salary, much higher for basketball than ice hockey, leading to consequent differences in lifestyle between players in the two leagues.

For the wives and families of hockey players, life is often unusual and uncertain, with very little opportunity to create a style that is completely their own. Because of frequent travel, wives are regularly left alone in cities with which they may not be familiar. Their husbands are often away for important events such as children's birthdays, or even the birth of a child. Because of player trades the families must move to new cities in order to be with the player, and wives have little opportunity to build friendships while their husbands have a readymade network of "friends" on the new teams. The women I talked to also made it clear that they felt the management of their husbands' teams also had an influence on the way they lived their lives and the choices they were able to make.

There are similarities with other occupations. For example, Harrison and Laliberté's (1994) study of families in the Canadian armed forces indicates that they live similar lives to families of professional athletes. Other professionals in, for example, medicine or music, have careers which may affect the lives of their spouses and children. The major differences lie partly in income level, but primarily in the circumstances surrounding player trades. A trade is a matter of urgency, and a player must often make the move to a new team within hours, leaving little time for preparation and even less for making choices. Also, women married to professional athletes must cope with their husbands' celebrity. Sometimes the women are incorporated into this celebrity, but most players' wives feel invisible when they are in public with their husbands since all of the attention is directed to him.

On the surface, wives of professional athletes appear to live quite glamorous and traditional lives, but this study of hockey wives suggests that these lives are actually less glamorous and less traditional than might be expected. The women were almost completely incorporated into their husbands' careers. The following examines the circumstances of this incorporation focusing on player mobility and trades, management influences, and the effect of player travel on his home life. I also look at the way in which the husbands' celebrity affects their wives' attempts to maintain their own identity, and the way in which it affects their relationships.

Incorporation into husbands' careers

While I was doing the interviews it began to be apparent that I and the wives I was interviewing were incorporated into our husbands' careers in a number of ways. For example, the women were expected to engage in charity work on behalf of the team, and to follow team rules against traveling with their husbands, or meeting their husbands in cities where the team was playing. The women whose husbands had been traded during the season at some point in their career noted that the majority of work involved in moving fell to them. Some of the women had even interfered with the natural birth of their children, having the baby induced in order to accommodate their husband's hockey schedule and allow him to be present.

Trades

Player trades were the overriding topic during the interviews. They were continually the subject of rumor and speculation, both in the media and among players and their families. Trades are always possible, and may occur with little or no advance notice during the season. Because of this, wives are responsible for all of the jobs involved in moving. When discussing a trade the women often spoke in the first person plural ("When we were traded to . . ."), or even the first person singular ("When I was traded to . . ."), suggesting how completely they have been incorporated into their husbands' careers. The following is typical:

> It's harder on the wife every time you get traded because the day he's traded he's on the plane; everyone told me that, and I didn't believe it. He's with his new team and he's getting to know them, and he's done and he loves it. It's really . . . incredible how quickly they bond, basically. Now you're back there and you're closing up the house and you're trying to sell it . . . you can't [move to the new city] yet because there's no house, but he's with his friends . . . And you have no friends in [old place] because you're not on the team any more, and you have no friends in the new place 'cause you're not there yet.

The social support for the husband, the isolation for the wife, and the responsibilities involved in moving, are all typical of trades, and may even occur at the most inopportune times:

> We got traded the day [child] was born so not only was it a shock to me having a new child in my life, it was also a shock to know that I was moving to another city. I had the baby, and they phoned while he was at the hospital with me and said he got traded. He drove me home from the hospital and then he left to come here. He delayed coming for two days.

Another woman noted that, because her husband was always traded late in the season, she waited until the season ended before moving:

> So [my husband] was always involved with the physical move each time, but the preparation prior to the move would have fallen on me. You put the house up for sale, arrange the move, close the bank accounts . . . you know, making all the physical changes.

These comments reveal the importance of the league schedule. Games must, if at all possible, be played at the stated date and time. Fans, the media, gamblers, sponsors and advertisers all depend on the schedule. The team management – once a trade is made – wants to field a full team, and take advantage of any benefits that may accrue from the new players, as soon as possible. Wives provide the domestic and reproductive labor that allows players to have a home and family – a very traditional female role. But they are further incorporated into their husbands' careers by providing the work that allows him to move quickly to the next team.

Management influences

All but two of the women interviewed stated that they were directly influenced by their husbands' employer in some way. Some noted that wives were expected to bond as a team, "just like the players." Others suggested they would feel uncomfortable traveling to see their husbands play in another city because of management rules implicitly prohibiting this. Most noted the demands on their time to be involved in charity functions:

> It's part of the deal and I think it affects . . . if you say no, or cause turmoil or whatever, it affects your husband. I think management knows everything that goes on in that "wives' room" [a lounge provided for players' wives, partners, and children, for use during a home game], who complains and who doesn't.

This woman believed that doing charity work and "behaving" while in the presence of team members and management was simply part of the job. While she could not articulate how it would affect her husband's career, she sincerely believed that it could have a negative impact. Another stated:

> I feel obliged to do it . . . yeah, I do. I know what it's like here and I know it's in your best interest to be nice about it and do what you can. I''m not saying he's going to get traded over it if you don't, but I think . . . I think a team likes . . . I think management likes to see you're doing what you can for the team. And I guess that kind of comes with it.

Thus wives are seduced by the "for the good of the team" philosophy, but also by the idea that their husbands' careers could be influenced by their contributions:

> Yeah, you have to do it. I think it's part of his job that you do that. You know, I don't think you have to work overly hard, but you have to be there.

The women described their participation as if they were also contracted by the team. With regard to the "unwritten" rule that women were not to travel to other cities to watch their husbands play, the following was typical:

> There's a real feeling that if you did go you would have to try to be invisible. You wouldn't want to be seen at the hotel they were at . . . You know hockey has some very strong attitudes, and I guess attitudes would be the word as far as management and coaching generally is concerned. I wouldn't want to affect my husband in a negative way by trying to accompany him or watch him play in another city because I know, and I have seen the effect that can have on a player in the eyes of management if they see a wife or girlfriend.

Two of the women I interviewed had experienced negative reactions from management after traveling to watch their husbands play:

> And then they got into some pretty big trouble about it because they lost both games, and management was pretty sour that it was the first round of the play-offs, and they just kind of said it's just not what you do. I'll never go again, unless it's play-offs and management pays our way. You know how they do that sometimes. Then I'll go, but I'll never do that again.

The other stated:

> We went, but we got in trouble. [Husband] is different, I think, than a lot of players. He doesn't mind if I come along and if somebody has something to say about it, too bad. And that is probably the reason we got in trouble.

She went on to say, though, that if her husband had been a "rookie" she would have been more attentive to the "rules," suggesting that management has more influence over younger players due to high job insecurity.

Spouses of many types of professionals are incorporated into their partners' careers, but there are few cases where the incorporation is as complete as in professional sport. The lives of players' wives are controlled in many ways by their husbands' employer and the nature of his work. The women have difficulty maintaining careers of their own because of the ever-present potential of a trade. One woman commented:

> It's hard you know. I just don't think you can really have a career. I juggle everything myself. You can't really put roots down.

Thus, players' wives often identify completely with their husbands' careers, and can become consumed by it because of the responsibilities they assume.

Player travel

Professional hockey players must travel frequently to different cities across North America. One possible consequence of the tyranny of the league schedule is missing the birth of a child. Several of the interviewees had accommodated the schedule by having their babies induced at a convenient time in the season, so that their husbands could be present at the birth. Taking time off work was not even a consideration for the players. Job insecurity is high, and a player's vacation time is in the summer. One interviewee laughed sarcastically and said, "You wouldn't want to take them away from a road trip." She was well aware that many people not involved in hockey would consider it ludicrous to induce labor to accommodate the father's work schedule.

All of the women in the study who had children, or were pregnant, had considered the procedure. But some of the women who had been induced commented that they would never do it again, preferring to go through the birthing process alone next time:

> The first one I induced so he could be there, and that was hell. Like it was eight hours of really hard labor because I was induced so he could be there, which I'd never do again.

The usual reason for inducing labor is because the husband has a long road trip scheduled at the approximate delivery date. But the schedule still has to be met:

> I mean, you get induced to have a baby so he's there to watch, and then he's on a flight as soon as the baby is born 'cause he's gotta get outta here.

Some who have been induced have decided that the risks outweigh the benefits and would not do it again. Others regard the procedure with little or no trepidation:

> I was induced . . . He wanted to be there. So I looked at the schedule and that was it . . . I mean, I knew he was home.

Another woman organized all her doctor's appointments around her husband's schedule, so that he could be there:

> I usually take my little [team] schedule to my obstetrician and say, OK, let's see, when do I want my appointments for this and that.

Job insecurity is high, and many wives do not want to interrupt their husband's career when it is possible to continue his routine and be present for the birth of a child as well. Even some of those who are uncertain about it will undergo the procedure in order to accommodate their husband's career.

At one time women were discouraged from participating in sport and physical activity because of the belief that they would damage their reproductive systems (Lenskyj 1986). Now women may induce childbirth, a practice that could possibly affect their reproductive systems, so that men can stay involved in sport. This is yet another factor that contributes to the incorporation of wives into their husbands' careers. There is very little in the lifestyle of wives of professional hockey players that these women can identify as their own. At times, even their identity is taken from them.

Since this study was completed I have had a child, and had my labor induced. There were other factors that contributed to the procedure in my case, but I must admit that I did not want to be alone for the birth of my child. I was elated when the doctor said that she was considering inducing the birth. My husband was about to leave on a five-day road trip, and I wanted to make sure that he was there to support me. I was in a new city, the doctor was new, and I was not even sure that I could find my way to the hospital when not in labor, let alone in an emergency. Fortunately, the birth went well. My husband did leave for a five-day road trip the day after he brought the baby and me home from the hospital. He did not even miss a practice.

Celebrity

A characteristic that is particular to professional athletes (and, of course, many in entertainment and politics) is the public nature of their profession and the celebrity attached to those in professional sport. Spouses often become an adjunct to this celebrity. The women in this study often found it difficult to maintain relationships, not just because they had to move often, but also because people perceived them differently. The women also suggested that their husband's celebrity amplified their difficulty in establishing their own identity.

Maintaining an identity

The women in this study recognized that it is possible to lose their own identities when so much of their life is consumed by hockey. It was important for them to be seen as individuals, but for many this was difficult to accomplish. Most had met the men who were to become their husbands when they were quite young, usually in high school. Some felt that they never really had an identity of their own:

I've lost that along the way. I've lost my own identity, but then again at nineteen what kind of identity do you have anyway? You know, I've yet to have my own identity . . . I'd have to accomplish something pretty big to go beyond a hockey wife.

Some women have learned to cope with the public image associated with their position. When people tell her that she is lucky to be married to a professional hockey player, one woman responds, "It's him that's lucky!" This woman tries not to let her husband's celebrity define her identity. Another comments:

I don't mind, because the people who identify me as his wife are not my friends; they're just people on the street and whatever, and that's fine.

The interviewees tried to maintain their own identity by refusing to define who they are simply by their husband's career. They know that they contribute greatly to that career, but none of the women felt satisfied simply to be an adjunct to their husband or his career. The majority did not find the lifestyle enjoyable, but knew that it would not last forever and were content to define their husband's career in hockey as a stage in their lives – one that would probably be over by the time they were thirty.

It is apparent that if a woman relies heavily on her husband's career for entertainment, or to replace her own desires, she may become discontented with her lifestyle because, as one stated, "the novelty wears off and then the husband is just gone." Another noted:

You know these girls who think it's so "glamorama" to be married to these guys . . . I want to say, come spend a week with me and I'll show you what it's really like. This is the reality of it, not going to a hockey game all dressed up. You know that's not reality; this is the reality.

Thus, the glamorous image of being married to a celebrity is not reflected in reality:

I live this life as much as he does. I think he lives the better part of it, though. They get to travel. They get to go out to nice places. They get the glory of it, you know, all the benefits.

Despite their incorporation and immersion into their husbands' careers, the women who have maintained their identity were not satisfied to be defined by his career or celebrity.

Because of my research in this area, and my critical approach to the realities of being a player's wife, I have often been asked (in seminars and classes I have spoken to) why I choose to live a lifestyle that appears to go beyond even the traditional role of wife. I have the potential to have a career, but it would certainly not be as lucrative as my husband's. I take comfort in my accomplishments, however little monetary return they provide. I also view hockey as a stage in our lives, and look forward to it ending. It is possible that I will then become the primary income earner.

My husband does enjoy playing hockey, but he feels limited by the inability to choose where he will play, and he does not like to move frequently. His career imposes limits on us both, and together we have decided that financially it makes sense for him to play hockey for as long as is possible (and while he is healthy). We both understand that hockey is not a secure job, and that is why I continue to build my resumé and we both continue with our education.

Relationships

Relationships with others was an important means by which these women attempted to maintain their own identities, but they found it difficult to establish and maintain them because of their husband's celebrity. The following is a typical comment:

> I meet a new friend, I have to train them all over again. It's like they're so excited that [husband] plays in the NHL, they act stupid. They ask stupid questions. They're not themselves and it takes them a long time to be normal around him. It seems for them, or even our children's teachers in school, they have a hard time talking to me because they're, you know . . . it takes a while and then they realize you're normal and he's normal.

This woman is not necessarily wary about relationships, but it does take time to get past the celebrity. Other women were more concerned and guarded about the relationships outside hockey:

> I think when you initially make friends outside the game there's a period where you're cautious as people approach you, or you approach people with respect to your business, because it's a public business and a public profession and you are more guarded when you first make friendships outside of the sport, until you get to know people better.

All of the women noted that their friends involved with hockey understood their lives better, but most wanted friendships outside the sport as well. They wanted to have friends who were not simply friends because their husbands did the same job, and they wanted friends who did not just want to be their friends because of the celebrity. They were well aware that celebrity easily attracts pseudo-friends and hangers-on who may just want to use them for contacts, to obtain tickets, or to suggest ways to invest or spend their discretionary income.

Conclusion

The women in this study appear to lead very traditional lifestyles in which they are responsible for domestic work, childbearing and rearing, and emotionally supporting their husbands. This fits in very well with the tradition-bound and authoritarian world of professional sport, where players are treated like children, and traditional gender relations are assumed. Wives who attempted to maintain a more modern and equal relationship with their husbands, who continued their own careers, or felt that it was their right to visit their husband during his free time away from home, would be a real problem in this world. Thus, the women find that they become incorporated into the world of their husband's career, and find it a struggle to maintain their identities. They all look forward to the day when they are past the "stage" of professional hockey and can begin to lead more normal lives.

References

Harrison, D. and Laliberté, L. (1994) *No Life Like It: Military Wives in Canada*, Toronto: James Lorimar.

Lenskyj, H. (1986) *Out of Bounds: Women, Sport and Sexuality*, Toronto: Women's Press.

LEARNING EXERCISES AND RESOURCES

Projects and discussion topics

1   Foley's opening chapter in Part 3 highlights the community-wide importance of social rituals associated with high school sports. What rituals were associated with the major sport(s) at your high school? Who was involved, and how were they involved? Were there micro-politics involved in such things as community support, team selection, access to funds and facilities (for practices and games)? Were these rituals involved in the reproduction of class, race, and gender relations in the school and community at large? How? Compare the characteristics of your school with those of others in the class or in your discussion group, and with Foley's description of North Town High School.

2   Interview a participant in a non-mainstream, alternative (resistant) sport or physical activity (e.g., snowboarding, skateboarding, ultimate frisbee, etc.). Develop a list of similarities and differences between the values, norms, beliefs, meanings, and social relations in the interviewee's sport and a more mainstream sport. Are there any pressures to incorporate the interviewee's sport into the mainstream, and how are they evident? When do athletes in these alternative sports allow themselves to be incorporated into mainstream versions of their sports? Develop some hypotheses about the conditions under which incorporation is most likely to occur.

3   Women's physicality is being expressed through increased participation in a wide range of contact and high-risk sports and physical activities. These women are stepping outside the traditional boundaries, stereotypes, and constraints associated with dominant forms of femininity in society. Nancy Theberge (Chapter 14) provides a fascinating account of how women ice hockey players negotiate their physicality. Interview a female participant in a contact or high-risk sport to determine how she feels about her participation in such an activity. Ask her to describe other people's reactions to her participation. Also ask her what she thinks about rule modifications for women in the sports that she plays. Use the information from your interview and those done by your fellow students to outline how women negotiate physicality in contact and high-risk sports.

4   It is often argued that sport overcomes racial and social barriers between people. However, Douglas E. Foley (Chapter 15) points out that his relationship with his high school football teammate, Jay White Hawk, went no deeper than most white–Indian friendships in most towns. Review the race relations on teams in which you,

and others in the class or your discussion group, have participated. How integrated or segregated were your teams? Did any integration spread beyond the boundaries of sport participation to other aspects of social life? What factors influenced the social relationships that developed between players on your teams?

5   The coach of a major university sport team hires you to design a programme to deal with some of the problems being experienced by the athletes. Specifically, how is it possible to be a celebrity athlete and a regular college student, attending classes and carrying out course assignments, at the same time? Is it possible to regulate and modify some of the negative consequences of celebrity? How might the players be encouraged to live up to their dreams of being professional athletes while at the same time keeping a keen sense of the reality that very few will make it and that they have to be prepared for the rest of their lives? Develop a set of specific recommendations to be implemented for the team.

6   Many individuals have had encounters with well-known athletes – requesting their autographs, meeting them at camps, clinics, athletic banquets, or in other settings. In the class or in your discussion group, compare the similarities and differences you have experienced in your encounters. Do experiences vary with or depend on the sport, the fame of the athlete, the stage of his or her career, or other factors? Putting yourself in the place of the athlete, and using Crosset's information in Chapter 17 about LPGA golfers, how might you respond to fans?

7   Design a research study to examine the lives of: (a) the wives of athletes in a men's professional team sport other than ice hockey; or (b) the husbands of a group of women professional athletes involved in, for example, tennis, golf, basketball, or figure skating. How would you do the study? Given what you have learned from Wendy Thompson in Chapter 18, develop at least three hypotheses that identify the results you expect in your study.

Films and videos

Film and video annotations are provided by Steve Mosher, Department of Exercise and Sport Science, Ithaca College, Ithaca, NY 14850, USA.

Feature-length films

● *The Loneliness of the Long Distance Runner* (1962), 104 mins, Warner Home Video
The first, and perhaps the best, "angry young man" sport film, *The Loneliness of the Long-Distance Runner* tells the story of Colin Smith (Tom Courtenay), a high-school dropout overwhelmed by his poverty and hopelessness. Smith's first attempt at petty theft lands him in reform school. While serving his time he displays a natural talent for cross-country running and is soon being groomed by the headmaster (Michael Redgrave) for a big race between rival schools and potential Olympic fame. Seemingly holding all the cards, the headmaster tries to inculcate the indifferent athlete with the ideology of "sport building character," "hard work getting you ahead," and "there can be no greater honor than representing one's country at the Olympic Games." Dripping with teenage angst, this film convincingly works its way to a showdown between the headmaster and the rebel.

Smith's Pyrrhic victory offers a great opportunity for discussions about the costs and benefits of the individual taking on the system, highlights the issue of resistance and rebellion, and raises questions about social control and whether we participate for ourselves or others. Vastly superior to the similar *All the Right Moves* (1983). Heavy British working-class accents may require attentive listening by those unfamiliar with them.

- *Pumping Iron II: The Women* (1985), 107 mins, Vestron Video
  The sequel to his better known *Pumping Iron* (1976, which introduced Arnold Schwarzenegger to North American audiences), George Butler's *Pumping Iron II* is a documentary that also explores the culture of bodybuilding. This time, Butler focuses his camera on a women's competition at Caesar's Palace in Las Vegas. In addition to studying the grueling training rituals and weird idiosyncrasies of the competitors' quest for body perfection, this documentary also explores issues of drug use and the hyper-voyeuristic nature of women's bodybuilding. It may be the best video case study of positive deviance in sport. The film shows real people struggling to define a new sport, and negotiations over what is "feminine" and how much muscle is appropriate for women to have.

Educational program

- *The Ultimate Athlete: Pushing the Limit* (1996), 100 mins, Discovery Channel Home Video
  Produced and directed by Scott Hicks, director of the acclaimed *Shine* (1995), *The Ultimate Athlete* tours the world to offer a variety of settings where athletes are pushing the limits of performance. With impressive footage from the Santa Monica Track Club, gymnastic training centers in China, the running grasslands of Kenya, and the ritzy tennis academies of Florida, this film constantly weighs the question of what price a child (or in some cases the parents) is willing to pay for athletic glory. One of the few documentaries to juxtapose the preachings of such coaching gurus as Tom Tellez and Nick Bolletieri with the views of sport science scholars such as Susan Brownell, Jay Coakley and John Hoberman, *The Ultimate Athlete* allows viewers to reach their own conclusions.

Additional books and articles

- Birrell, Susan and Richter, Diana M. (1994) "Is a diamond forever?: feminist transformation of sport," in Susan Birrell and Cheryl L. Cole (eds) *Women, Sport, and Culture*, Champaign, IL: Human Kinetics. pp. 221–44.

The title of Birrell and Richter's study is a clever pun, questioning a traditional and stereotypical view of a desire by women to become engaged and get married, and linking that view with the baseball/softball diamond. The pun goes further because this is a study of women who are questioning the traditional practices of baseball. Susan Birrell and Diana Richter spent four years studying a women's softball league in Iowa. They found that the women wanted to develop their skills, play hard, and challenge their opponents. But they were dissatisfied with aspects of the game that linked it to the dominant (masculine) sport culture in the USA. For example, they did not like the practices of putting down opponents and overemphasizing winning. They did not like injury-producing practices or social exclusion and elitism based on skill. Over the period of the study, the players began to transform the game into one that felt more comfortable to them. They emphasized a process (rather than outcome) oriented approach to the game, along with the collective, supportive, and inclusive aspects of softball as a team sport. Finally, they infused their play with an ethic of care (p. 408). This process of resistance to the dominant sport culture is somewhat different from the processes described by Becky Beal in her study of skateboarding (Chapter 13). While new sports are the most usual way of expressing resistance, Birrell and Richter show that transforming the norms and values of an established game is also a form of resistance.

- Freedman, Jim (1988) *Drawing Heat*, Windsor, ON: Black Moss Press.

Although Jim Freedman is an anthropologist, this study of one of the smaller professional wrestling circuits is much more descriptive than interpretive. However, the book follows an important tradition in sociology by taking us behind the scenes into a relatively closed world and describing the characters and experiences of those who are living the life. Studies of pool hustlers (Ned Polsky 1969, *Hustlers, Beats and Others*, New York: Anchor) and the race track (Marvin Scott 1968, *The Racing Game*, Chicago: Aldine) are among the best known in this tradition, but there are also other studies of wrestling from before the time when everyone knew that the matches were fixed. It is always important to be reminded that the professional wrestling caricatures we see at the arenas and on television are actually real people working hard at their jobs, and Freedman's sensitive study does just that.

- Klein, Alan M. (1993) *Little Big Men: Bodybuilding Subculture and Gender Construction*, Albany, NY: State University of New York Press.

Alan Klein, who wrote Chapter 9 on Dominican baseball in Part 2, also spent seven years studying the strange world of competitive bodybuilding, mostly at its center in Southern California. Like Freedman (above) and others, Klein provides an insightful behind-the-scenes look into one of the relatively closed worlds in sport. But his study goes further to provide a vivid reminder of the contradictions between public image and private reality that is characteristic in so many of these worlds. Like the men described by Messner (1992; see Additional Books and Articles, Part 2, p. 125), male bodybuilders, who apparently represent the ideal of a type of dominant masculinity, seem to be very insecure about their masculinity. Some of the other contradictions in this world reveal why they are insecure. The public image of rugged individualism is denied by the private reality of a feudal structure in competitive bodybuilding where the competitors are the serfs in the kingdom of the Weiders (the family that has controlled much of bodybuilding around the world). The public image of health and fitness is denied by the reality of drug abuse and extraordinary dietary practices such as bingeing, starving, and dehydration to the point of near death. Finally, the public image of heterosexual masculinity is denied by the reality of engaging in homosexual hustling in order to obtain drugs and pay for training costs. Resolving such contradictions is the key to living the life in such subcultures.

- Klein, Alan M. (1997) *Baseball on the Border: A Tale of Two Laredos*, Princeton, NJ: Princeton University Press.

Alan Klein returned to baseball and Hispanic culture in his most recent study. He takes us to the Southern border of the USA with his case study of a baseball team called Los Tecolotes de los dos Laredos (not just the Laredo Owls, but "The Owls of the Two Laredos"). The study of a single semiprofessional baseball team located in the twin towns of Laredo, Texas and Nuevo Laredo, Mexico – one on each side of the Rio Grande – provides a unique insight into the nature of nationalisms and internationalisms in a globalizing world. The local people say that the river joins and the river divides, and the data collected in Klein's study revealed the truth of that statement. Players and fans came from both countries, and Klein's field work shows how the players worked to mediate their differences in language, nationality, and culture. As with Foley's examination of white–Indian relationships in his hometown (Chapter 15), we again see the way in which sport becomes part of the struggle to resolve differences between people. It is a struggle that seems to have an equal chance of success and failure because, just as sport can be socially constructed to minimize social differences between people, it can also be constructed to exacerbate and exploit those differences.

- Pearson, Kent (1979) *Surfing Subcultures of Australia and New Zealand*, St Lucia: University of Queensland Press.

Although this is an older study, it provides a useful example of sport subcultures research because it deals with two contrasting surfing subcultures, one which reproduces the dominant culture, and one that resists it. Surf lifesaving is a sport unique to Australia and New Zealand, derived from the techniques of rescuing swimmers in heavy surf. Pearson describes how the norms and values of surf lifesaving are completely in accord with the dominant sport culture, and while he does not use the language of reproduction, it is easy to see how the sport contributes to the reproduction of class and gender relations. In contrast, board surfing has long been associated with resistance to the status quo, particularly in its connection to the 1960s counterculture. Pearson develops the contrast between these two subcultures and their participants over a whole series of dimensions involving the norms, values, beliefs, meanings, and social relationships in the two sports. (See also, Doug Booth 1995, "Ambiguities in pleasure and discipline: the development of competitive surfing," *Journal of Sport History* 22(3): 189–206; Doug Booth "Surfing 60s: a case study in the history of pleasure and discipline," *Australian Historical Studies* 26(103): 262–79, for a more explicit connection of these two subcultures to the themes of reproduction and resistance.)

- Stebbins, Robert A. (1987) *Canadian Football: The View from the Helmet*, London, ON: Centre for Social and Humanistic Studies, University of Western Ontario.

Although Bob Stebbins is an expatriate American sociologist who has never played Canadian football, he shows us the insights that can be developed by systematic interviews and observations. Stebbins looks at three levels of the Canadian game – junior (club), university, and professional. He explores the connections between those levels, along with players' experiences at each level. While his study gives an insider's view similar to the views provided by Freedman (1988) and Klein (1993) above, he also explores the connections between the game and Canadian culture. In his analysis he particularly notes the threat to the Canadian professional game from the hugely popular National Football League in the USA. He concludes with recommendations for the survival of the Canadian game.

Part 4

TRANSITION EXPERIENCES
Facing life beyond the playing field

Sport participation, especially in high performance sports, is not forever. At some point, athletes must change or terminate their sport participation. Changes or termination may be "forced" by injuries. Athletes may be "cut" from teams or unable to qualify for participation, or they may lack the resources to continue their training and competition. For example, athletes may lose corporate or personal sponsors, or face the necessity of obtaining jobs to support themselves and their families.

Changes or termination may also be voluntary. Athletes may realize that their skills no longer enable them to compete successfully or meet their own performance expectations. Some athletes terminate their playing careers because they feel it is time to seek alternative career opportunities or develop new competencies, relationships, and identities. Others may retire because they are tired of intense training, bored with the limited experiences available to them through sports, or anxious to focus their attention on family relationships and responsibilities.

Changing or terminating sport participation often occurs in connection with the same processes that underlie becoming involved in and doing sports. Changes in participation are grounded in decision-making processes, and these are tied to the lives, identities, life courses, and social worlds of the people involved. The chapters in Part 4 illustrate that it is difficult to explain changes in sport participation without knowing about at least four sets of factors:

- the general circumstances surrounding the changes;
- identity issues related to the changes;
- developmental and life course issues at the time of the changes;
- the availability of resources for making transitions to other roles or activities.

The research findings discussed in these chapters suggest that we can understand the problems and processes which people experience when they retire from competitive sports if we know how sports fitted into their lives and whether playing sports has limited or expanded their identities, relationships, experiences, and resources. If sport participation has limited these, problems are more likely. If it has expanded them, transitions to life beyond the playing field usually involve positive experiences combined with relatively minor problems.

The first chapter in Part 4 illustrates how athletes often resist changing or terminating their playing careers, even in the face of pain and injury. Kevin Young and Phil White (Chapter 19) provide compelling evidence to show that we must understand the dynamics of "doing sports" if we are to understand the dynamics of making the transition from being an athlete to living life off the field. Their in-depth interviews with 28 high performance athletes (16 men, 12 women) help us to understand that athletes often resist changing or terminating their sport participation because their identities are so deeply tied to being athletes, displaying their physical skills, and maintaining the respect of fellow athletes.

Young and White focused their interviews on how athletes experienced and made sense of pain and injury in their sport careers. They found that athletes concealed pain and played through injuries. Changing or terminating careers was a last resort for most of them. It seemed that as these athletes became immersed in the highly masculinized subculture of high performance sports, they learned that athletes never quit, and that quitters are not athletes.

Young and White make the case that high performance sports are grounded in the values and experiences of men for whom the ability to perform physically is central to their sense of self, and for whom physical performance involves conquering the odds, opponents, and even one's own body. This way of playing sports and the processes of self-identification that accompany it are encouraged and maintained by a vocabulary through which men and women athletes learn to conceal pain, differentiate pain from injury, ignore the pain and injuries of others, and objectify injured parts of their own bodies.

This study suggests that high performance sports constitute a subculture in which members learn a special vocabulary and then use it to "talk injury" in a particular way. As people become a part of this subculture they learn to view their own bodies in ways that enable them to engage in risky and aggressive behaviors, and then to maintain sport participation in the face of the pain and injuries caused by those behaviors. This subculture serves as the context in which both men and women form their ideas of what it means to be an athlete and what it takes to claim an identity as an athlete.

Young and White's chapter does not deal directly with terminating sport participation and getting on with the rest of life, but it helps us to understand why some athletes find it so difficult to end their active playing careers, even when such a decision is in the best interest of their health and well being. Furthermore, it helps us to realize why many athletes continue to play sports until their injuries become so serious that they are forced to stop playing.

Chapter 20 by Anna Dacyshyn is based on a project in which she interviewed women who had been high performance athletes in swimming and gymnastics. Her analysis focuses on seven former gymnasts whose average retirement age was 18 years old when she talked with them. She devoted her attention to the gymnasts because they were more likely than the swimmers to have serious problems making the transition out of their sport careers and getting on with the rest of their lives. The swimmers retired at an older age and seemed to connect their retirement from sports with other transitions in their lives during young adulthood. The gymnasts retired before age 20, and Anna was interested in whether their transition problems were related to a combination of age-related developmental issues and the organization of competitive gymnastics. Anna's ultimate goal was to see if there was a need for special programs to assist gymnasts with their transitions out of the sport.

Dacyshyn found that transition problems for gymnasts were linked primarily to a long-term, exclusive emphasis on athletic performance in their lives. This highly specialized emphasis and the long hours of training that began during childhood interfered with a more balanced life that could have promoted holistic developmental experiences through late childhood and adolescence. In the absence of holistic developmental experiences, retirement was generally associated with feelings of disorientation, identity loss, and social alienation. Retirement came at a time when the young women had not yet developed the emotional strength and maturity to deal with the unresolved issues associated with not achieving many of the goals they had set for themselves. Furthermore, the young women had spent so much time in the gym that they did not have the experiences or the sense of personal control and autonomy they needed to construct a vision for their futures apart from gymnastics.

Retirement for the five youngest gymnasts seemed to come before they had a chance to discover who they were or who they could become outside the gym. The two gymnasts who did not experience major adjustment problems were both 23 years old at the time of the interviews. Their retirement seemed to have occurred at a point in their life course when they had the emotional and identity resources to make the transition into the rest of their lives without feeling as if they were in "nowhere land."

Each of us connects with the rest of the world through our identities. We present ourselves to others through these identities, and others recognize and interact with us through them. Dacyshyn's research suggests that when young people focus their entire lives on being an athlete in a particular sport, they may not have the chance to develop the range of identities needed to connect meaningfully with the rest of the world when they retire from sports. This is especially likely to occur when coaches and parents rigidly structure athletes' lives over many years.

The third chapter in Part 4 is written by psychologist Derek A. Swain. His research emphasizes the notion that retirement from high performance sports is a process that occurs gradually over a relatively long period of time. Swain conducted multiple in-depth interviews with ten men who were former professional athletes from a range of sports. None of these men had million-dollar contracts, but they were accomplished athletes in each of their sports. During his interviews Swain discovered that retirement for these men involved a transition process which began during their active playing careers, well before they took the field for the last time.

These men initiated this process when they realized that they could not play forever, and that there was life after sports. They anticipated problems as they ended their careers, but they were often ready for retirement because they had become increasingly weary of training and competition and sensitive to the toll that sport participation was taking on their bodies. They began to seek new career alternatives and to plan for the future. They viewed retirement with mixed feelings, but after it occurred they gradually accepted it and became settled in their new lives after sport.

Swain reports that these former athletes did experience a strong sense of loss as their careers ended. They felt alienated and worried about their futures, and it was difficult for them to give up the celebrity status they had as athletes. But they appreciated the new opportunities and improved health that came with retirement. They also enjoyed the chance to connect in new ways with their families. Overall, the former athletes were ready to move on to other things in their lives, but they also made efforts to stay connected with sports on a recreational level or in various supporting roles in sport organizations. This enabled them to preserve part of their sport-related identities as they developed additional ones through new relationships and activities.

Swain also found that the wives or "girlfriends," and other family members of the former professional athletes sometimes had problems adjusting to their loss of celebrity status when the athletes retired. This reminds us that athletes often receive emotional and social support from others during their playing careers, and through the retirement process. The experiences of those who provide this support have seldom been acknowledged. What happens in their lives as the athletes they live with go through the retirement transition? In the final chapter, Bette McKenzie provides one, highly personal reply to this question. Her answer is very consistent with the information presented in Thompson's study of the wives of ice hockey players (Chapter 18).

Bette McKenzie is not a social scientist, but she has had a lifetime of experiences connected with sports. Her insights based on those experiences help us to understand the ways in which the people in athletes' families are involved in and impacted by an athlete's playing career and retirement.

McKenzie's father had been a player in the National Hockey League. As a girl and young woman she was known as "Johnny Pie's daughter." This status was attractive because it gave her access to advantages unavailable to many others of her age. Her identity as the "daughter of an NHL player" dominated her childhood and adolescence. Then as a 19-year-old college student she began dating a man who was a rookie offensive lineman for the New England Patriots in the National Football League. At 20 she dropped out of college and they were married. Almost immediately her life became structured by the demands of her husband's career and the glow of his celebrity status as a high-profile professional athlete. Her experiences were much like the professional ice hockey wives' experiences reported by Wendy Thompson in Chapter 18.

After realizing that others knew her only through her connection to a professional athlete, McKenzie decided to return to college, earn a degree, and find out who she was outside pro sports. Building on the contacts she had made through sports, she gained entrance into two good colleges, one near the home where they lived during the season, and one near the home where they lived in the off-season. When her husband was traded to the Los Angeles Raiders in 1987 she decided to stay in New York with their 3-year-old son. She was pregnant with twins and in her senior year of college at the time. She knew that if she did not complete her degree that year, she might have a long wait for graduation. She earned her degree in Art History in 1988, about the same time that her husband was cut from the Raiders. Over the next few years, Bette's desire to be more than an ex-player's wife, and the difficulties they both faced in connection with her husband's transition into life beyond the NFL contributed to their divorce.

After the divorce Bette was able to use sports and her sport-related connections to develop new identities on her own terms. She co-founded and continues to operate a Speakers' Bureau through which she books business people, entertainers, and professional athletes. She began to use to her advantage the resources and contacts gained from years of being a "daughter of the NHL" and a "wife of the NFL." She began to train and compete in road races and triathlons. One of her new goals was to run the Boston Marathon. In the process of developing these new identities she was able to redefine her past in terms that complemented her new life and her visions for the future.

Bette McKenzie's autobiographical chapter shows that retiring athletes are not the only ones who face transitional challenges. Spouses and children also face them. After years of providing social and emotional support to athletes and living in the shadow of their reflected glory, these spouses and children must also get on with life beyond the playing field. Hopefully, McKenzie's chapter will inspire social scientists to do research on this process as it occurs in athletes' families. At this point, research on this topic has never been done.

After reading the four chapters in Part 4 and reviewing dozens of studies on transitions out of sports, we have concluded the following things about what happens when athletes move from the playing field into the rest of their lives:

- When people terminate competitive sport careers, they do not abandon all connections with sports; in fact, many play different and less competitive sports or move into other sport roles such as coach, program organizer or administrator, sports businessperson, etc.
- Retiring from a career as an athlete is usually part of a process involving changes and transitions in the rest of a person's life, such as changing schools, earning a degree, getting a job, getting married, becoming a parent, or seeking new learning experiences.
- Transitions out of sports into the rest of life are most likely to involve problems when athletes have no identities apart from sports, or lack the social and material resources needed to enter other careers, activities, and relationships.
- The spouses who have lived with and provided support for elite athletes may face their own challenges and problems in connection with the athletes' transitions into the rest of their lives.

19

THREATS TO SPORT CAREERS

Elite athletes talk about injury and pain

Kevin Young and Philip White

Kevin Young and Philip White know sports injury. As former rugby and soccer players at English and Canadian schools and universities with subsequent experiences in jockdom, both authors have had their fill of minor and major injuries, rehabilitation programs, and lasting aches and pains. For over a decade, Kevin Young has suffered from a lower back problem (two disc "bulges") that began when he played university rugby in Canada, and which has familiarized him with the world of anti-inflammatory drugs and painkillers. Among other injuries, he has also experienced two broken fingers, three broken noses, a broken ankle, and ligamental damage to both knees. White's athletic career, which includes top level rugby on both sides of the Atlantic and professional soccer in Canada, has also been punctuated by numerous injuries including two broken fingers, cracked ribs, chipped teeth, torn hamstrings, four concussions (including two "overnighters"), three MCL (knee) injuries, and repeated separated shoulders. At the age of 42, his hips were described by a surgeon as "like those of a 65-year-old." At the time of writing, chondromalacia (irritation of the undersurface of the kneecap) prevents Kevin Young from jogging as far as he would like, and Philip White's daily runs have had to be suspended because of recurrent leg cramps.

Our research into injury experiences stems from mutual frustrations with our damaged bodies and from our shared interest in research on sport and gender. But in the course of casual discussions it became evident that our experiences with physical limitations and ongoing pain, caused by intense involvement in violent games at school and university, were far from isolated or unusual. Rather, Kevin Young's chronic back problem and Philip White's ongoing shoulder problem (following a complete separation twelve years ago) seem to be quite normal in the social circles within which we have lived and worked. For example, both of us have family members who have suffered similar, and possibly worse, sports injuries during their playing years that continue to impact their lives. Two immediate male colleagues, both former university football players, have had to endure chronic neck and back pain following the routine poundings suffered during their careers. One has had surgery to fuse some of his vertebrae and the other visits a chiropractor each month to control his pain.

From our discussions, which later led us to conduct more systematic research, it also became evident that we were both ambivalent about the physical damage incurred during our athletic careers. On the one hand, we both derived a great deal of enjoyment and satisfaction from playing sports like rugby – the thrills and spills, the competition, the comraderie, and (dare we say it) the affirmation of our masculinity. On the other hand, there was always a side of us that suspected that we had caved in to the types of pressure put on many young men (and increasingly women) to expose their bodies to levels of risk that could be considered excessive.

Our work is ongoing, but this chapter draws from the early phases of our research into the injury experiences of athletes. The first phase involved studying the experiences of elite male athletes. It made sense to us to begin research on this topic, and with men, because very little had been done previously that focused specifically on what male athletes thought about their injury experiences, and because we thought that our own experiences might help us to understand those of our subjects. The second phase involved a parallel study of female athletes. In the first two phases of the research the lead role was taken by Kevin Young who had undertaken a number of previous studies using qualitative methods. Interviews with male athletes were conducted by Kevin Young, Philip White, and Bill McTeer, with Kevin Young subsequently analyzing the data. Kevin Young conducted all of the interviews and analysis of data in the study of female athletes. A third and comparative phase is underway to look at the extent to which there may be gender similarities and/or differences in the meanings attached to sports injury.

Our research began with two small exploratory samples. We wanted to look at how involvement in sports which carry a high risk of injury, and the experience of injury itself, affect how participants think about themselves in relation to masculine and feminine identities. Sixteen male athletes and twelve female athletes were interviewed. All of the men had experienced extremely painful injuries. They were either currently or formerly elite-level participants in football, kickboxing, downhill ski racing, track and field, ice hockey, and tennis.

The aggregate picture represented by a simple injury count among the male subjects read like an emergency room nightmare. It included fractures to most bones, a ruptured spleen, concussions, a lacerated kidney, a punctured testicle, shoulder and other joint dislocations, torn ligaments, heart attack, and a stroke. Long-term results of these injuries included carpal tunnel syndrome, chronic pain variously located, a removed kidney, partial paralysis, tendinitis, arthritis, and body parts kept in place with braces, plates, pins, and other devices. These subjects, then, clearly represented seriously injured athletes.

The women were involved in at least one of the following sports: rugby, basketball, downhill skiing, football, and bodybuilding, although most had also participated in several sports simultaneously and other sports not listed here. All of the women had competed at least at the collegiate level, three being national athletes. All had experienced at least one major injury (including broken ribs, noses, cheekbones, legs, and ankles, separated shoulders, dislocated knee caps, and herniated discs), requiring eight of them to undergo reconstructive surgery. Again, our small female sample represented seriously injured athletes.

We built these samples using the "snowball" method, which means that we started with friends and acquaintances and then used them to establish further contacts. We wanted to interview people from varying social backgrounds, but in the end were unable to explore social class, age, or minority group effects as thoroughly as we would have liked. All but one of the subjects were white, and all could broadly be categorized as middle class.

Although the subjects were asked to talk freely about their experiences, a number of issues were tackled consistently in all of the interviews. For example, we asked about subjects' early involvement in sport as children and their relationships with significant others around sport. We also asked about their earliest recollections of sports injury and how these experiences affected their bodies and health, their image of themselves, and their relationships with others. But for the most part, we asked our respondents to tell us how they experienced and made sense of pain and injury in sport. We also explored what we call "injury adjustment" – how injured athletes deal with their problems in a practical way and move on with their lives. So far, this work is far more developed with our male samples, and this is reflected in the chapter.

Our analysis involved reading the transcripts of the interviews and identifying recurrent themes and consistent experiences and views. Although we discovered surprisingly little variability in our "readings" of the transcribed interviews, we recognize that, as with other qualitative work, our findings represent our own interpretations of the meanings of sports injury expressed by the subjects. Because of the nature of the methodology, we cannot claim with certainty that our interpretations are absolutely reliable. However, as former university-level participants in the kinds of aggressive sports many of our subjects play, or have played (football and rugby, specifically), and with each of us having experience in what Messner and Sabo (1990: 14) call the "very limiting, often painful downside of sport," we felt confident that our decoding of the data was accurate.

Talking injury

Our interviews suggest that if there is a difference between the ways that male and female athletes in our samples appear to understand pain and injury, it is only a matter of degree. It became apparent that both male and female athletes subject themselves to risk even while injured and suffering from pain. In accepting injury and complying with what remains a central component of high level sport – "no pain, no gain" – several strategies were used by athletes. At this stage of our research, it is clear that both men and women adopt similar techniques to displace the impact of pain in their sports lives. Although it is considered to be appropriate male behavior to continue to play with pain, or not to admit to pain, we found that elite athletes of both sexes hold similar beliefs. This is reflected in locker room slogans like "you don't make the club sitting in the tub." Many athletes even hold tolerance of pain in high regard. As D—— suggested:

> On the football team you expect your neck to hurt or your back to hurt and as long as you can keep playing things aren't that bad. I think that's your thinking. Plus, after the season things get better. A few weeks later you can start to move your head again.

In what follows, we summarize the interpretive strategies that male and female athletes appear to use in "talking [about] injury." These strategies emerged as common themes in the ways that athletes dealt with pain, such as hiding it, disrespecting it, unwelcoming it, and depersonalizing it.

Hidden pain

Much like coping mechanisms associated with illness more broadly, some male athletes denied their pain, suppressing its physical and mental impact on the body. J——, for example, risked severe and possible fatal injury by playing football with internal bleeding caused by a ruptured spleen. As he explained, ignoring pain had always been a part of sport for him, even as a child athlete having badly injured his leg:

> Then, I responded the same way that I responded with the present injury because I would just try to hide it, and you know the doctors tell you what not to do or not to play or whatever. And I remember playing hockey with the boys, you know, like after school or something, and that I was always goalie. And I remember playing with this broken leg. You know, taking shots off the leg and it would be you know, right in the shin.

J——'s views on injury spoke both to a philosophy of hiding pain, and to norms requiring that pain not be revealed to football teammates:

> I bite my tongue and sometimes if it's really bad I moan once or twice. But sometimes it gets pretty bad and hard to bear. If the guys were around it was a different story but if my girlfriend was there I kind of got more sympathy. When I was recuperating, it was hard. When I was starting to "rehab," I would grin and bear it.

Similarly, among female athletes, L——'s case is classic. Here, she describes her responses to a dislocated kneecap:

> The first thing I remember is being very scared after hearing the "pop" and the feeling of no control as I hit the ground. I knew immediately it was my knee, but tried to deny it. I hunched over my leg grabbing my shin and waiting for the referee, which seemed like ten minutes, to notice a player was down. I kept telling myself that it was only some pulled muscles, and even when my leg went into contractions, I refused to believe it was bad. I didn't give in and actually waited the entire game. It was the first step on the way to admitting defeat and acknowledging my injury.

Rather than being confined to notoriously rough team sports such as football and hockey, the willingness to conceal pain was evident in over twenty sports represented by the subjects, including high jumping, squash, and downhill skiing. The general consensus was summarized best by M—— who, despite chronic foot pain aggravated by racquet sports, noted, "I sort of live with it. I block it out somehow."

Disrespected pain

No athletes in our sample were able to convert "pain into pleasure," as some body-builders claim to be able to do (Smith 1989: 82). Rather, our conversations demonstrated that injury tolerance is possible because of an attitude of irreverence towards what K—— called "everyday pain." This was especially clear in the manner that several subjects (all male football and hockey players) differentiated pain from injury. While the former included, in T——'s words, "mostly soreness and aches" (but which nevertheless often required prescription drug treatment and even surgery), the latter implied either unbearable suffering or manifestly unplayable body conditions, such as a broken limb set in a cast.

Like many athletes in the study, D—— had spent several years on painkillers, even using them in the off-season to reduce his permanent pain:

> We have this term in football. People refer to it as a difference between pain and injury. If you can walk or you can run to any degree, you know, they look at your injury in terms of percentages. If you're at 70 percent and it's better than your second stringer's 100 percent – then you're playing. So, you tend to take a couple of painkillers and tape her up nice and tight and ice before you play, and away you go.

Almost a decade of playing football had led J—— to express similar indignation about the routine hazards of his sport:

> Last year I ripped my "trap" and separated my shoulder . . . Every now and again it flares up and then I take a bunch of Tylenol and forget about that pain. That's probably the most pain I have. But is that injury?

On the matter of "disrespected pain", women did not go as far as men in differentiating pain from injury, although the capacity of female athletes to feel irreverent, even indignant, about pain remained evident if less extreme. As a result of spending up to six hours a day training, D——'s lower leg and ankle pain had been severe for some time. Until she suffered an incapacitating injury, her coping mechanism involved denial and a daily dose of painkilling drugs:

> I never skated or played basketball without constant pain. However, this just made me push harder to beat it. I was often sore and stiff. The pain, while playing, was often enough to make me cry once I got home (never at the rink!). I dealt with it through the use of painkillers and denial.

Among women athletes, D——'s story was common: V—— "blocked out the pain;" L—— became "annoyed and irritated" by it; and G—— became "resentful and bitter."

Unwelcomed pain

That pain is so frequently concealed by athletes is also partly attributable to the fact that it is poorly received by teammates, coaches, and others. In brief, our male subjects were critical of the negative impact of injury on teammates, and described the display of injury or pain as a "demoralizer." As D—— described:

> There's always that pressure because, I mean, you don't want to tell your quarterback you're injured because he'll have reservations about getting you the ball if you're a step slower. Plus it puts more pressure on him because he's got more on his mind. It's a matter of just don't tell anybody else about yourself and just do your job, basically.

The rules of masculinist sports culture also require that intense pain is controlled and masked. There were several accounts of this. J—— reported that after breaking his leg, the pressure to "play through it" came from peers, his hockey coach and even his father:

> With my femur, I remember vividly just going up the wall and kind of having my head down and getting hit from the side. I know it was my left leg and all I felt was my left leg wrapping around my right leg. Then I fell down. I tried not to show pain and lay there on the ice. I was trying to get up and I remember just falling back down again. And then I remember the coach coming up and trying to help me up and he said, "Come on, you can get up, you're tough," or whatever, and just trying to stand on it, but there was no way. I remember my dad even giving me shit. Even going through the dressing room no one would help me take my equipment off. That was, oh Jesus, something was wrong with my leg here. And we were in a small town and there was no stretcher, so I had to get put in the back of our van and taken to the nearest hospital.

When asked to explain the apparent negligence of those surrounding him, J—— hinted at the constraints of his "enforcer" role: "No one really thought it was anything serious because . . . of the tough guy label." Similarly, after tearing ligaments in his knee (subsequently requiring reconstructive surgery and a half year of physiotherapy), hockey player K—— recalled being told by teammates not to ice the swelling and not to "be a pussy."

Even at the amateur level, being hurt appears to be unwelcomed by coaches. D——, for instance, expressed concerns over his university football coaches' lack of support for his and others' suffering: "Really, they see it as more of an inconvenience." M—— came by this knowledge more explicitly and recalled several kickboxing coaches telling him not to display any physical distress to them. In the words of one of his coaches: "I'm not bringing a towel to your corner. So don't even bother thinking about stopping."

Female athletes also reported concealing pain to avoid alienating teammates and coaches. This is an indication of the unwelcomed character of pain in sport. In D——'s words: "The other players at the club pretty much ignored the injury and downplayed its seriousness. It wasn't 'cool' to admit your body wasn't finely tuned and healthy, so I downplayed it." So unwelcome are pain and injury that sanctions are sometimes imposed on athletes for declaring them. R——, a former school swimmer and varsity basketball player, was surprised to find herself being disciplined after deciding to quit as a result of bilateral knee injuries:

My parents wanted me to quit. They didn't agree with my basketball coaches who pushed training beyond what was physically reasonable for that age group and development. My swim coach was concerned and barred me from the pool. My basketball coach in Grade 10 had me pulled into the principal's office for refusing to go to practice, even though I told him I'd quit because I was going for surgery.

Other women also spoke of "feeling obliged" to demonstrate, and even fake, courage and gameness in the face of physical risk.

Depersonalized pain

Depersonalized pain entails using a particular way of thinking and speaking about pain and injury. If pain has to be acknowledged it is usually a specific body part that is seen to have "given out." Given athletes' generally excellent health and their posture of physical invulnerability, injury is unsurprisingly often understood by players as a form of bodily betrayal. In fact, injured parts are referred to as objects. In K——'s words: "It's like it's not a part of you. Like it's a totally different portion or something." As further testimony to this depersonalization process, subjects frequently referred, for example, to an injury of the knee or the shoulder, and were often reluctant to explicitly acknowledge that the injured body part was their own. In general, we found that athletes were humbled, even embarrassed, by the vulnerability of their bodies.

As a result of these ways of knowing injury, body damage itself is often articulated by male and female athletes alike through the use of impersonal and techno-rational terminology. Legs become "iced," knees "scoped," ankles "strapped," aches and pains "killed," and mechanical glitches (pulls, strains, tears, breaks) simply "fixed," often artificially. Remarkably, J—— noted that the pain from his ruptured spleen was "just like squeezing an orange," except rather than juice "a little bit of blood came out." Referring to a skiing accident which resulted in him "actually living on half a kidney . . . one kidney was totally ripped open and the other was lacerated," G—— described his injury as "the equivalent of dropping two eggs on the floor – one cracked, one smashed."

Transition experiences and adjustment to injury

Efforts to suppress pain and injury, however, are often unsuccessful because their effects can disrupt the lives of players beyond sport. Seriously injured athletes ultimately have little choice but to deal with their problems in a practical way. Although at both amateur and especially professional levels there are medical services designed to address the physical aspects of injury (sports medicine clinics, rehabilitation centers, physiotherapy), athletes seldom receive assistance in working through the emotional and psychological side effects which, ironically, may be even more traumatic. However, while we found the emotional and psychological effects to be profound in the short term, all but two of the men we interviewed later sought out and played alternative sports. Our data (again, far more developed with male athletes than with females) suggest that in assessing the relationship between sport, gender, and injury, it is useful to distinguish between short-term and long-term adaptations. We do this below by briefly discussing the initially traumatic impact of injury and pain, and the subsequent techniques that men adopt in order to reframe, and recover from, compromised notions of self.

Dependent as they are on fit and physically powerful bodies, injury often confounds male athletes. Among other things, injury may involve hospitalization, missing competition, social dislocation from the team, even retirement. But equally upsetting for men unaccustomed to feeling physically vulnerable (Rutherford 1992) are experiences such as unwanted weight gain or loss, rejection by teammates and coaches, and depleted sense of personal worth. In other words, athletes are forced to recognize, perhaps for the first time, that the physical body and its skills are centrally tied to one's identity and to one's social relationships.

For both triathlete J—— and skier G——, niggling minor injuries had never been enough to threaten their feelings of invincibility. When asked about taking unnecessary risks, G——, for example, remembered that there "was a belief that you were bullet proof." So when G—— hurt his knee and lacerated a kidney in a bad fall, and J—— suffered a heart attack during the biking leg of a triathlon, rethinking the place of sport in their lives and their self-image was unavoidable. As J—— put it, the process was a troubling one to his "inner self." "I've always prided myself on being healthy and strong and it was really confusing feeling weak." For others, coming to terms with injury was similarly demoralizing. K—— described his initial response to tearing knee ligaments as "pretty close to the biggest down of my life," and recalled the mental adjustment being "much tougher" than the leg pain. D——'s broken collarbone was reported as "a very big loss," and J——'s broken femur "fully devastating."

Predictably, the magnitude of adjustment problems was often determined by the nature and extent of injury. J——'s experiences with heart attack during a triathlon, and his subsequent stroke were highly traumatizing. Not only was he left partially paralyzed and without speech, but his medical difficulties were followed sadly by family breakdown, and what J—— described as a "downward spiral" personally:

> Funny, I was feeling less of a man. I was married. The doctors inserted a tube in my penis to control the urination and I couldn't control my bladder and I was pissing on myself all the time. I felt just inadequate for maintaining my lifestyle with my wife and I suggested to her that we get separated and we did. For me, it was a non-verbal period. I couldn't explain my feelings. It was really frustrating. I felt like a baby. And in the hospital and the physio gym, I couldn't crawl because I'd get sore with my broken rib and my separated shoulder and I couldn't verbalize and I couldn't walk. I just felt like a baby.

J—— was not the only one, however, to understand his injury as demasculinizing in the short term. T——, for instance, saw his shrinking body as a betrayal making him "less attractive and less manly." "You just feel incompetent . . . not being able to do things. You just feel helpless." M——'s diminished fitness level made him try other activities, even gingerly early on, "to try to maintain that image" of himself. For I——, simply having to adjust to a less rigorous bodybuilding routine because of carpal tunnel syndrome also affected his "confidence, self-esteem, and mood." Crucially, we found that the difficulty brought on by adjusting to injury was strongly linked not only with the psychological reassessment anyone might face under similar circumstances, but also to feelings of lesser adequacy as a male.

Perhaps most remarkable about challenges to notions of invulnerability is that on the whole they are extremely short-lived. Despite the severity of these athletes' injuries, all but two returned to essentially risky sports. The two not returning were physically unable to: one is still recovering from stroke-induced paralysis, and the other is constrained by only having the use of one half kidney. It appears that the dominant model of sport with its emphasis on forceful male performance and its promise of "masculinity validation" (Sabo and Panepinto 1990: 115) is so meaningful in the lives of some men that injury becomes more constituting than threatening. This may be demonstrated in several ways.

K——'s recovery from knee surgery depended on him overcoming the psychological hurdle of whether he "could take a hit again:"

> I felt good after I came out of my surgery. I thought I'd worked hard in physio. I thought [I'd] done basically everything that I could've done to make myself better. People told me that the next year I skated with a limp. I still cross over one way better than the other. I still always turn to one side. That's just something that maybe came out of habit more than anything from being maybe timid on it for the first little while. The best thing that happened to me, I think, was that in the first game I played I just got hammered. I just got nailed. I got up and I felt great. I felt like nothing went wrong and after that I thought that was a big sort of camel's back to get over. I mean it would've worked out better if I had maybe hit the guy, but all in all that was a big step for me.

With the knowledge that he could once more dole out and take pain, K—— returned to hockey more confident than ever. This was much the same for J——, for whom temporary disablement was a catalyst to a stronger, tougher self:

> I know that through hard work I can basically overcome anything and I proved that at a young age with my femur. You know, you've broken the biggest bone in your body and it's supposed to be a very serious injury and I've never had any, you know, complications with it since. So I knew that through hard work I would be able to come back, and at the end everything would be alright.

Finally, while for J—— the six weeks it had taken to recover from his spleen injury had shaken his confidence, the effect was only temporary. His main recollection was how rehabilitation "re-energizes" and provides an opportunity for "a brand new start." Despite still having to use anti-inflammatory and painkilling drugs frequently, J—— saw his time away from sport as so "reviving" that he returned to football with an even more zealous commitment to the "pain principle": "I could even learn to play with a little more pain."

Reframing injury as purposeful appears to be a result of both the machismo and fatalism of athletic culture, and of a broad acceptance of the notion that sport is a "character builder." J——'s belief that "everything happens for a reason" was tied to his and others' focus on the beneficial attributes of having to deal with the adversity of pain and disablement. When asked how he responded to injury in the short and long term, for instance, T—— noted how his initial feelings of anger and self-pity were ultimately superseded by a revelation that "in the long run it (injury) will make you a better person."

Although not all athletes spoke directly of recovering identity from injured bodies, all but one indicated that enduring pain while rehabilitating was linked to self-improvement. For some, this meant rethinking their lives (taking slightly less risk, being more prepared, living for more than the moment), but for most it meant regaining bulk, strength, confidence, and self-image – factors all demonstrably tied to reconstructed masculinity in the post-injury context (White and Young 1997).

Conclusions

These are some of the main types of "injury talk" that we discovered both male and female athletes engaging in, although sometimes with different emphasis. Each of the strategies more or less involved the suppression of emotion except frustration and anger. Our sense is that such strategies represent cornerstone principles of the dominant masculinist model of sport, and are adopted for a number of reasons: to show courage and character; to consolidate membership and kudos in the group; to avoid being benched; and, to help make sense of compromised health in a lifestyle that demands and reveres fitness.

Our findings also suggest some striking similarities in the attitudes of elite athletes to physical danger, aggression, and injury. The ways that both females and males talked about sport was full of the language of conquest (winning, beating the odds, overcoming pain). Female athletes seemed as willing as men to expose themselves to physical risk, and both women and men were relatively uncritical about such things as being pressured to perform aggressively, or to play with injury.

Though our research is still in its early stages, in addition to raising critical questions about what sport offers to males, we think that it raises some important questions regarding what sport has to offer to the large numbers of females now participating in physically risky sport. On the one hand, women are clearly participating more and more in traditionally male-exclusive sports. On the other hand, much of this involvement, rather than contributing to a deliberate reconstruction in the meanings of sport, appears to be consolidating very traditional and masculinist sports structures which are full of violent, excessive, and health-compromising qualities and attitudes.

Our work also raises further questions about the lived contradictions for women and men regarding the supposed healthfulness of sport and the actual experiences of pain and injury in sport. Sport-related norms prescribing tolerance of pain and playing while injured call into question what our culture requires of athletes who want to succeed in sport regardless of sex. Our research with male and female athletes leads us seriously to query these norms and to ponder the negative health consequences of much of modern sport. We believe that a critical challenge of sport might be to modify dominant thinking about ways that the body may be exploited and damaged and, perhaps more controversially, how we as athletes sometimes consent to the abuse of our own bodies.

References

Messner, M. and Sabo, D. (eds) (1990) *Sport, Men, and the Gender Order: Critical Feminist Perspectives*, Champaign, IL: Human Kinetics.

Rutherford, J. (1992) *Men's Silences: Predicaments in Masculinity*, New York: Routledge.

Sabo, D. and Panepinto, J. (1990) "Football ritual and the social reproduction of masculinity," in M. Messner and D. Sabo (eds) *Sport, Men, and the Gender Order: Critical Feminist Perspectives*, Champaign, IL: Human Kinetics. pp. 115–27.

Smith, E. (1989) *Not Just Pumping Iron: On the Psychology of Lifting Weights*, Springfield, IL: Charles C. Thomas.

White, P. and Young, K. (1997) "Masculinity, sport, and the injury process: a review of Canadian and international evidence," *Avante* 3(2): 1–30.

20

WHEN THE BALANCE IS GONE

The sport and retirement experiences of elite female gymnasts

Anna Dacyshyn

This study grew out of my personal interest in the topic of sport retirement. After being an elite athlete on the Canadian National Diving Team and then experiencing my own transition from sport, I had first-hand experience with the dramatic change of lifestyle and identity transformation that often is associated with retirement. I knew the feelings of loss and sadness that were associated with saying goodbye to a life-time passion and to lifelong goals and dreams. I did this study because I wanted to contribute to our understanding of issues faced by high performance athletes as they retire from active competition.

When I began designing my thesis at the University of Toronto my goal was to do a research project that had practical implications. My review of past research indicated that many athletes experience retirement as a difficult time of adjustment. Retiring athletes often feel anger, confusion, decreased self-confidence, and concern for the future, they generally feel alone and unique in their experience (Danish *et al*. 1993). Some suffer more serious difficulties such as depression, eating disorders, substance abuse, and even attempted suicide. Programs to assist retired athletes have been implemented in Canada and the USA, but their main emphasis is on career planning. They have not been designed to provide emotional support or a context in which athletes can share their feelings as they make the transition out of their competitive careers and into the rest of their lives (Donnelly 1993; Pearson and Petitpas 1990). So I designed an experimental program to provide emotional support and a context for expressing feelings to a small group of retiring athletes as they made the transition from competitive sports into the rest of their lives. My goal was to study the effectiveness of this type of program.

My original sample consisted of five athletes. There were four swimmers (men and women) and one female gymnast. I conducted an initial interview with each athlete about his or her transition. All of the swimmers seemed to be experiencing remark-ably easy transitions, while the gymnast was quite distressed and described her transition as very difficult. Because the swimmers did not need the program I wanted to study, I abandoned my original thesis idea. But there were still questions that I wanted to answer. For example, what factors accounted for the fact that the swimmers were having such easy transitions, while the gymnast was experiencing serious difficulties? My thesis advisor, a sport psychology consultant to the Canadian National Gymnastics Team, knew many other retired gymnasts who had experienced difficult transitions. We wondered if there was something about this group of athletes that made them particularly vulnerable to difficult transitions. The retirement transitions of female gymnasts had not been studied previously. This was surprising because gymnasts begin competing and then retire at much younger ages than most other athletes. We wondered whether the age factor had an impact on their retirement transitions. These questions led me to revise my thesis topic so I could study the retirement transitions of elite female gymnasts.

I wanted to use qualitative methods so I could capture the deep personal experiences involved in retirement from sport. Qualitative methods appealed to me because they offered a window into the lived experiences of people, into their thoughts, feelings, and inner worlds. I used my coach's contacts with former gymnasts to assemble a sample of seven gymnasts who had retired recently. Interviewing these athletes was enjoyable and enlightening. Their stories were fascinating. They shared personal and meaningful experiences and had a great deal to say, not only about their transition out of sport, but also about their experiences during their careers and living the life of an elite athlete. They offered important and insightful information about the social world of elite gymnastics.

What stood out most clearly in my interviews were the accounts of the profound challenges these athletes confronted at such a young age. The testimonies of these young people speak to the need for more research designed to enhance the experiences of future gymnasts as they move through and end their competitive careers. I learned that career planning may not be the central issue for all athletes making the transition from sport. Some athletes do need programs designed to provide support and guidance in dealing with difficult emotional and psychological adjustments. More important, we need to ask critical questions about a sport system that emphasizes performance at the expense of the holistic development of young people. As long as the sport system remains as it is, retirement transitions are likely to be traumatic for many athletes.

My study was based on in-depth interviews with seven former elite female gymnasts (rhythmic and artistic). At the time of the interviews, the participants had been retired for different lengths of time, ranging from six months to five years, and were between 16 and 22 years old. All of the participants had trained on a year-round basis and devoted 20 to 30 hours per week to training. The average age at which they left competitive gymnastics was 18 and their average career length was 10 years.

The interviews were designed to collect information on the participants' thoughts, feelings, and opinions regarding their transition experiences. The athletes were contacted by phone and asked if they were interested in participating. If they were willing, we arranged a convenient time and location for the interview. Two of the interviews were conducted over the phone because the participants lived in another province.

Everyone I contacted agreed to be interviewed. In fact, many of them welcomed the opportunity to talk about their experiences and were pleased that someone was interested in their well-being since leaving sport. Those who were in the midst of their transitions and still adapting to the adjustments found it helpful to tell their stories. One participant who was experiencing a particularly difficult transition told me afterwards that our conversation was "therapeutic."

The interviews were non-directive and semi-structured. At the outset I explained to the participants that I was interested in hearing about their retirement experiences. This allowed them to talk freely about the aspects of their experiences that they, rather than I, considered important and meaningful. Follow-up and probe questions were asked to encourage the interviewees to elaborate or clarify a point. The interviews lasted between 45 minutes and 2.5 hours. I audio-taped all the interviews so that I could analyze them for themes and patterns.

Backgrounds and general experiences

I begin with a brief description of each of the former gymnasts in the study, combined with an overview of the general nature of each young woman's retirement transition. Pseudonyms have been used to protect their identities.

Allison, an 18-year-old high school senior, was only six months into retirement and finding the adjustment to life without gymnastics very difficult. She was forced into retirement due to a severe injury and was struggling with the fact that her career was over before she ever had the chance to achieve her goals. Furthermore, her injury prevented her from participating in other activities. This further frustrated her and made the transition even more difficult. When I asked her if there were any good parts to retiring she said that "The only good part about retirement is that I'm not in so much pain. I can sleep, I can walk, I don't have to be on medication. But other than that, it's pretty tough."

Two of the young women, **Molly** and **Alex**, were interviewed two years after they retired but still felt that they were "in transition." Molly had lived and trained away from her hometown until she retired at 17 years old. After retiring, she returned home and has lived there for the last two years. She described her retirement as "really, really difficult for the first year." During this first year, she had to adjust to a new school and make new friends, in addition to adjusting to life without sport. She described feeling lost, and not knowing what to do with herself during the first year. Although life had become somewhat settled since then, she described her current state as "adjusted, but not particularly happy. I always find myself coming back to gym, or thinking about it – thinking I might start again." She still felt a void in her life and at times she felt panicky when not occupied. She also said that she worried about the future and had a sense of being out of control.

Alex also experienced difficulties two years after retiring at 20 years old. At 22 she still felt as if her life "revolved around retirement and this state of confusion." She also felt out of control since retiring, and was unsure of the direction of her life. On the positive side, she did feel a sense of liberation and freedom now that she was not under the rigid control of her coach.

Sandra was 17 years old and in high school at the time I interviewed her. She had been retired for nearly one year. She felt somewhat ambivalent about retirement. On the one hand, she said she was generally happy to be out of gym, as if a huge weight had been lifted off her shoulders. She explained that she had not enjoyed gymnastics during the last stage of her career, and that training and competitions had ceased to be fun. On the other hand, she said she would not have retired if it had not been for an incident with her coaches that she described as "traumatic." This incident left her feeling angry, betrayed, and unwanted. She explained that she has been extremely depressed immediately following retirement, but that she was starting to feel happy again.

Laura, a 20-year-old university student, described her retirement as "an important and painful time in my life." She considered her transition to have lasted for about one year after retiring. During that time she felt very out of control. However, at the time of the interview, two and a half years after retirement, she felt that her transition was complete. She said that she had worked through everything and was happy with her new life.

Only two respondents felt they had relatively easy transitions. **Michelle**, 23, had a smooth transition in part, she thought, because she "hated" gymnastics by the time she retired. Also she was able to maintain her involvement in the sport at a much less intensive level which she felt eased her transition considerably. **Melissa**, 23, also had a smooth transition and seemed unique in that she deliberately tried to keep a balance in her life while she trained.

In summary, five of the seven young women described their transitions as very difficult, while two respondents felt their transitions were relatively easy. Each of the former gymnasts experienced both positive and negative emotions throughout their transitions. All of them described missing some elements of their involvement in sport and five expressed feelings of loss of control, frustration, anger, betrayal and fear. On the positive side, nearly all of them said they enjoyed a sense of freedom from their rigid schedules and relief from the stresses and demands of being an elite gymnast. They were especially happy to be away from the dietary restrictions and the constant pressure to be thin.

Sport is life and life is sport

One of the dominant themes that emerged from the interviews revolved around the notion that "Sport is life and life is sport." This statement highlights the extreme importance of sport in gymnasts' lives. To appreciate the dramatic change in lifestyle and identity that retirement sometimes involves, it is necessary to understand the time and energy that these athletes devoted to their sport and the meaning that gymnastics held for them.

The participants of this study started gymnastics between 3 and 6 years old, and most were training intensely by the age of 8 or 9. They trained between four and six hours a day, logging 20–30 hours per week. Allison had an exceptionally rigorous schedule. As young as 8 years old she trained seven days a week, 5–7 hours per day.

Although all the gymnasts had been students while they were athletes, their focus and identity were clearly immersed in sport. Allison explained this in the following way:

> I'd just always be thinking about gym. I can remember going out for lunch with my friends, and not hearing anything they said . . . even at school, I'd be sitting in class and separate myself from the rest of the class. I'd be off in my own little world, thinking about gymnastics.

Given their intense involvement from such a young age, some of the participants in this study literally did not know life without sport. Alex expressed this by saying that

"My whole life revolved around sport. So now my whole life is revolving around this retirement and this confusion."

Retirement and being in Nowhere Land

The athletes' testimonies revealed that their transitions out of sport often involved processes of disorientation and reorientation. According to the gymnasts' accounts, retirement seldom involved simply withdrawing from sport and moving on with the rest of their life. Rather, in between retiring and the next phase of their lives, most of the young women seemed to experience a time of uncertainty and disorientation. After listening to them describe this time, I labeled it as "Nowhere Land." The adjustment process also involved identity changes. First there was the shift from the identity and orientation of "athlete" to a state of disorientation and loss of identity. Then the former athletes experienced a period of reorientation and the development of a new definition of self.

The concept of "Nowhere Land" arose from the five athletes' descriptions of feeling disoriented and confused after their retirement. They felt out of control because there was no direction to their lives and they were uncertain about where to focus their energies next. Molly felt as though she was "kind of just floating around." Allison explained that "I feel like I'm between worlds."

The loss of identity and the struggle to find a new one was another important aspect of the retirement transition. Allison explained in the following words:

> I'm still very uncertain as to who I am. I still think I need to find myself without gymnastics. Because I hid behind my gymnastics and my gymnast identity. That was my protection. And now it's not there. I don't know who I am. I'm someone less an athletic identity. So I'm trying to find myself.

On a similar note, Laura said, "All my friends were associated with gymnastics, and everyone I knew, knew me as a gymnast, and I was no longer that. So who was I?"

The young women generally felt an enormous void in their lives after retiring from gymnastics. Three of them described an intense desire to recreate their gymnastics experience. They hoped to devote themselves to another activity that would give them the same sense of satisfaction and fulfillment. Allison craved "all of it – the competition, the intensity, the stimulation, the fame, the attention, the athlete–coach relationship and pushing my body to exhaustion." Alex and Molly expressed similar sentiments, explaining that two years after retiring they still searched for something to replace gymnastics. Alex said, "I have to find something that affects me that much, and is that much of a passion for me." Molly explained that "I'm just kind of floating around. I always find myself coming back to gymnastics. I'm just hoping to get another focus . . . I'm adjusted but I won't be happy until I actually get into [another activity]."

Insights gained from deconstructing past experiences

The former gymnasts often described their transition experiences as a time of thinking and analyzing. They deconstructed past experiences and looked at them in a new light, which often led to a new insight or understanding. Some examined and began to question the culture of elite sport that they had fully internalized and used to guide their behavior. For example, Allison reflected on her relentless determination to train through a serious and debilitating injury, despite the risk of causing permanent nerve damage. She described her final years in sport in the following way:

> The last two years were really difficult. I would go to therapy before gym, and then I'd go to gym, and go to therapy after gym so I could go to bed at night. Then I'd wake up in the morning, and I'd be sore after sleeping. Then I'd go to therapy again so I could train. And it's funny because I didn't clue in that this wasn't normal behaviour. I just accepted it. It was like "OK if this is what it takes to train, then that's fine." I really did believe that everybody was in this amount of pain [as me] training. I just thought this is what is expected. They always say that sport goes along with blood, sweat and tears, so I thought this was part of the tears. I was on anti-inflams and painkillers to try to get ready for nationals. I was basically just numbing the pain. I knew the pain was still there, getting worse. But I didn't care. I just kept telling myself "I can handle it". And I kept working.

Once in retirement, Allison began to question her commitment to the notion that athletes "play through pain" and "never give up." She explained her new way of looking at things in the following way:

> It worries me that the thing that kept me in sport sometimes was that I was competing with myself: "How much pain can I tolerate?" I just wanted to see how much pain I could handle. And the more I handled the better person I was, the better athlete I was. And now I see that's wrong. But to me, that was everything.

The other young women had reflected on their careers and realized that they lacked power and control over their lives as athletes. They lacked control over their training and competition regimes and were denied opportunities to make decisions. Most had trained at some point in their careers with coaches who dictated what was to be done in training and competition. For example, Michelle said: "At [club] nothing was controlled by me. I did everything I was told. I was a robot. That's what most of us were like and it really undermined the activity." They also lacked control over their bodies. Most had coaches who dictated how much they should weigh and what they should eat. If coaches wanted them to lose weight, they dictated how it was to be done and at what rate. The gymnasts who had lived with their coaches for a period of time also felt that they even controlled their lives outside of the gym, including which courses to take at school and which friends and boyfriends to have. Looking back on her life in sport Molly commented:

> You need to have some input and control over your training because it's your life, your career. Otherwise you get into the problem I got into: where they start to take control over your whole mind set, your whole life. And it carries on outside sport as well. You have to have your own mind, your own goals.

Retirement, then, allowed the athletes to look at their experiences from a different perspective and prompted some of them to question what they had learned in sport. Alex felt an important part of her transition was learning to take control of her life again. She summed it up as follows:

> Since retiring, I've had lots of time to think about my experiences and figure things out – figure out which things I learned were beneficial and good for my well-being and which (of the) messages I had learned were not necessarily so good for me.

Dealing with repercussions of the sport experience

The flip side of analyzing and examining their experiences from a cognitive perspective was to work through the resulting by-products, such as feelings of loss, anger, regret, or disappointment. Those who harbored such feelings, who left the sport with unresolved conflict or unfinished business seemed to have longer, more difficult transitions.

Allison's transition seemed to be particularly difficult because it represented the loss of her hopes and dreams – dreams in which she had a deep emotional investment – as the following quote demonstrates. She said, "It didn't matter that I might not be able to walk later. The only future I thought about was the future that involved my sport. All I cared about was doing gymnastics." Despite the years of hard work and sacrifice, the injury thwarted the accomplishment of her goals, and her exit from sport left her feeling regretful and angry. Even more frustrating, her injury now prohibited her from trying all the activities she had planned to explore once her gymnastics career was over.

Three athletes had difficult relationships with their coach(es) or left because of conflict. They spoke of coaches who verbally abused and manipulated them and these experiences left scars. Molly said: "My coach was verbally abusive. Once he yelled at me and told me how worthless I was for 45 minutes." Alex described her transition as a time of healing and processing years of unexpressed anger. She explained that her coach yelled at her regularly in practice while she never challenged her coach in any way or expressed anger in return for fear of the consequences. She said:

> I never expressed any anger or talked back. It was like [coach] was the one on top and I was only the little pawn on the bottom. She had total control over me. Coach could say whatever she wanted, she could get angry at me and vent her anger on me, and even walk out on me. And I would just sit there and take it.

Alex's anger surfaced once she was out of the sport. She explained that for many months after retiring she had disturbing dreams in which she confronted her coach.

The interviews indicated that an important byproduct of the experience in gymnastics was a long-lasting preoccupation with weight and a poor body image. A major theme to emerge from the gymnasts' accounts was the emphasis placed on body size and weight and the constant stress this posed. Many rated it as the biggest stress associated with being an elite gymnast. Throughout their careers coaches, judges, and sport officials strictly monitored their weight and many were in a constant battle to "control" their weight and suffered from poor body images. Some struggled with eating disorders.

Once retired, they were: free from having others monitor and control their weight; free from the ordeal of daily weigh-ins and monthly "fat tests;" and free from having their weight publicly displaying on the gym wall, or from being punished if they were deemed "overweight." However, they were not free from the burden of their own dissatisfaction with their bodies and constant self-monitoring. Many remarked that the preoccupation with weight and body image did not simply disappear after retiring, nor did eating disorders. If anything, a few noted, the preoccupation worsened:

> I haven't been on a scale in a long time. I'm too scared. I'm terrified. The last time I stepped on a scale I cried because I had gained a bit of weight. Gaining weight is very scary for me. I'm very, very self-conscious about my body. I get so down on myself. I do have a poor relationship with food now. Food is the enemy. When I was in gymnastics, I thought about food all the time − how much to eat, when to eat, don't have too much. I'm so used to seeing food as the enemy.

Lack of support from sport organizations

Some of the participants made comments about the lack of support that they received from the sport organizations with which they had been associated during their competitive careers. For example, one former gymnast said:

> There isn't anything developed or any programs that support and follow up with retired athletes. Because I really am nothing now. I mean nothing. I'm of no importance to the sport. And I feel like I gave so much to the sport and the administration used me up to whatever I could give them and now I'm out and I'm just used up and forgotten. And that's upsetting.

The social implications of leaving sport and the perceived availability of social support are important aspects of the transition experience.

Conclusion

The data in my study contribute to our understanding of the retirement experiences of a particular group of elite athletes. While all the former gymnasts spoke of both positive and negative aspects of retiring, only two of the seven respondents found their transitions to be easy and uneventful, requiring minimal adjustments. The remaining five gymnasts described their retirement experiences as difficult, marked by feelings of disorientation and loss of control.

A common theme that emerged from the interviews was "Sport is life and life is sport." It represents the degree to which the athletes' lives revolved around gymnastics and lacked balance. The athletes' identities were also clearly immersed in sport. Consequently, retirement evoked feelings of disorientation, loss of identity, and the feeling of being in "Nowhere Land."

My sense is that the vulnerability of these female gymnasts during the retirement transition was associated with the age at which they began their intensive sport involvement. Most of the interviews indicated that these young women literally did not know life without gymnastics. They lacked alternative roles, activities, and interests and, as a result, had little to fall back on once gymnastics was gone. This suggests that retirement might be less traumatic if coaches, parents, and administrators work to see that athletes are exposed to a whole range of recreational, social, educational and cultural experiences. It is also important that athletes be discouraged from making sport the only context in which they derive a sense of personal worth. Sport and competition schedules should be arranged to allow athletes to live a more balanced life while they are competing.

My data also suggest that the meaning of retirement influences an athlete's response to it. The nature and extent of adjustments required during the retirement transition are related to a combination of the nature of sport experiences, the quality of the coach–athlete relationship and the circumstances surrounding the decision to retire. During their transitions, the gymnasts dealt with emotional and psychological issues. They coped with the painful emotions that resulted from dashed hopes and dreams. They were often left with a negative body image and a preoccupation with weight.

As they moved through the transition process the former gymnasts often benefited from deconstructing their past experiences and re-evaluating the values and attitudes they had acquired as elite athletes. This deconstruction and re-evaluation enabled them to deal with the social, psychological, and emotional impact of retirement.

Overall, my data indicate that some retiring athletes need an intervention and support program that goes beyond traditional concerns with career counseling and planning. While career issues are important to many athletes as their competitive careers come to an end, they are not the only important issues. When elite athletes retire at a young age, career planning does not appear to be a crucial issue in their lives. Even older athletes who have formulated career plans may still need assistance in dealing with difficult emotional issues. Athletes should be prepared for the feelings of loss, disappointment, and concern for the future that are often associated with major life transitions (Murphy 1995). Therefore, sport organizations should seriously consider sponsoring intervention programs designed to provide retiring athletes with emotional support and a context for discussing feelings as they experience the transition out of sport competition and into the rest of their lives.

References

Danish, S., Petitpas, A., and Hale, B. (1993) "Life development intervention for athletes: life skills through sports," *The Counseling Psychologist* 21(3): 411–29.

Donnelly, P. (1993) "Problems associated with youth involvement with high-performance sport," in B. Cahill and A. Pearl (eds) *Intensive Participation in Children's Sports*, Champaign, IL: Human Kinetics. pp. 95–124.

Murphy, S. (1995) "Transitions in competitive sport: maximizing individual potential," in S. Murphy (ed.) *Sport Psychology Interventions*, Champaign, IL: Human Kinetics. pp. 334–45.

Pearson, R. and Petitpas, A. (1990) "Transitions of athletes: developmental and preventive perspectives," *Journal of Counseling and Development* 69: 7–10.

21

MOVING ON
Leaving pro sports

Derek A. Swain

This chapter is based on a study I completed for my doctoral degree in counseling psychology at the University of British Columbia in 1990. I conceptualized the study during a research methodology course as my classmates and I considered various research topics. As emerging psychologists, we had an interest in experiences that marked transitions in people's lives. I had recently reviewed other studies on transition experiences associated with career development and unemployment. Apart from my academic interest in these topics, I also had a personal interest in them because I was in a career transition myself.

The specific focus on sports careers had personal meaning for me. Although I had never been a physically accomplished athlete, sports had been a very significant part of my life. Through high school, university, and my early professional career, I had been involved in sports administration. In fact, my last meaningful occupation had been as a college athletic director and basketball coach, a position that had been swept away by government cutbacks.

I wanted to do a qualitative study because I saw little value in surveys or quantitative experimental work that attempted to collapse human experience into numbers and categories. I wanted to do research that would bring some color and depth to the understanding of human experience. My master's thesis involved an historical study of sport, so I had confidence in my ability to write clearly, an important consideration in doing qualitative work. My recent training in counseling methodology gave me confidence in my ability to interview people, not simply asking questions but observing, listening to what was said and what was not said, probing for deeper meanings and implications, and making sense of the dialogue. So, as I tried to understand the experience of leaving a career in professional sport, I had a research topic and a methodology that allowed me to meld personal experience with academic interest and practical skills.

My initial investigation of past research on retirement from sport suggested that transitions out of sports were full of negative experiences. The academic literature reflected the assumption that retirement from sport was a universal, major, and traumatic life crisis, an experience involving deep feelings of loss and disillusionment which was considered analogous to that of the dying person. The popular press also painted a dismal picture of the former athlete as a sorry and cast-off figure who was unable to cope with a world outside sport. These descriptions did not fit my understanding of the experience of leaving professional sport, nor did they fit the general experience of career transition which, although sometimes very distressing, is not universally traumatic and, on the contrary, might even be positive.

The early investigations of the experience had employed largely quantitative methodologies with an emphasis on measurement of variables which might contribute to the perceived problems of psychosocial adjustment to career termination. Rather than seeking a general understanding of the experience, the survey studies perpetuated assumptions about athletes and their careers. They relied primarily on non-representative anecdotes and literary accounts that may well have been more sensational than the norm. As I read further, I became encouraged and excited by the more recent literature in which authors had begun to challenge those assumptions and had suggested that qualitative studies might be more appropriate when investigating the dynamics of retirement from sport.

Similar conclusions were being reached in the more general research on career development and transitional experiences. Early studies had been concerned with the objective adjustment to change, focusing on measurable factors in an effort to determine causal influences. But more recent literature emphasized the complexity of human experience. Turbulent social, economic, technological, and political conditions had eroded occupational certainties and challenged traditional assumptions about career development. Notions of continuous employment, with careers following a rising trajectory to age-based retirement, were no longer appropriate if, indeed, they ever were. And it was becoming apparent that transitional experiences were highly complex. My sense was that to understand these experiences, I needed a contextual approach that considered situational factors plus the individual's subjective experiences consisting of the explanation or meaning which the individual applies to the event. Qualitative research, I decided, would best yield that understanding.

This chapter describes the experiences of people who chose to leave their professional careers. It is rich in biographical information as it follows the individuals' lives from childhood to current experiences. Unfortunately, athletes who were forced from their careers due to factors such as crippling injury or non-renewed contracts, were not available to the study. Their experiences could well be examined using a similar methodology.

One way to gain information about the experiences of others is a simple case study approach of interviewing people and recording their comments. However, problems arise in validating those records, ensuring that they are accurate representations of what the people intended to say. Another problem involves developing a relationship in which the interviewees feel comfortable sharing their stories. This is a particular concern when dealing with public figures such as professional athletes who have learned to be very guarded. As jockey Danny Williams told me, he had kept his personal struggles to himself, not even including his mother or his girlfriend because "we were taught not to tell anyone. Keep it to yourself . . . You don't tell anybody because if they tell someone else, it will hurt your career."

To address these issues, I used ethnographic techniques in my interviewing. Briefly, this meant that the participants in the study were going to be much more than "subjects." They were to be informants who were guaranteed an opportunity to review my interpretations of their words and they were invited to comment and help me build a synthesis of their experiences. Thus, I would meet with each participant at least three times. The first was for a general, tape-recorded interview in which they were asked to describe their experiences in approaching, attaining, and leaving their careers. I would provide comments and questions to support and clarify each description. The second interview gave them the opportunity to review, reflect on, and critique the biographical narrative that I had written based on the first interview. The third session was similar to the second, except that now they were to help me critique and refine a general story that was a synthesis of the experiences of all the informants. This was the most challenging part of the research as I tried to identify clusters or themes of experience.

People became participants in the study in an opportunistic and snowball manner. I found leads about people who might be good candidates for the study and sometimes those people would refer me to others. I wanted to have a mix of athletes from both team and individual sports. Those people who were available to me came from the sports of hockey, football, racquetball, and thoroughbred horse racing. A total of ten male athletes was involved and, in some cases, members of their families also contributed. All these athletes might be considered "journeymen," extremely well paid relative to their non-jock peers, but not multi-million dollar superstars.

Major findings

Instead of seeing withdrawal from pro sports as a single "problem" event, it was more helpful to adopt a "process" perspective through which the experience could be viewed over a period of time. In a life story, numerous events and subexperiences are likely to take place simultaneously, or vary with the individual according to specific circumstances. However, in synthesizing the ten individual stories it was possible to identify a sequence of events, a general story which describes and helps us understand the commonalities in the experience of withdrawing from professional sport, as well as unique points of difference. In the general story, the sequencing of experiential units reflects the apparent shifts in emphasis or focus within the common experience. Like all stories, this one has a beginning, middle, and ending.

The beginning of the story

In brief, the general story indicates that withdrawal from sport was a process over time, which frequently began soon after the athletes became engaged in the career. Among the numerous background issues relevant to the individual stories is the degree and manner in which the athlete might have become enmeshed in the unique lifestyle of the pampered celebrity in which, as Dave Hindmarch noted, "the game makes it easy for you to stay a kid" because so much of one's life is organized by management. The lifestyle may be very fast paced, promoting irresponsibility through an excessive round of parties, sex, drugs, and alcohol. While some athletes might feel alienated by the superficiality of celebrity status, always being on show as the "guest," others, such as hockey player Gary

Lupul, may remain unchanged because "there's things [about] the limelight you kind of shy away from."

In general, a nagging sense of the impending and inevitable end seemed to persist throughout an athlete's professional career. From the start, these athletes recognized the rare opportunity to be a professional, that the highly competitive selection process regularly terminates careers with the changing seasons of sport, and that careers are very vulnerable to sudden changes in health, performance, and management. The impermanent, transient nature of a professional career is commemorated in the stories of the old-timers, the mythology of the sport, and the rumors generated and spread by sometimes worried, sometimes malicious sportsmen and the ever-eager news reporters. It is reinforced by frequent observations of the rapid changes in the careers of others. Although many may not apply the norm to themselves, athletes often knew that successful careers are brief, rarely lasting beyond five years.

A variety of personal experiences can remind the individual that his own career is provisional. Personal setbacks provide one set of examples. Jockeys constantly monitor their weight and any sudden gain is cause for anxiety and worry that they might not be able to reduce. Any perceived decline in health, performance, or opportunity to compete can set an athlete to wonder about the longevity of his career. Mobility within the sport, the "suitcasing" of team trades or demotion to the minor leagues, reminds the athlete that he is a commodity with variable value and marketability. This point is further reinforced through struggles over contract negotiations. Personal successes provide other examples. The high incomes may bring awareness of discrepancies with the average working public. The achievement of personal goals, such as being named an all-star, can cause the athlete to wonder if his career has peaked. As time goes by, advancing age and the very longevity of a career remind the individual that time is running out on both his career in sport and the opportunity to address other life tasks and interests.

The personal potential for withdrawal becomes apparent. Frequently, athletes reported an increasing weariness toward the end of their careers. They grew tired of the physical wear and tear, the abuse of their bodies through preparation, competition, and travel. Some, like Terry Lombardo, found the sports environment became oppressive and confining. For others, there seemed to be at least one particular experience, a catalytic event, which led to serious consideration of the potential for retirement.

Nevertheless, the athletes typically found some reason to re-immerse themselves in the career, developing new hope for survival in professional sport. This process has also been observed in the business world. When downsizing appears imminent, instead of preparing for change and considering personal career options, employees frequently invest themselves more fully in the quest for corporate survival, often deceiving themselves with optimism.

The potential for withdrawal eventually became more immediate, more urgent, frequently arising in the context of an enlarged perspective on the self and the profession. For example, Darcy Rota did not want to be a "one-dimensional" person focussed only on hockey and Dave Hindmarch realized he was living "in the fast lane", a temporary lifestyle which was far from the norm. The athletes were eventually confronted with both internal and external pressures for change. Their emerging personal values, including interest in family, health, and quality of life, were diverging from those of the sports world. For example, Dave Hindmarch recognized that further injury might lead to permanent disability. This was a threat to his future lifestyle because "down the road I'd like to be able to go out and play catch with my kids and I'd like to be able to do other things in life . . . There's more to life than just chasing a puck around the rink."

At this time, the athletes frequently became concerned about perceived limitations for life after sport. Their concerns revolved around issues such as education, transferable knowledge and skills, social contacts, job opportunities, and financial considerations. This experience caused confusion and indecision, and marks the most difficult and trying component of the story, particularly because athletes did not want to leave their careers prematurely. For example, Gary Lupul spent nearly four months of anxious, sleepless nights grappling with his hockey career and Mark Patzer described himself as being near suicidal in wrestling with the thought of leaving horse racing.

The middle of the story

In the middle of the story, the athletes frequently sought direction in their careers, scrutinizing the profession more carefully and uncharacteristically reaching out to others for ideas and support. For example, Mark Patzer began to re-assess the long-term health consequences of a jockey's restricted body weight. Despite the general taboo against talking about personal concerns, the athletes began to seek the support and advice of medical doctors, family members, mentors, and other trusted individuals. Eventually, a culmination point arose, resulting in a decision to withdraw. For example, football player Al Wilson realized that his young back-up player was ready to assume his position. Frank Barroby was frustrated by his efforts to lose weight in the jockey's sauna and simply went home to a good meal. Darcy Rota felt the pain of a previous injury and knew the risk in continuing to play hockey was too great.

The athletes typically felt relieved once they had committed themselves to withdraw because they were weary of indecision and confusion and often were weary of the physical and emotional demands of the career. Mark Patzer found that within a week of his decision he felt "100 percent better." Other athletes, like Darcy Rota, reported that they gained confidence in having made the right decision. When Danny Williams won his last race on "Wanderkind," his best horse, he knew "this is it! . . . It's time! It's time!" The decision to withdraw concluded the most difficult part of the story and led to steps to launch a new career.

The athletes pursued a variety of new career opportunities. Some were planned, such as Steve Clippingdale's departure from hockey to join his father's printing business, and Lindsay Myers' preparations to become a stockbroker at the conclusion of his racquetball career. Some opportunities were unexpected. As Terry Lombardo left the racetrack he was offered a construction job by a social acquaintance. Some opportunities allowed continued involvement with another dimension of professional sport. Darcy Rota was offered a management position with the Vancouver "Canucks" and Frank Barroby was invited to train a string of horses. Some new careers were difficult to reach. Hockey player Gary Lupul began to lose his self-confidence because he did not know how to go about finding a job:

> The hardest thing is, whom do you go to? Who do you talk to that can lead you in some directions? When you don't even have a clue what to do . . . You don't know who to talk to or who to tell you where to go. It's tough!

He eventually found a temporary position as an assistant to a realtor, which provided an income and an opportunity to consider future directions. Likewise, Danny Williams found temporary work as an exercise boy at the track.

The ending of the story

The story ended with the establishment and acceptance of a post-sport career and life-style. This involved becoming established in a new position, adjusting to a new lifestyle, developing new perspectives, immersion in life activities and interests other than sport, and feeling settled with life.

In adjusting to a new way of life, athletes reported a variety of difficult or trying experiences, as well as a number of easy or supporting ones. Among the difficult experiences are a sense of loss of some of the features of the athletic career such as: intense physical activity; challenge and competition; thrilling atmosphere; performing in front of large crowds; seasonal rhythms and the routine of the lifestyle; and association with other athletes and celebrities. On some occasions, athletes experienced quite a strong yearning for features of their former careers, but these were frequently fleeting, wistful moments of wondering what it would be like to have the opportunity to participate again. Some, particularly the jockeys, were frustrated because they did not have the opportunity to continue participation in their sport on a recreational basis. Without regular, vigorous physical activity, some former athletes felt frustrated because they had yet to find an outlet for their energy. Others, such as Al Wilson, slipped into a level of inactivity which they regarded as unhealthy.

Sometimes former athletes experience a sense of alienation or separation from other people. For example, Gary Lupul found that he could not enjoy participation in recreational hockey because other participants would not accept him as just another recreational player. Lindsay Myers ended his career as the top professional racquetball player in Canada and considered that he would not find any pleasure in recreational play. Terry Lombardo found difficulty in sharing stories about his career because he was afraid that other people would not understand or appreciate his experience and might even think that he was boastful. In another example, Al Wilson considered that his age and, particularly, his sense of independence, made him a poor candidate as an employee.

There were many other difficulties reported by the athletes. These included lack of direction, guidance, or counseling services to assist with career planning. The athletes also reported difficulties related to insufficient finances, a sense of frustration and stagnation due to underemployment or inability to accomplish goals. Some had a sense of social failure due to lack of employment status and a lack of marketable skills. They were worried about and feared an uncertain future. Some experienced other misfortunes such as divorce, death in the family, and even sabotage of a business.

Sometimes other people in the athlete's life experienced difficulties with his change in status. For example, some wives and girlfriends were reported to have difficulty accepting that they no longer enjoyed their celebrity status when the athlete left his sport. In another example, Dave Hindmarch's father reported an unusual disinterest in the National Hockey League during the year following his son's retirement.

Former athletes also experienced a number of pleasant or facilitating experiences that counteracted difficulties. For example, many found that second careers provided excitement and challenge, as well as enjoyable working relationships. In addition, even though it often took time to select and establish themselves in long-term second careers, many found alternative business and employment opportunities readily available.

Even when these were only temporary positions, such as exercising horses, laboring, or part-time sales, they were opportunities to earn an income while considering other possibilities. These positions also served as bridges between careers, providing individuals with the opportunity to shed the "ex-athlete" status which some found to be demoralizing. Simply having a plan, even in the short term, was helpful in bolstering the individual's sense of confidence and optimism.

Other facilitating experiences included the continued appreciation of good health and physical activity that might have been placed in jeopardy by continued participation in professional sport. There was the enjoyment of the physical challenge and camaraderie found in recreational sport. There was the realization that the individual was no longer expected to perform for others and respond to public attention. There was the enjoyment of a family lifestyle and time to spend with loved ones; the continued support of family, friends, mentors, and teammates; and the continued involvement and inclusion with the sport organization. On balance, it would seem that former athletes found the facilitating experiences outweighed the hindrances in establishing a new lifestyle.

In reflecting on the decision to withdraw, the athletes were typically glad that they quit when they did, even though they were reluctant to do so at the time. From a distance, they seemed to find new meaning in sport. They usually had fond memories of their professional years and often experienced a new appreciation for the respect and regard that they received from other athletes and the general public. However, they also realized that in some ways professional sport was a dream world that provided a lifestyle consisting of income and public attention which is unrealistic in comparison with everyday life. Darcy Rota said that the career can be like "a gravy train," probably not comparable to anything else in regular life but a very temporary experience from which athletes must move on. It can provide fun, excitement, variety, and thrills but, beneath the glamour, professional sport is a "grind" of very hard work that is both physically and emotionally demanding. Frequently, former athletes acknowledged that they now realize that in the latter part of their careers they had less drive or motivation than in their younger years. Some still wonder how they were able to handle the professional lifestyle for as long as they did. This was especially true for the jockeys who had to fight their growing bodies. Some of them reported that the meaning of their sport had changed dramatically. For example, Danny Williams said: "When I started [riding], it was everything I'd ever wanted . . . (now) all I think is what I went through to ride – the suffering and the torture."

These former athletes often look back on their careers as valuable learning experiences. While they often learned helpful skills (such as patience, tolerance, and other "people" skills) which carried over into later life, many also learned important principles and attitudes. For example, they frequently gained a new appreciation of their health and they realized that, because they have much longer to live, there are other goals in life more important than sport. Many now realize that the commitment and dedication given to sport can be used to achieve those other goals.

Their timely withdrawal from sport allowed them to preserve health, self-respect, and the regard of others. It also allowed them to develop other competencies and to express a more nurturant dimension of themselves as their interests turned toward their emerging family lives. Most have found the transition to a new career and lifestyle relatively easy, frequently accepting a more modest lifestyle than they had experienced as professional athletes and usually finding some means to continue their participation in sport in a recreational or leadership capacity.

For these people, being settled in a post-sport career involved a sense of resignation to the realities of life. Al Wilson wanted to play football for the rest of his working days but he accepted that this was impossible. Terry Lombardo knows that thoroughbred racing still holds an attraction for him and so he avoids temptation by staying away from the track. Darcy Rota wanted to continue playing hockey but he recognized that it is important for people to move on.

Feeling settled in life after sport seems to involve a sense of satisfaction both with what one has accomplished in sport and with what one is currently accomplishing in the new career. In terms of sport, satisfaction appears to involve the ability to reflect with pride on what was accomplished, particularly acknowledging that the individual "gave his best shot" at the career under the available circumstances. It involves the ability realistically to appraise and appreciate the individual's own efforts and to cherish fond memories of his involvement. Rather than bitterness over lost opportunities and perceived injustices, it also involves the ability to accept that the past is concluded. As Dave Hindmarch noted:

> The biggest thing is not to leave it with resentment . . . Different people go into the game with different values and different priorities. I think it's important that you examine the ones that are important to you and . . . realize that hockey's not the end of your life. Even if you're the luckiest player in the NHL, you're not going to be playing past thirty-five. So, you've got lots of life left.

Satisfaction in new careers involves contentment with the available challenges, opportunities, rewards, and accomplishments. In some cases, athletes see the potential for more satisfaction in their new careers than they experienced in their old ones. For example, Danny Williams has been surprised to find greater satisfaction in training horses than in riding them as a jockey. Some athletes do not look for comparable satisfaction. For example, Terry Lombardo and Al Wilson have simply resigned themselves to the assumption that nothing in life will be as rewarding as their athletic experiences.

Summary

My interviews indicate that among the former athletes I interviewed the withdrawal from professional sport was a process that frequently began soon after they became engaged in their playing careers. Over time, the athletes were confronted with both internal and external pressures for change. Although they often became concerned about perceived limitations and experienced a period of great confusion and indecision, the athletes did not find this experience to be traumatic. In reflecting on the decision to withdraw, the athletes were typically glad that they quit when they did, even though they were reluctant to do so at the time. Their withdrawal allowed them to preserve health, self-respect, and the regard of others. It also allowed them to develop other competencies and to express a more nurturant dimension of themselves as their interests had turned toward their emerging family lives.

Former Canadian Football League player, Al Wilson, provided a summary observation that the decision to withdraw from a sports career may appear more dramatic than other career transitions because professional sport commands so much energy, emotion, and public attention, but the experience generally is far from traumatic. He also provided an observation suggestive of future research into the experiences of those individuals who do have great difficulty in leaving professional careers. Reflecting on the experience of a former teammate, Wilson noted, "People who were troubled in [sport] were troubled outside [of sport]. It's no surprise . . . His career ended and life's a bitch. Well, it was a bitch when he was playing." Perhaps the trauma in leaving professional sport has more to do with the individual's life as a whole than with the particular experience of ending a playing career.

22

RETIRING FROM THE SIDELINE

Becoming more than "hockey's daughter" and "football's wife"

Bette McKenzie

This chapter is based on personal experience rather than research. I have been connected closely with sports for my entire life. As a child I grew up in a "professional sports family" because my father played in the National Hockey League (NHL). Then I married a man who played in the National Football League (NFL). Now I deal with professional athletes as I arrange their speaking engagements through my consulting business. I train as a recreational athlete in my spare time.

Jay Coakley and Peter Donnelly asked me to write this chapter because I have lived through two transitions out of sports: first, my father's, then my husband's. I know firsthand that the transition out of sport affects the families of athletes who end playing careers, especially when those careers have shaped the structure and rhythm of family life. Spouses and children often experience their own transitions when athletes make their transition into life off the playing field. When the transitions are difficult for the former athlete, they are often difficult for the athlete's spouse and children. Family relationships may be affected.

This chapter focuses on a part of my experience as the daughter of a pro hockey player and the wife of a pro football player. I focus on identity issues and the challenges I faced when I made my own transition to life outside the direct influence of professional sports.

The retirement of a professional athlete often puts incredible strain on his marriage and other close relationships. The transition from the intense and highly focused world of professional sport to the rest of life can be full of difficulties. It involves the loss of identity, status, and stature. It demands maturity, creativity, and effort as the retired pro works at forming a new identity. Due to the challenges faced in this transition, many athletes retire only to stage desperate attempts at comebacks, despite advancing age and debilitating injuries. During this transition it is often the wife who must hold the marriage and family together.

In my case, this transition process did not go smoothly. It was stressful, emotionally draining, and probably the main cause of our divorce. In the end I was left wondering who I was and how I would survive. I was no longer the wife of a celebrity. I no longer enjoyed a large income. I am sure many other wives of pro athletes have similar experiences. Breaking away from the seductive world of professional sports and the identity that comes with it is not easy. It is not easy for the athletes. It is not easy for their families. It was especially difficult for me.

Hockey's daughter

My father is John "Pie" McKenzie, a former professional hockey player for several teams, most notably the 1971–2 Stanley Cup champion, Boston Bruins. During my childhood I was often referred to as "Johnny Pie's daughter." I never objected to this, even though my name was altogether omitted. It was not especially important to me then. Being referred to as "Pie's daughter" connected me with someone very special, someone who was respected and well liked by nearly everyone I met. As a child this made me feel special too.

My identity was positive and secure in those early years. I never chose the fame and celebrity that came with being the daughter of a professional athlete, nor did I object to it. Being associated with the cult of celebrity that surrounds many professional sports in the USA brought wonderful privileges and favorable treatment. I enjoyed that. For example, when I was 10 years old Bobby Orr, a hockey legend and a teammate and good friend of my father's, gave me and my two younger sisters, Jackie and Lori, brand-new, red suede ice skates. When we put them on we were extremely proud and I am sure quite precocious, especially since we were skating on the ice of the Boston Garden, under the flashing, colored lights used for figure skating performances. I remember feeling like Peggy Fleming that night.

My parents divorced when I was 12 years old. I believe that my father's career and the wild lifestyle associated with it played a major role in the break-up of their marriage. My mother raised my three sisters and me. I did not see much of my father during those years because he was playing hockey for the Hartford Whalers in Connecticut.

Looking back, I realize that this must have been a difficult time for my father as well. Because professional athletes can be traded virtually any time, there is always the threat of being forced to make another transition and start over again somewhere new. When I was a teenager, my father was playing hockey in Connecticut while his children were living north of Boston, 120 miles away. Had my parents still been together I am sure we would have moved too, even in the middle of the school year. During my childhood I moved five times, from Canada to Pennsylvania, and then to New York, Chicago, and eventually to Boston. I was extremely grateful to have the chance to complete high school in the same town north of Boston.

Football's wife

At a time when most young people test and forge their own identities as they go off to college or start careers, my identity became entwined with another professional athlete. During my second year at a small state college in Massachusetts I met Brian Holloway, a rookie offensive lineman for the New England Patriots in the National Football

League (NFL). We dated for a year and married in 1982. I was 20 years old and had completed only two years of college.

The privileges of being married to a professional athlete were even more attractive than when I was the child of a professional athlete. As a child I enjoyed the benefits of my father's celebrity status in a passive manner, as if they were gifts. Now, as the wife of an NFL player, I could take advantage of those benefits in a more active way. For example, Brian's endorsement contract with Nike entitled me to order any shoe, sweat suit, or other Nike apparel that I wanted at no charge. For a 20 year old this was an impressive perk.

Other perks included free dinners at good restaurants, complimentary trips including an all-expenses paid cruise in the Caribbean, and four consecutive trips to Hawaii for the NFL Pro-Bowl. The wives of Pro-Bowl players flew first class on tickets provided by the NFL. And there was plenty of spending money for our meals. This was a lifestyle others just dream about, and I was living it in my twenties because I was the wife of a National Football League player.

Life as the wife of a professional athlete was full of seductive perks. But it was not too long before I realized that these did little to help me answer on my own terms the question, "Who am I?" I began to realize this on the day I gave birth to our first son, David. David's timing was bad. He decided to enter the world on an NFL "game day," Sunday, 4 December 1983. The coach gave Brian the day off to be with me during the delivery, but missing the game was difficult for him. In fact, while he was with me his mind seemed to be more on the game plan than on the labor and delivery. After several hours of watching the distracted behavior that indicated his preoccupation with the game, I became angry and said, "Go and play the game!" He did, and fortunately for him my labor was so long that he made it back to the hospital in time to see the birth. His teammates dedicated the winning game ball to our son.

The headline in the next morning's newspaper read, "Brian Holloway's young wife delivered a nine-pound baby boy." After nine months of pregnancy and many hours of hard labor, my first name never appeared in the article. I was reminded vividly of my childhood. When I was a child known as "Pie's daughter," I had not been bothered that to most people I had no first name. But as an adult I had different feelings; now it bothered me.

This experience, combined with the rest of my personal history, opened my eyes to three important things. First, the game would always be my husband's number one priority, as it is for most pro athletes. Second, in the world where I lived most of my life, I was an afterthought at best, and my existence was acknowledged only because of my connection to my NFL husband. Third, in this world, I was easily replaceable. Realizing these things made me insecure about who I was. I needed an identity that was separate from my identities as an athlete's daughter and an athlete's wife.

I was not alone in this realization. Other wives of professional athletes told me that they had similar experiences and feelings. Like me, many of these women never developed identities apart from sports. Even when they tried, their efforts were sidetracked or obscured by the glare of their husband's celebrity status.

Some felt pressures to look, dress, and act in a certain way. Others felt like a showpiece or a social accessory on the arm of the hero – just another trophy to be displayed in connection with his achievements as an athlete. Many felt insecure because of the rumors about other women eager to step in and take their place on the hero's arm. Self-esteem among many of these women was low. They resented being second to football and living in the shadow of their husband's celebrity status. Even my own mother looks back on her life and remembers being resentful of the attention and adulation received by my father as she raised four children after their divorce.

Back to school

My feelings of insecurity were compounded because I felt inferior for never having finished my college education. Brian had graduated from Stanford, and his family valued education highly. Several members of his family had earned advanced degrees from prestigious universities. So I set the goal of completing college in the hope that it would help me develop my own identity and overcome some of my insecurity.

After setting this goal, I decided that I did not want to return to the small state college I had attended before marrying Brian. I hoped that I might be accepted into an Ivy League caliber university. Unfortunately, my grades were not Ivy League grades. This is where the connections in the world of sport came in handy. Being the wife of a professional football player did give me access to powerful people. Through my husband's influence, an interview was arranged for me with then governor of Massachusetts, Michael Dukakis. Governor Dukakis met me at the state house for a brief interview during which we discussed my goals. A letter of recommendation, bearing the governor's signature, was sent to Wellesley College and Williams College, both prestigious institutions. It was not long before I was accepted at both. During the football season I studied at Wellesley, near our home in Boston, and during the off-season I attended Williams, near our farm in the Berkshire Mountains of upstate New York. I worked hard and in 1988 I earned an Art History degree from Williams College.

Divorce

Marriage difficulties had begun in 1987 when Brian was unexpectedly traded to the Los Angeles Raiders in the middle of the season. I was pregnant with twins at the time, and in my last semester of college. We already owned two homes in New England, so Brian moved to Los Angeles for the last four months of the season while I stayed in the east with our 3-year-old son, David. It was a difficult situation for all of us, but I felt it had to be that way if I wanted to complete my degree. Dropping out now and going back at some later date with three children to care for was not an option in my mind.

Then things got even worse. In October of 1988 Brian was cut from the Raiders. He came home but had a difficult time making the transition from professional sports to a nine-to-five work schedule. His energy level was high and not well suited to his new life off the field. Nor was I adjusting well to the changes in our lives. Perhaps we would have benefited from marriage counseling, but we never pursued it. After several years and the birth of another child we divorced.

New beginnings

Time and distance have given me the chance to reflect on and come to terms with many of my identity issues. For the first time, I now have an identity that I can call my own.

Ironically, but not surprisingly, that identity is still connected with sports, but the connection now reflects my choices and concerns.

In the summer of 1996 I began running in road races, including "ironman" competitions and half-marathons. I have developed a passion for weight training and one of my goals is to compete in the Boston Marathon. Sports have always been a part of my life, but now I am a part of that world on my own terms. I take pride in my accomplishments. They have helped me physically, emotionally, and spiritually. They have enabled me to become empowered as I have made new discoveries about who I am and what I can become.

Another irony is that I have used my access to celebrity athletes to develop my own business. Through the connections I made as the daughter of a NHL player and the wife of a NFL player, my business partner and I have established and nurtured the Berkshire Speakers' Bureau. We book speaking engagements for professional athletes, entertainers, and business people. I have worked with sport celebrities such as Mike Ditka, former television commentator and now coach of the New Orleans Saints in the NFL; Pat Riley, now coach of the Miami Heat in the NBA; golfer Tiger Woods; former major league pitcher and author, Jim Bouton; and many others.

It is not easy to break away from the world of professional sports and the identity that it provides. The identities associated with that world still follow me like a shadow, especially when others discover, "You're Johnny Pie's daughter!" or ask, "Weren't you married to Brian Holloway?" I now know that those identities will always be a part of who I am, but I also know that I am much more than that.

Like many former athletes, I have set aside the identities which were grounded in the world of professional sports and I am pursuing life on new terms, on my terms. As I do, I continue to come up with new answers to the question, "Who am I?"

Editors' note: We first talked with Bette McKenzie after reading a feature article written by columnist Robert Lipsyte in the *New York Times* ("Married to the game: one more athlete's wife picks up the pieces of her life," 1 June 1997, pp. 19–20 in Sports). The article recounted how Bette, daughter of "Pie" McKenzie, a former hockey player with the Boston Bruins, was undergoing a divorce from her husband, Brian Holloway, a former football player with the New England Patriots. Bette disclosed to Lipsyte that, "My mother always told me not to marry a pro athlete. She said they have affairs and they leave you." We were intrigued by life experiences that matched so closely those outlined by Wendy Thompson in Chapter 18, and we were struck by the fact that her husband's retirement from professional football appeared to be implicated in the events that led to the divorce proceedings. As Bette explained, "As long as he had football, as long as he had the outlet of being a warrior at war, it wasn't so bad. But all that energy, all that intelligence needs a channel. Once he figures [retirement] out, there is no limit to his potential." This article and Bette's chapter raise the possibility that the difficulties experienced by the family members of retiring athletes may be influenced by the very same factors that influence difficulties among the athletes themselves. We outlined these factors on p. 197.

LEARNING EXERCISES AND RESOURCES

Projects and discussion topics

1 Many athletes in high performance sports resist retirement, even in the face of painful and serious and/or chronic injuries. Talk to two or more athletes in high performance sports and ask them to explain why they or their teammates would continue their sport careers despite pain, injury, and threats to their physical well being. What is it about some forms of sport participation that encourage many athletes to resist retirement from playing careers?

2 The chapters in Part 4 deal with transitions out of competitive sport careers into the rest of life. Identify someone you know who played varsity high school sports but does not play varsity college sports. How has s/he made the transition from playing competitive sports to what s/he is doing now? Is sport participation still part of his or her life? What else has changed in his or her life? Are the changes consistent with what you might have expected on the basis of readings the chapters? Why or why not? (If varsity sports are not emphasized among your fellow students, ask someone who has competed in elite amateur sports and has since retired from top competition.)

3 Talk with two athletes who are currently participating in intercollegiate sports or elite amateur sports. Ask them about what they anticipate when they retire from their active playing careers. What challenges do they think they will face in their lives beyond the playing field? Do they think their sport careers will help or hinder them as they make this transition? In what ways might they help? In what ways might they hinder?

4 The chapters in Part 4 suggest that the ease of making the transition out of competitive sport careers into the rest of life will vary from one athlete to another. What are the social factors that might be associated with an easy and successful transition? What are the social factors that might be associated with a difficult transition? Would you expect variations by age, gender, race or ethnicity, social class, or type of sport? Present two hypotheses about social factors affecting transitions, and support your hypotheses with personal experience and/or materials from the articles.

5 There has never been a large, systematic study of the spouses and children of athletes who are terminating long-term sport careers. As an expert in the sociology of sport you have been hired to direct a major research project on this topic. You have a large amount of money for the study. Indicate who you would include in the study, and explain why. Identify the five main question areas you would include in your

in-depth interviews with those included in your sample. Explain why you selected each of the five question areas and indicate what kinds of hunches you have about what you will discover through the interviews.

6   Choose a sport or a group of athletes in which you would expect a relatively high rate of problems associated with athletes' transitions out of their competitive sport careers. Design a "transition assistance program" for the athletes in that sport or that group. What would be involved in your program? Explain why each component of the program has been included. What problems does your program address, and why would you expect your program to be successful?

Films and videos

Film and video annotations are provided by Steve Mosher, Department of Exercise and Sport Science, Ithaca College, Ithaca, NY 14850, USA.

Feature-length films

- *Everybody's All-American* (1988), 127 mins, Warner Home Video
  What does an athlete do when his glory days are over? In many cases, not much. Such is the case of Gavin Grey (Dennis Quaid), the "Grey Ghost" – football All-American and sporting hero. Adapted from well-known sports writer Frank Deford's novel, *Everybody's All-American* painfully shows the gradual disintegration of the big man on campus as he moves through a relatively uneventful professional football career into the restaurant business and finally to selling "himself." While not entirely successful as a story, this film is a rich character study that becomes even more powerful for students when viewed together with Irwin Shaw's short story *The Eighty Yard Run*. Gavin Grey, Christian Darling and, arguably, even the real-life Joe Dimaggio (the self-proclaimed "greatest living baseball player") show both the intoxicating appeal of athletic glory and the numbing reality that it is a glory all too brief.

- *The Turning Point* (1977) 119 mins, CBS/Fox Home Video
  This potentially overwrought and sentimental film is about a woman (Shirley McLaine) who gives up ballet for marriage and motherhood, and then tries to come to terms with her daughter's (Leslie Browne) choice to make ballet her career. Her life is further complicated when she is reunited with her estranged friend and fellow dancer (Anne Bancroft) who chose stardom over marriage and motherhood. While the mother worries about her child paying too great a price for fame, her friend wonders about life's opportunities missed. Partly based on Browne's own life, this film presents the dilemmas often encountered by young women athletes. The damned-if-you-do, damned-if-you-don't paradox plays well in a setting not traditionally explored in sports movies about women and only hinted at in *A League of Their Own* (1993). Ultimately the question raised for students is why does our society force women to make these difficult choices while men can have it all.

Shorter film

- *Sticky My Fingers, Fleet My Feet* (1970), 24 mins, Pyramid Films
  John Hancock's marvelous fiction film about Norman, the middle-aged touch football star who is humiliated by the teenage nephew of a fellow player. The teenager is not even good enough to make his high school team (he's the manager). Norman's buddies play for fun, Norman plays to hang on to his youth. A wonderful treatise on why we persist in playing sports long after we have lost our skills.

Additional books and articles

- Coakley, J. (1992) "Burnout among adolescent athletes: a personal failure or social problem?," *Sociology of Sport Journal* 9(3): 271–85.

After analyzing data from fifteen in-depth interviews with young former athletes, all but one from individual sports, Coakley concluded that burnout was grounded primarily in the organization of the high performance sports in which these young people had played. Burnout occurred when the young people felt they had lost control over their lives and had no chance to develop and nurture selves apart from the sport they played. This combination of having no control and having a unidimensional identity was associated with high levels of stress and a decline in the fun which the athletes experienced in their sports. As stress increased and fun decreased, they burned out. Therefore, burnout was connected with how sport programs were organized and how sport experiences were connected with developmental issues during adolescence. When being a young athlete interferes with developing desired identities apart from sports, and precludes establishing the autonomy and independence so important during adolescence, burnout is likely. Coakley concludes that burnout is best prevented by finding ways to empower athletes in high performance sports and to change the social organization of the sport contexts in which they train and compete.

- Koukouris, K. (1994) "Constructed case studies: athletes' perspectives of disengaging from organized competitive sport," *Sociology of Sport Journal* 11(2): 114–39.

Konstantinos Koukouris (1994) is a physical educator from Greece who wanted to know how and why people who have been committed to sports decide to end or seriously reduce their participation. After analyzing questionnaire data from 157 former athletes in track and field, rowing, and volleyball, Koukouris identified 34 who ceased or reduced sport participation between the ages of 18 and 24 years old. In-depth interviews with these young adults enabled him to construct case studies illustrating the process of "disengaging from sports." The stories told by the former athletes indicated that they consciously made the decision to end or change their participation. Many went through a period of time during which they stopped playing and then started again more than once. Their decision was caused primarily by the need to find a job and support themselves, but was also connected with an assessment of their sport skills and their chances to move to higher levels of competition. As they graduated from high school or college, they felt they should be responsible for their own lives. But their jobs and their lifestyles as adults interfered with training and competition. As serious training ended, they often sought other ways to be physically active or connected with sports. Problems occurred, but most had positive transition experiences.

- Messner, M. (1992) "Out of the limelight: disengagement from the athletic career," in Messner *Power at Play: Sports and the Problem of Masculinity*, Boston: Beacon Press. pp. 108–28.

Mike Messner's interviews with thirty former elite athletes indicated that men who had played sports seriously since early childhood often faced problems in connection with the termination of their competitive careers. They missed the structure that sport provided in their lives, and the camaraderie with fellow athletes. Messner concluded that these athletes faced two major challenges during their transition: the task of redefining their identities through activities and relationships not connected with sport participation; and the task of re-establishing supportive relationships with friends and family members on terms unrelated to playing sports. Messner also found that men from low income backgrounds had more problems because they lacked material and cultural resources to facilitate the transition. Men from middle-income backgrounds had fewer problems because they had more material and cultural resources and were in better positions to use their sport-related social contacts to find opportunities unrelated to sport participation.

- Wheeler, G. D. *et al.* (1999) "Personal investment in disability sport careers: an international study," *Adapted Physical Education Quarterly* 16 (forthcoming).

Building on a study he had done with Canadian paralympic athletes, Wheeler and his fellow researchers gathered data through interviews with 40 athletes from Israel (N = 17), the UK (N = 11), Canada (N = 9), and the USA (N = 3). Data indicated that patterns among athletes with disabilities were similar across the four cultures. The athletes tended to become deeply involved in their sport participation, and often experienced a high level of success in a relatively short time. Through sport they found meaning, developed a sense of personal competence, and established an identity as an elite athlete. Their intense investment in sport participation and their sport identity brought both rewards and costs. Withdrawal from participation and the transition into the rest of life presented challenges for many. About one in ten experienced serious emotional problems during this process. Retirement often came quite suddenly and was accompanied by a process of reinvesting time and energy into other activities and relationships. There was a focus on reconnecting with family members and friends, going back to school, and getting on with careers. However, most stayed connected with sports and sport organizations as coaches, administrators, or recreational athletes. Those who aspired to return to competition often encountered difficulties during the transition, but most of those interviewed accepted and adjusted to the termination of their competitive careers. However, most also endorsed some form of counseling intervention to assist paralympic athletes with their transitions out of sport and into the rest of their lives.

INDEX